A Theology of Flourishing

A Theology of Flourishing

A Theology of Flourishing

The Fullness of Life for All Creation

Paul J. Schutz

Maryknoll, New York 10545

Founded in 1970, Orbis Books endeavors to publish works that enlighten the mind, nourish the spirit, and challenge the conscience. The publishing arm of the Maryknoll Fathers and Brothers, Orbis seeks to explore the global dimensions of the Christian faith and mission, to invite dialogue with diverse cultures and religious traditions, and to serve the cause of reconciliation and peace. The books published reflect the views of their authors and do not represent the official position of the Maryknoll Society. To learn more about Maryknoll and Orbis Books, please visit our website at www.orbisbooks.com.

Copyright © 2025 by Paul J. Schutz.

Published by Orbis Books, Box 302, Maryknoll, NY 10545-0302.

Scripture texts used in this work, unless otherwise noted, are taken from the New Revised Standard Version Updated Edition. Copyright © 2021 National Council of Churches of Christ in the United States of America. Used by permission. All rights reserved worldwide.

All Vatican documents are available online at Vatican.va.

All rights reserved.

No part of this publication may be reproduced or transmitted in any form or by any means, electronic or mechanical, including photocopying, recording, or any information storage or retrieval system, without prior permission in writing from the publisher.

Queries regarding rights and permissions should be addressed to: Orbis Books, P.O. Box 302, Maryknoll, NY 10545-0302.

Manufactured in the United States of America.
Manuscript editing and typesetting by Joan Weber Laflamme.

Library of Congress Cataloging-in-Publication Data

Names: Schutz, Paul J., author.
Title: A theology of flourishing : the fullness of life for all creation / Paul J. Schutz.
Identifiers: LCCN 2024055820 (print) | LCCN 2024055821 (ebook) | ISBN 9781626986145 (trade paperback) | ISBN 9798888660690 (epub)
Subjects: LCSH: Life—Biblical teaching. | Well-being—Religious aspects—Catholic Church. | Christian life—Catholic authors.
Classification: LCC BS680.L5 S38 2025 (print) | LCC BS680.L5 (ebook) | DDC 233—dc23/eng/20250118
LC record available at https://lccn.loc.gov/2024055820
LC ebook record available at https://lccn.loc.gov/2024055821

For my parents,
who taught me how to walk with God
and empowered me to discover my most authentic self;
and who showed me, with food, laughter, and openness to others,
that God created all things to flourish.

And for Nikko,
who showed me infinite patience, compassion, and care
and encouraged me amid numerous struggles;
and who, with brilliant creativity and limitless love,
made space for this work to flourish.

Contents

Foreword by Elizabeth A. Johnson ... *xi*

Acknowledgments ... *xv*

Introduction: Why We Need a Theology of Flourishing ... *xix*

Part I
Foundations:
Approaching a Theology of Flourishing

1. Two Seeds for a Theology of Flourishing ... 3

A Seed Is Planted: Grace Jantzen's Ecofeminist
Philosophy ... 4
From Necrophilia to Natality, Death to Birth ... 6
Seedlings Sprout: The Symbol of Creation
Functions ... 10
Losing Creation, Reimagining Creation ... 13
A First Bud: A Preliminary Understanding of
Flourishing ... 17

2. Approaching a Theology of Flourishing
Method and Context ... 21

The Method That Guides This Study: A Hermeneutics
of the Fullness of Life ... 22
Situating a Theology of Flourishing: Preliminary
Commitments and Limitations ... 27

viii *Contents*

Part II
Explorations:
Tracing the Thread of Flourishing
through Scripture and History

3. **Abundant Life in the Order of Creation**
Hebrew Bible Foundations for a Theology
of Flourishing   35

     Framing the Interpretations: Biblical Creation Texts
         as "Cultural Cosmologies"   36

     Genesis 1   37

     Genesis 2—3   48

     Interlude: Flashes of Flourishing, Disobedience,
         and Sin within Covenantal History   54

     Psalms 19 and 104   56

     Proverbs and Wisdom   62

     Key Insights for the Path Ahead   64

4. **Revolutionary Love for "All Things"**
New Testament Foundations for a Theology
of Flourishing   67

     Christological Context: Creation, Incarnation,
         and Flesh in John 1 and Colossians 1   68

     From Vision to Praxis: Creation, Life, and Love
         in the Pauline Corpus   71

     The Gospel of Matthew: Revolutionary Love and the
         Flourishing of the "Least of These"   79

     1 John: Incarnation, Love, and Enfleshed Care
         for All Things   84

     Key Insights for the Path Ahead   89

5. **Creation, Deification, and Flourishing in Early**
Christian Thought
Irenaeus, Athanasius, and Gregory of Nyssa   93

     Irenaeus of Lyons   95

     Athanasius of Alexandria   102

Contents   *ix*

Gregory of Nyssa   105
Key Insights for the Path Ahead   111

6. Creation, Life, and Love in and beyond the Medieval Period
Hildegard of Bingen, John Duns Scotus, Julian of Norwich, and Nicholas of Cusa   113
Hildegard of Bingen   115
John Duns Scotus   124
Julian of Norwich and Nicholas of Cusa   133
Key Insights for the Path Ahead   143

7. Rahner and Beyond
Twentieth-Century Foundations for a Theology of Flourishing   145
Toward a Cosmic Christianity: Rahner's
Evolutionary Christology   146
Rahner's Transcendental Anthropology—
A Closer Look at Humanity   151
Love of Christ, Heart of Creation   159
Beyond Rahner: Critique, Development, and
the Birth of Political and Liberation
Theologies   161
Toward a Theology of Flourishing   169

Part III
Integrations:
A Theology of Flourishing in Vision and Praxis

8. A Theology of Flourishing
Envisioning Christianity for the Fullness of Life   173
Contours of a Theology of Flourishing   175
Implications for Theological Discourse   201
Resituating Sin and Salvation   203
Onward, toward a Praxis of Flourishing   204

x

9. Dialogue, Discernment, Decision
A Framework for Flourishing 207
Dialogue as Method of Attunement and Context
for Discernment   208
Discernment: Discovering the Spirit's Will
in Relationship with God and Creation   215
Decision: Self-Actualization that Reaches to
the Ends of Creation   220

Conclusion: Toward a Praxis of Flourishing 225
Christianity as Contemplation in Loving
Action   226
Amor Mundi: The Praxis of Flourishing   230
Four Test Cases for a Theology of Flourishing   232

Index 243

Foreword

ELIZABETH A. JOHNSON

Flourishing as a word, a concept, a goal is currently having its moment in the sun. Derived from the Latin *florere*, "to flower or blossom," it is being used in fields as diverse as biology and chemistry, anthropology and philosophy, psychology and sociology, business and politics to describe the optimum functioning of an individual or system. Religious studies is party to this trend, as witnessed by multiple uses of the term in studies of sacred texts, interpretations of beliefs, reasonings of ethical arguments, and analysis of rituals and spiritual practices. Most often, its usage focuses on the well-being of our own species, as seen in the Human Flourishing Program at Harvard University or the Humanities and Human Flourishing Project at the University of Pennsylvania. Increasingly, a growing ecological awareness expands the scope of interest to include the well-being of ecosystems, animals, plants, and microbes and our planet's land, water, and air that support us all.

In this book, a work of Christian theology, the author turns a searchlight on the meaning of flourishing as such. Is it a brand-new idea or does it have precedent in scripture and tradition? What would change if the concept of flourishing were at the center of theological understanding and if the reality of flourishing were the goal of ethical practice? What would shift if we *xii* Foreword

saw that the holy mystery of God whom we must love with all our heart, soul, mind, and strength actually intends that all creatures should flourish, including human beings as part of the community of creation? How would loving our neighbor as ourself assume a terrible concreteness if each one's flourishing were in fact the focus of our love? Answering these questions via a multi-pronged analysis demonstrates the powerful potential of this complex term to refresh our theological imagination with practical results.

At its core the book takes a strong stand with a saying of Jesus Christ that draws a contrast between his own intent and a criminal's activity: "The thief comes only to steal and kill and destroy. I came that they may have life and have it abundantly" (Jn 10:10). Life in abundance, flourishing, the very opposite of failure to thrive, is the gift. Here, in a nutshell, Paul Schutz argues, can be found the purpose of creation, the reason for the incarnation, the goal of the ongoing work of the Spirit in the world, and an attractive pattern of Christian life, thought, prayer, and praxis.

To be sure, for long eras the Christian tradition placed its main emphasis elsewhere. As commonly understood, sin abounded while grace did not so much superabound as needed to be gained in increments by repentance and right observance. Suffering was to be borne patiently even when caused by unjust social structures. This world was a vale of tears, of less importance than the salvation that was hoped for beyond the world, from the world, once life on earth was over.

Although it is difficult to write the history of a period that is still under way, even a cursory glance at many different types of contemporary theology reveals how they have departed from the vale of tears paradigm in a striking way. In many locales, Irenaeus's beautiful insight that the glory of God is the human being fully alive implicitly guides reflection on doctrine and ethics even when not directly referred to, while ecological wonder and concern broaden the axiom to include God's glory at stake

Foreword xiii

on earth and its creatures fully alive. By proposing a vision for Christian thought and praxis that takes flourishing as its starting point and center of gravity, this book lends robust strength to such a change of direction.

The idea is not without an honorable ancestry. Sequential chapters reveal its lineage in key passages of both testaments of scripture and chart its development in select theologians of the early Christian, medieval, and twentieth-century eras. This method of tracing threads through the vast tapestry of accumulated Christian texts buttresses the case for the meaning and value of an idea whose time has come. Flourishing was indeed present even if marginalized.

In developing the concept theologically, Schutz offers an insightful argument. While creation and incarnation provide the foundation for a theology of flourishing today, in practice such a theology is fundamentally *pneumatological*. Forgetting the Spirit, marginalizing the Spirit's ways in theological discourse and liturgical practice, corresponds closely with the suppression of the paradigm of flourishing in theological history. A beautiful metaphor illustrates this connection with panache: the Spirit, Giver of life, "makes all things and keeps them in existence from moment to moment, not like a sculptor who makes a statue and leaves it alone, but like a singer who keeps her song in existence at all times."[1] Creation goes on continuously as a live musical performance! While the musician keeps singing, the music lasts. When she stops, the show is over. Centering on the importance of fullness of life for all creatures goes hand-in-hand with a revived appreciation of the whole mystery of the living God, who is Love, present and active in every moment.

Retrieving and arguing for this paradigm does not lead to a romantic vision of life. A theology of flourishing has teeth.

---

[1] Herbert McCabe, OP, *God, Christ, and Us*, ed. and intro. Brian Davies (New York: Continuum, 2003), 103.

xiv *Foreword*

Keenly aware that finitude, to say nothing of destructive sinful actions and sinful social structures, limits the range of thriving at any given moment, this pattern of thinking names and tangles with the injustice of racism and other violent, patriarchal, heterosexist, ableist, and colonialist systemic evils of society. It also gives warrant for critique of church teaching that prevents whole groups of baptized people from flourishing. In addition, all creation is groaning, uniquely so today due to human action. This theology mounts a full-scale press against destruction of ecosystems and extinction of species while generating care for our uncommon common home. In sum, salvation is a matter of this world, a matter of flourishing.

Poet Sue Ellson has remarked that words we know but are not in regular use are like musical notes in our everyday language; once used, they make our ears stand up and listen. This book demonstrates with great insight that *flourishing* is one such word. In the face of the terrible destruction of war, poverty and hunger, prejudice and exclusion, grief and depression, it announces the living God's intent that life should bloom. With twenty-first-century sensibility, the term carries forward ancient prophetic visions of rich harvests and a bountiful table open to all; justice for the oppressed and comfort for the broken-hearted; swords beaten into plowshares and no more training for war; streams of water in a dry place and the desert breaking into bloom; praise arising to the God of our salvation, "the hope of all the ends of the earth and of the far distant seas" (Ps 65:5).

Make this category the center of theology, and a path of faithful discipleship comes into view at once strong, attractive, and hopeful. Reading the signs of these critical times, this book mounts a courageous argument that such should be the case. Therein lies the challenge.

Acknowledgments

Flourishing happens in relationship, and it's my great pleasure to acknowledge the people and communities that helped this work come to fruition. My first thanks go to the people of St. Mary Catholic Church in Evansville, Indiana. The time I spent working and praying in community at St. Mary led me to become a theologian and, although I didn't know it at the time, sowed the seeds of this book's central thesis. Special thanks go to Rev. Stephen P. Lintzenich, former pastor of St. Mary, who showed me what it looks like to empower others, practice radical hospitality, and seek justice in faith. Steve also was the first person to suggest that I consider graduate studies in theology. Special thanks go also to Sr. Darlene Boyd, SFCC, my partner in making joyful noise, and to the members of the St. Mary choirs and symphonia. The music we made still enlivens my heart. Thanks, too, to the members of the once-indomitable Liturgy Committee—especially David Bower and Susan Hagan—who taught me what authentic, living worship looks like, and to all those who contributed to the parish's liturgical life. To my fellow staff members, Sr. Barbara Lynn Schmitz, OSB, Lee Griggs, Pat Fitzsimmons, and the fabulous Georgia Kerswick, whose high heels are surely clicking about in heaven as she prepares God's table for Eucharist: thank you for teaching me what it means to build and serve a flourishing family of faith. Finally, deepest thanks go to my friend and collaborator Dr. Cindy Bernardin, whose artistic sensibility, boundless creativity, and contemplative heart showed me what it means to attune a community to the Spirit's stirrings and respond in love toward all. I think that's what flourishing is all about. To the whole St. Mary community, thank you. You changed my life.

Great gratitude goes also to my teachers and mentors from the Fordham University Department of Theology. Both inside and outside the classroom our work together sharpened my thinking and deepened my commitment to justice. Special thanks go to Ben Dunning, Brad and Christine Hinze, Jeannine Hill Fletcher, Michael Lee, Telly Papanikolaou, Michael Peppard, and Tom Scirghi, who broadened my intellectual horizons and accompanied me through challenging periods of personal growth. The same is true of many wonderful friends and colleagues from my Fordham years. They are too numerous to name, but I must mention Heather DuBois, Jason Steidl-Jack, Eric Martin, Brendan McInerny, Mary Kate Holman, and Maria Terzulli, who remain companions in laughter, love, encouragement, and inspiration.

I could not have completed this manuscript without the support of my colleagues at Santa Clara University. I remember with gratitude the love and encouragement I received from the late Paul Crowley and Teresia Hinga. While writing, Teresia's favorite creature—the hummingbird—often buzzed by my window, especially, it seemed, when I was struggling with anxiety and finding it difficult to write. Seeing the birds reminded me of Teresia's smile and Paul's laugh, which motivated me to keep on. Cathleen Chopra-McGowan, Karen Peterson-Iyer, Nicholas Hayes-Mota, Eugene Schlesinger, Rob Scholla, Haruka Umetsu Cho, and Bryson White gave generously of their time to talk with me about key aspects of my argument. Haruka and Gene also provided feedback on chapter drafts that clarified and enriched my thinking and encouraged me greatly. My research assistants Claire Lindstadt and Sasha Eros discovered and analyzed countless sources and shared vital perspectives on the meaning of flourishing. Sasha also read and offered invaluable

Acknowledgments xvii

feedback on the entire manuscript. Thank you all for your gifts of time and perspective. Thanks go also to the baristas at 7Leaves and Cocola in San Jose, who unknowingly accompanied me and provided much-needed coffee and pastries throughout the writing process.

Thanks, too, to Robert Ellsberg and the team at Orbis Books for believing in this project. Your flexibility, encouragement, and openness to my vision made this work possible. Special thanks to my editor, Thomas Hermans-Webster, for talking through my argument, providing perceptive editorial suggestions, and holding me in prayer amid the challenges of writing.

For the last eight years, three people have constituted my core writing community. They offered exceptional support to me while I worked on this manuscript, as well. First is my longtime mentor and friend Terrence Tilley. With characteristic candor and good humor, Terry provided critical feedback that sharpened my logic and clarified my main claims. Thank you, Terry, for believing in this project—and in me. Second is my dear friend and colleague Jessica Coblentz, whose editorial brilliance helped me reimagine key parts of this book, opened my imagination to new ways of framing the story of flourishing I've tried to tell, and encouraged me to keep on writing when I wasn't sure I could go on. Thank you, Jess, for your incomparable insight and unflagging support. It's my honor to be your colleague and friend. Third is my inimitable Doktormutter and friend Elizabeth Johnson. I'll never forget the genuine interest and excitement Beth showed when I proposed the idea of writing a theology of flourishing a few years ago. That excitement remained a source of inspiration as I completed this work. Beth also provided incisive feedback on the manuscript and reminded me that sometimes we just have to step back, take a breath, and *rewrite*. On top of all this, she generously contributed a foreword to this book. Having a mentor like Beth, who listens and shares wisdom with a spirit of generosity and really believes in her students' potential, is, like Wisdom *xviii*   *A Theology of Flourishing*

herself, more precious than gold. Thank you, Beth, for believing in me and showing me what it means to be a theologian.

Finally, I wouldn't know what love or flourishing means without my dear family, especially my parents and brother. Since my childhood, your love has shown me what it means to have faith in a God who is love and who calls us to love others. Thank you for always being there for me and letting me flourish (even when I was really annoying). And to my beloved Nikko, whose creative brilliance helped to shape key parts of this book, thank you for making space for me to write. When I didn't think I could do it, you told me to lock myself away and keep working. When anxiety and innumerable distractions tried to keep me from writing, you stood by, abounding in patience, and urged me on. Thank you for everything. I couldn't have done this without you.

Above all, I thank God for walking with me, guiding me, and keeping me safe throughout my life. This book is an expression of my faith in you, the love who made all things, holds all things in being, and intends all things to flourish. Thank you for giving me the gift and the joy of life in your presence.

Introduction

Why We Need a Theology of Flourishing

*The thief comes only to steal and kill and destroy. I came
that they may have life and have it abundantly.*

—JOHN 10:10

This fall, while leading a workshop on Ignatian pedagogy at
the university where I serve, I was asked what gives me joy as a
teacher and scholar. After thinking for a moment, I responded
that what brings me joy is seeing students—and colleagues—
come alive in community as we engage new ideas and imagine
together what the world can be. This question remained on my
mind and in my heart as the day went on. By evening, I found
myself connecting my work as a teacher and scholar to a commitment I've held for as long as I can remember, a commitment I
likely learned from the love I experienced, even amid significant
hardship, throughout my life: God really is *love*, and, as love, God
creates a world in which all creatures are made to flourish in the
fullness of life, each according to its own kind.

As I reflected, I kept returning to the years I served as director
of worship at St. Mary Catholic Church in Evansville, Indiana.
When I started work there, I was only twenty-four years old—

xix

xx *A Theology of Flourishing*

fresh off two years teaching at Crazy Horse High School on Pine Ridge Indian Reservation. My time living and working on the reservation, amid a community experiencing what was, for me, unimaginable poverty and oppression, sharpened my understanding of justice and showed me what authentic community looks like—what it means to show up for others and seek solutions to complex socio-ecological problems. I was pleased to find similar commitments at St. Mary.

The parish ran a huge array of justice and outreach ministries: an on-site food pantry, a cutting-edge program for LGBTQ+ Catholics, Saturday soup kitchens, interfaith prayer services, community-organizing initiatives, and more. But what I experienced there went deeper. Sunday after Sunday I saw something I'd never witnessed in all my years as a Catholic—and probably never will again. I saw a diverse group of people *come alive* in a collective encounter with the living God. To quote the church's liturgical tradition, I saw "people of every race, language, and way of life" experiencing self-actualization in relationship with God and others—I saw them *flourish*.[1] Even more, I saw people discerning, as I also discerned, who God intended them to be. And out of this encounter I saw the members of our community, individually and collectively, become radically attuned to the needs of the world, discovering what it meant for them to seek justice and foster the flourishing of others. I never expected St. Mary to be the kind of community it was. At twenty-four, I just thought I was taking a job. But the love and joy I experienced in union with God and others in a small parish in a small city in southern Indiana changed me in ways I still cannot articulate.

Linking this experience to my present vocation, I realized in a way I had not before that my desire to make my classrooms

---

[1] "Eucharistic Prayer for Masses of Reconciliation II," 1975 *Sacramentary for Mass*. Although this text has been retranslated and revised, this form of the text was in use when I served at St. Mary.

Why We Need a Theology of Flourishing xxi

(and even meetings!) spaces of joy and life, where people are free to be the beloved persons they are, speaking from their experience, naming injustices, giving voice to too-often unspoken hopes about what the world can be, is my way of expressing what I've always believed Christianity to be about: a faith that fosters the self-actualization of persons and communities in relationship with God and each other and opens people up to new ways of seeking justice and serving the needs of all. Christianity is, indeed, a faith that fosters the fullness of life for all creation.

But what does it mean to live? Or better, what does it mean to experience the fullness of life—in a word, to *flourish*? Within the intertwined traditions of Christian theology, spirituality, and praxis, the answer to this question rests on the foundation of relationship with Christ, or "life in Christ" (Gal 2:20). Yet traditionally, fullness of life in Christ typically has been understood in terms of heavenly salvation beyond earthly existence—an afterlife. When linked to the idea that creation is fallen, *dis*-graced, understanding fullness of life only in terms of heavenly fulfillment leads naturally to the idea that salvation is about righting a wrong, paying a debt, or overcoming the sinful conditions of earthly existence to achieve a kind of union with God that is not possible in this world.[2] Riffing on Gerard Manley Hopkins' poem "God's Grandeur," we might even ask if the fullness of life is imaginable in a world "seared with trade; bleared, smeared with toil"; a world with soil barren from centuries of human trampling, and in which humans trample upon each other; a world in which human hearts are often "shod" by indifference, numbed to the suffering of other humans and the whole creation. Perhaps we humans hope for heavenly salvation because we often live

---

[2] For a detailed treatment of models of salvation in relationship to creation, see Elizabeth A. Johnson, *Creation and the Cross: The Mercy of God for a Planet in Peril* (Maryknoll, NY: Orbis Books, 2018).

xxii *A Theology of Flourishing*

in comfortable denial of the fact that most of the problems that plague life in our world are of our own making.

At the same time, generations of liberation and feminist theologians have pointed out that the material conditions of creaturely life—embodiment, finitude, suffering, sociality—provide crucial context for understanding the meaning of salvation in a way that integrates the fullness of life in this world with hope for eschatological union with God.[3] Such integration necessarily entails naming and denouncing oppression, violence, marginalization, ecological degradation, and all forms of sin—personal and social—as contradictory to the proclamation of a God who created all things and desires their fulfillment. For only by taking seriously the suffering, violence, and degradation that so often characterize creaturely life can Christians come to authentic hope that moves us to action for the justice, peace, and liberation that make flourishing possible.

Yet, even in majority-Christian contexts, these conditions hardly ever exist in a fully realized way. Only rarely, it seems, do Christians feel motivated by their faith to radical action, to practices of revolutionary love, on behalf of God's life-giving intentions for all creation. In light of the perdurance of social injustice and ecological degradation today, Christian theologians must reflect anew on the concrete impacts of traditional models of creation and salvation. We must take another look at the

---

[3] Gustavo Gutiérrez offers an illustrative early statement: "From this point of view the notion of salvation appears in a different light. Salvation is not something otherworldly, in regard to which the present life is merely a test. Salvation . . . is something which embraces all human reality, transforms it, and leads it to its fullness in Christ. . . . Insofar as it constitutes a break with God, sin is a historical reality. . . . And because sin is a personal and social intrahistorical reality . . . it is also, and above all, an obstacle to life's reaching the fullness we call salvation." Gustavo Gutiérrez, *A Theology of Liberation: History, Politics, and Salvation,* rev. ed., trans. Sister Caridad Inda and John Eagleson (Maryknoll, NY: Orbis Books, 1988), 85.

Why We Need a Theology of Flourishing   *xxiii*

central claim of our tradition, that is, that Jesus Christ took flesh and entered the created order to "save."

How do theologies that view creation as corrupted by sin and soteriologies that cast salvation primarily in terms of heavenly union with God apart from material reality relate to the ever-present reality of indifference to injustice and worldly misery? Put another way, is the promise of salvation in an otherworldly heaven *sufficient* to make Christians agents of love and justice in this world on the model of Jesus himself? Or does this model of Christ's saving work incline Christians to see creation as merely a means to an end—or a holding cell we occupy while awaiting release to something better? Further, if Christ's proclamation is not just about heavenly salvation, what does the promise of abundant life mean for the here and now, as all creation moves toward God within the conditions of finite, material, embodied existence? In light of the suffering, injustice, and degradation that plague our world, we discover in these questions an urgent need to retell the story of creation and salvation once more, to discern and actualize God's life-giving intentions for creation—intentions that are revealed in creation itself, in the Word made flesh, and in the Spirit's stirrings in human hearts and, indeed, in all things.

This book wagers that taking flourishing as the starting point and center of gravity for Christian theology and praxis has the potential to orient Christians to experience creation and everything therein as made for abundant life and to act in faith on behalf of the flourishing of all things. As *an embodied process of self-actualization whereby creatures come to live in the fullness of what they are in relationship with God and other creatures,* flourishing summarizes God's basic intention for creation. Making flourishing the starting point for theological discourse will guide Christians toward a shared vision of what the world can be if, in faith and action, we embrace from the very first moment God's primary intention for creation: that all creatures may flourish in the

xxiv   *A Theology of Flourishing*

fullness of life.[4] It is my deep hope that such a theology—a theology of flourishing—will foster positive perspectives on materiality, embodiment, and the cosmos as a whole, leading Christians to recognize that God loves all things in their beloved particularity. Further, inspired by the Spirit's work of renewing all things and drawing them to fulfillment in relationships of justice and peace, a theology of flourishing aims to lead Christians to perceive all instantiations of injustice and degradation as contradictions to God's life-giving will. This theology grounds a stance of protest and a praxis of love that cultivates material conditions that do not "quench the spirit" (1 Thess 5:19) but enable the realization of the Spirit's aims within the concrete conditions of creaturely life.

In this way, too, a theology of flourishing has the potential to avoid spiritualizing the idea of salvation, thus enabling indifference toward suffering. Instead, a theology of flourishing challenges Christians to attune ourselves to suffering and to enter more deeply into the cares of the world, recognizing the intrinsic connection between the cry of the earth and the cry of the poor and integrating action for social and ecological justice into a holistic socio-ecological paradigm.[5] All in all, I humbly hope that setting flourishing at the center of theology—making God's life-giving intentions the point of departure and center of gravity for theological reflection—will guide us toward a more faithful rendering of the meaning of creation, sin, and salvation, wherein creation is seen as richly blessed, not fallen, and sin is seen as a contradiction to the fullness of life for which all things are made, the essence of salvation. All this testifies to a need for flourishing to stand as a theological category in its own right, a

---

[4] This use of the term *self-actualization* must not be confused with the Enlightenment notion of a "self-made man" (gendered language intentional), a radical individual. Throughout this text I use *self-actualization* to describe the process of prayer and discernment by which a creature becomes fully alive as that which God intends it be.

[5] See Pope Francis, *Laudato Si'*, no. 35.

Why We Need a Theology of Flourishing xxv

basis for retelling the Christian story from creation to salvation with God's life-giving will in our hearts and minds.

John 10:10—which Patricia Santos describes as "the biblical foundation of the vision of flourishing," Pablo Richard names a summary statement of "the basic actual divine will," and Ignacio Ellacuría dubs "the fundamental principle on which to base the new order"—provides the grounding vision for the theology of flourishing I propose.[6] In this passage, an excerpt from John's parable of the shepherd and the gate, Jesus states, "The thief comes only to kill and steal and destroy. I have come that they may have life and have it abundantly." Commenting on this passage Celia Deane-Drummond and Barbara Rossing note that the Greek *perisson*, translated "abundantly," evokes a sense of aliveness that overflows and spreads out.[7] Reading this verse in its narrative context, Craig Koester observes that to pass through the gate is to enter into a multilateral relationship with God and others that is characterized by abundant life.[8] Abundant life is, then, not so much attained as it is experienced and shared so that all may partake of the fullness for which they are created.

Although the promise of abundant life typically receives the lion's share of attention, the verse's contrasting image of the thief also raises crucial questions for theology: to what extent do theologies, ecclesial teachings, and the structures in which the church subsists form people to be "thieves"—agents of death,

---

[6] Patricia H. Santos, "That All May Enjoy Abundant Life: A Theological Vision of Flourishing from the Margins," *Feminist Theology* 25, no. 3 (2017): 235; Pablo Richard, "Theology in the Theology of Liberation," in *Mysterium Liberationis: Fundamental Concepts of Liberation Theology*, ed. Ignacio Ellacuría and Jon Sobrino (Maryknoll, NY: Orbis Books, 1993), 164; Ignacio Ellacuría, "Utopia and Prophecy in Latin America," in Ellacuría and Sobrino, *Mysterium Liberationis*, 306.

[7] Celia Deane-Drummond and Barbara Rossing, "The Eco-Theological Significance of John 10:10," *The Ecumenical Review* 65, no. 1 (Mar 2013): 85.

[8] Craig R. Koester, *The Word of Life: A Theology of John's Gospel* (Grand Rapids, MI: Eerdmans, 2008), 56.

theft, and destruction, rather than life? A theology of flourishing must maintain constant awareness of this negative possibility, denouncing forces that kill, steal, and destroy and announcing God's reign of life through a radical praxis of love on behalf of the fullness of life for all creatures, human and otherwise.

Taking John 10:10 as a grounding principle, this book contends that flourishing stands at the very heart of the Christian proclamation. Perhaps more boldly, this book argues that a careful retrieval of the doctrine of creation and a *ressourcement* of the theme of flourishing throughout the tradition suggest that flourishing is in fact constituent of a proper understanding of salvation, providing a foretaste of the fulfillment for which we humans hope and a basis for standing in solidarity with all creation in the here and now. Seen in this light, creatures are not so much saved *from* this world as we are saved *in*, *with*, and *through* it. For if God creates all things to flourish, and if Christ reveals the fulfillment of that intention, which continues to be realized through the Spirit's work among us, then hope for heavenly salvation must be understood in concert with, and never apart from, fullness of life in this world. Here, Christ's proclamation of abundant life takes on even deeper significance, revealing "something new, something fuller, something more life-giving" in line with the divine will of flourishing that is discernible, if not always recognized, in creation itself.[9] Guided by this vision, this book aims to chase the precious thread of flourishing through the tapestry of the Christian tradition, shedding light on an often-unrecognized strand of creation theology and soteriology that has significant implications for other aspects of Christian theology, spirituality, and praxis. In doing so, it aims to inspire Christians to live ever more fully as agents of abundant

---

[9] William R. Stoeger, "Our Experience of Knowing in Science and in Spirituality," in *The Laws of Nature, the Range of Human Knowledge, and Divine Action* (Tarnow, Poland: Biblos, 1996), 17.

Why We Need a Theology of Flourishing xxvii

life, protesting injustice and degradation and acting on behalf of the fullness of life for every member of the "splendid universal communion" God has made (*Laudato Si'*, no. 220).

Mapping the Road Ahead

The road ahead pursues the precious thread of flourishing from its hidden place in the tapestry of scripture and tradition on the way toward proposing a theology of flourishing in its own right. I have structured the book in three parts. The two chapters in Part I, "Foundations," establish theological and methodological foundations for the proposed theology of flourishing. Part II, "Explorations," traces the thread of flourishing through scripture and history. Within this section the third chapter considers the relationship among creation, life, and flourishing in the Hebrew Bible, while the fourth chapter contemplates the connection between creation, embodiment, and love in the New Testament. The fifth and sixth chapters undertake a *ressourcement* of key early Christian and medieval thinkers. These explorations emphasize the connection among creation, incarnation, deification, and the fullness of life in often-unconsidered sources of the Christian tradition. This historical study culminates in the seventh chapter, which uses the writings of Karl Rahner, Johann Baptist Metz, and Ignacio Ellacuría to bring the foregoing study of flourishing into the present.

In dialogue with contemporary thinkers utilizing a wide array of theological methods, Part III, "Integrations," proposes a theology of flourishing in its own right. The eighth chapter expounds the theology of flourishing toward which this book aims, and the ninth chapter proposes a framework of dialogue, discernment, and decision that actualizes the proposed theology in human life. The book concludes by proposing principles for a praxis of flourishing that fosters the fullness of life for all creation and applies these principles to four questions of contemporary concern.

Part I

FOUNDATIONS

Approaching a Theology of Flourishing

1

Two Seeds for a
Theology of Flourishing

In *Feminism and Ecological Communities: An Ethic of Flourishing*, Chris Cuomo observes that, although feminist theology and ethics are characterized by a commitment "to the flourishing, or well-being, of individuals, species, and communities," there remains an "absence of explicit discussions of flourishing."[1] Despite this absence, two ecofeminist thinkers—Quaker philosopher Grace Jantzen and Roman Catholic theologian Elizabeth Johnson—provide vital foundations for thinking about the significance of flourishing as a model of salvation and articulating how creation functions as a grounding symbol for a theology of flourishing. In dialogue with these thinkers, this chapter elucidates the fundamental commitments that ground the proposed theology of flourishing. After laying out these commitments, the chapter concludes by articulating the basic understanding of flourishing that will guide us on the road ahead.

---

[1] Chris J. Cuomo, *Feminism and Ecological Communities: An Ethic of Flourishing* (New York: Routledge, 1998), 62.

3

A Seed Is Planted:
Grace Jantzen's Ecofeminist Philosophy

Consistent with Cuomo's diagnosis of an unrealized need for explicit discussions of flourishing in theology, Patricia Santos observes that Jantzen's writings on flourishing remain "at the level of analysis and critique."[2] They reflect on flourishing's potential to address important theological and philosophical problems but rarely offer fully realized theological conclusions. Even so, Jantzen's observation that "it could be shown that 'flourishing' is the unacknowledged foundation of 'salvation' in the western theological 'text,'" establishes the basic trajectory that this book will follow.[3]

For Jantzen, flourishing is something of a suppressed "other" or contrapuntal corollary to salvation that, under different circumstances, might have occupied the heart of Christian theology, and in particular soteriology. Indeed, as Jantzen notes, while heavenly salvation and this-worldly flourishing are both valid metaphors for understanding Christ's redemptive work, flourishing receded to the margins of the Christian imagination as Christianity spoke increasingly of Christ's life, death, and resurrection as a divine response to the reality of sin. In flourishing's place stood a view of the world in which "the human condition must be conceptualized as a problematic state, a state in which human beings need urgent rescue, or calamity will befall. The human situation is a negative one, out of which we need to be delivered."[4] Correlatively, the calamitous

---

[2] Patricia H. Santos, "That All May Enjoy Abundant Life: A Theological Vision of Flourishing from the Margins," *Feminist Theology* 25, no. 3 (2017): 234.

[3] Grace M. Jantzen, *Becoming Divine: Towards a Feminist Philosophy of Religion* (Bloomington: Indiana University Press, 1999), 157.

[4] Jantzen, 161.

Two Seeds for a Theology of Flourishing

character of the human condition came to extend to creation as a whole: creation is fallen, a place of lack, where sin rather than grace abounds, and where salvation is needed to correct what sin—now an abstract force in competition with grace—has destroyed. As Jantzen concludes, in this history, heavenly salvation came to be taken as the literal meaning of redemption; flourishing fell away.

In Jantzen's analysis, this development also manifests a dominant aspect of the Western cultural imaginary: a "preoccupation with death" that she names "necrophilia."[5] A necrophilic imaginary corresponds well with a vision of humanity and creation as fallen and in need of salvation from the outside, in direct correspondence with the marginalization of flourishing in Christian thought and praxis. Within such a paradigm, Christ delivers humans *from* the conditions of finitude, mortality, and sin—from the world—through an assertion of power over death. To say that Christ saves is, then, to say that Christ provides an escape from the inevitable end of creaturely life. As Jantzen explains, the choice of personal salvation over a more holistic model of flourishing thus "reflects and reinforces the necrophilic imaginary and its obsession with domination, mastery, and escape."[6] In practice, this obsession conditions Christians to stand *against* world and flesh, inured to the oppression and violence wrought by a patriarchal, white supremacist, ableist, extractivist status quo.

Recognizing the political implications of the necrophilic logics that inform many traditional soteriologies need not devolve into a wholesale rejection of the idea of salvation as rescue from sin. Flourishing is, after all, a form of salvation. The world needs to be saved from indifference and injustice, and Christ's death

---

[5] Jantzen, 161.
[6] Jantzen, 157.

6 *A Theology of Flourishing*

and resurrection chart a path toward victory over these forces of death. Still, Jantzen invites us to consider alternative possibilities: What if theology started with flourishing instead? What if, instead of seeing Christ's "victory" as heavenly triumph over a fallen creation, we saw this "victory" as a starting point for confronting forces of death and working on behalf of God's reign in this world? For if forgoing a sole focus on heaven and developing a theology of flourishing "would lead to quite a different account of the human condition and our relation to one another and to God," as Jantzen suggests, we must ask what might happen if Christians came to see redemption as entailing a responsibility for fostering the fullness of life now, taking Christ's proclamation of life as constitutive of salvation.[7]

From Necrophilia to Natality, Death to Birth

In a preliminary response to questions like these, Jantzen offers "natality," the condition of being *born*, as an antidote to necrophilia and its inherent orientation toward death. She asks, "How if we were to treat natality and the emergence of *this* life and *this* world with the same philosophical seriousness and respect which had traditionally been paid to mortality and the striving for other worlds?"[8] Jantzen suggests that beginning with birth, with our entry into materiality, would reorient human energies away from "a futile struggle against finitude" and liberate us to "rejoice in the (limited) life we have as natals and act for the love of the world."[9] Living *from* our birth, not *unto* death, intrinsically orients humans toward an appreciation of materiality. Creation then appears as a graced place of love, wherein Christianity may foster what Jantzen—riffing on Hannah Arendt—terms *amor*

---

[7] Jantzen, 86.
[8] Jantzen, 2.
[9] Jantzen, 155.

Two Seeds for a Theology of Flourishing

mundi, love of the world.[10] Practically, shifting from necrophilia to natality also sets into motion other important shifts in understanding. For example, placing birth and flourishing at the forefront of the Christian imagination allows us to imagine "the divine [as] a goal of human endeavor, that against which human thought and conduct must be measured."[11] Put differently, making flourishing the foundation for human life conditions Christians to see God as the source and term of life, rendering human existence a graced process of becoming toward God through the world's mediation of God's presence and action. In this approach salvation becomes something that happens here in this world just as much as in a heavenly afterlife. And the self-actualization of creatures in this world, never apart from it, provides the surest sign of the fulfillment of God's intentions for creation. Describing the anthropological and theological implications of this turn toward flourishing, Jantzen writes:

> We could then see human beings as having natural inner capacity and dynamic, being able to draw on inner resources and interconnection with one another in the web of life, and having the potential to develop into great fruitfulness. Whereas with the metaphor of salvation God is seen as the Saviour who intervenes from outside the calamitous situation to bring about a rescue, the metaphor of flourishing would lead instead to an idea of the divine source and ground, an imminent [*sic*] divine incarnated within us and between us. . . . An imaginary of natality therefore suggests a symbolic of flourishing, of growth and fruition from an inner creative and healthy dynamic, rather than a theology which begins from the premise that the human condition

---

[10] Jantzen, 116. Arendt writes, "*Amo: Volo ut sis*—I love you: I will that you be." Hannah Arendt, *The Life of the Mind: Thinking and Willing*, vol. 2 (New York: Harcourt Brace Jovanovitch, 1978), 136.

[11] Jantzen, *Becoming Divine*, 12.

is a negative condition or crisis from which we must be rescued by an external saviour.[12]

Jantzen's analysis also raises the question of praxis: practically speaking, what manner of Christian life is produced by the respective logics of necrophilia and natality? As Jantzen sees it, "A symbolic of flourishing lends itself readily to a social and cultural order of justice and protest; while a symbolic of salvation easily becomes introverted and depoliticized—which of course means that it supports the status quo."[13] In other words, while traditional soteriologies make it possible for a person to "be saved" while remaining insulated from injustice and suffering,

> since flourishing involves the physical and communal realities of a person's life . . . a theology of flourishing could not content itself with looking piously to an afterlife where present injustices will be abolished, while doing nothing in the struggle for their abolition here and now. For this reason a symbolic of flourishing would not be able to avoid confrontation with issues of domination, whether in terms of poverty, class, race, sex, or any other form of injustice: since these are the things which prevent people and communities from flourishing.[14]

Jantzen's analysis of flourishing calls Christian theology and praxis to account for their complicity in and explicit perpetration of historical and contemporary violence and injustice. Yet more

---

[12] Jantzen, 161–62. Compare the theological development of these points in Grace Jantzen, "Feminism and Flourishing: Gender and Metaphor in Feminist Theology," *Feminist Theology* 4, no. 10 (September 1995): 81–101. This text predates *Becoming Divine* but contains a significant amount of text that appears in the monograph, rendered in more theological terms.

[13] Jantzen, *Becoming Divine*, 166.

[14] Jantzen, 169.

Two Seeds for a Theology of Flourishing 9

important, she embeds such complicity in the soteriological bedrock of the Christian tradition. Perhaps the greatest reason we need a theology of flourishing arises, then, from the fact that for generations Christian theology has spoken of personal salvation from sin and heavenly union with God while also perpetrating injustice, violence, and oppression—often in ways authorized by Christian institutions. Elaborating on this point, Jantzen asks how it is possible that the same people who colonized and destroyed lands and peoples, enslaved and exterminated people of other races and ethnicities, oppressed women, remained indifferent to dehumanizing hunger and poverty, and so forth, claimed also to be morally upstanding citizens in their societies, untroubled by the pain, death, and destruction they caused. Connecting the various facets of her analysis, she answers that because the symbolic system of the West is rooted in violence and domination, it tacitly expresses and reinforces the logic of necrophilia even while proclaiming victory over death.[15] This system includes Christianity and its understandings of salvation.

In contrast, a theology of flourishing activates a sense of responsibility for the well-being of creation in view of the realities of systemic and individual injustice and oppression. In so doing, a theology that begins from flourishing activates the Christian tradition to serve as a mechanism for social transformation, abolishing unjust structures and fostering "a standpoint arising out of a chosen solidarity" that cultivates the fullness of life for all.[16] This perspective, Jantzen reflects, elicits a "priority of the ethical over the ontological" that demands accountability "in the first instance to women's lives but ultimately to the pursuit of justice for all people and for the earth."[17] A concluding statement draws the threads of the foregoing analysis together in ways that express

---

[15] Jantzen, 234.
[16] Jantzen, 212.
[17] Jantzen, 212.

10 *A Theology of Flourishing*

the vision for which a theology of flourishing rooted in the life and love of Christ strives:

> The model of flourishing is one which assumes the interconnectedness of people, and indeed of the ecosystem: flourishing is impossible by oneself alone. It is not only the individual species but a whole rain forest which can be described as flourishing. Moreover, that flourishing is not once-for-all, but is growth and process, never static. The model of flourishing is therefore a model of *amor mundi*, love of the world and care for all within it, to set over against the competitive individualism reinforced by the model of personal salvation while the rest of the world goes up in flames.[18]

Seedlings Sprout:
The Symbol of Creation *Functions*

Jantzen's discussions of necrophilia, natality, salvation, and flourishing provide fertile ground for cultivating a theology of flourishing. Yet her work only gestures toward theology, remaining largely in the arena of philosophical critique. Thus, although she raises questions with theological implications, thinking about flourishing as the fullness of life in Christ requires deep consideration of flourishing as a theological category in its own right, in relationship to a broad range of theological loci, including creation, Christ, God, church, and anthropology.

Elizabeth Johnson's analysis of how theological symbols function complements Jantzen's thought and offers further resources for developing a theology of flourishing. In a well-known passage on the "symbol of God," Johnson writes:

---

[18] Jantzen, 165.

Two Seeds for a Theology of Flourishing

11

Speech about God shapes the life orientation not only of the corporate faith community but in this matrix guides its individual members as well. . . . As the focus of absolute trust, one to whom you can give yourself without fear of betrayal, the holy mystery of God undergirds and implicitly gives direction to all of a believing person's enterprises, principles, choices, system of values, and relationships. The symbol of God functions.[19]

By centering attention on the "symbol of God," or how we conceptualize and articulate who God is, Johnson reminds theologians and all Christians that our concepts, images, and categories will never attain to the essence of God. Attempting to capture the mystery of God in words is like trying to use a single candle to illuminate the whole universe. This reminder necessitates ongoing reflection on the symbols of Christian faith.

Further, like Jantzen's treatment of the interlocking relationships of salvation, escapism, capitalism, and patriarchy, Johnson inscribes as a hermeneutical principle that the adequacy of a theological symbol depends on its faithfulness to the sources of Christian faith and its material impacts.[20] In a theology of flourishing, the adequacy of a theological symbol is measured by how it *functions* with respect to Christ's proclamation of abundant

---

[19] Elizabeth Johnson, *She Who Is: The Mystery of God in Feminist Theological Discourse* (New York: Crossroad, 1991), 4.

[20] In *She Who Is*, Johnson's analysis of material impacts focuses on the correspondence between the exclusive use of masculine language for God and the oppression of women. Other theologians offer analogous analyses of theological symbols, considering the correspondence of the crucifixion of Christ and the experience of being Black in the United States, the link between stories of humanity's creation in Genesis and the experience of LGBTQ+ persons, the trajectory from theologies of creation that grant humans special status to anthropogenic ecological degradation, and so on. I will engage these developments in Chapter 8.

life. When a symbol kills, steals, or destroys—when it obstructs a creature's ability to live fully in relationship with God and other creatures—we must reconsider its adequacy, recognizing with Johnson that, in light of the incarnation, "it is impossible, or if not impossible at least incorrect and even blasphemous, to speak about God's stance as other than a passion for human and cosmic flourishing."[21] As Johnson suggests, all of this has to do with our ability to discern God's intentions for creation.

Indeed, because the symbol of creation "encompasses the manifold of humanity, earth, and God in a comprehensive vision," as Norman Wirzba observes, it grounds the entire Christian imaginary.[22] The symbol of creation establishes the basic trajectory for how Christians understand God's relationship to material reality and God's intentions for the world. The symbol of creation *functions*. Thus, as a theological symbol, creation orients theology toward certain emphases and away from others, such that we can see the symbol of creation operating beneath the surface of Jantzen's discussion of salvation and flourishing. For indeed, traditional ideas of salvation as escape from finitude and the confines of a fallen material order are predicated on a particular way of seeing creation. We choose to prioritize salvation over flourishing in part because we believe we inhabit a realm from which our only hope is escape rather than deeper entry: hopeful, loving embrace; acceptance; the work of resistance that brings about an end to injustice and heralds the reign of God. Thus, the symbol of creation provides a basis for understanding God's intentions in view of Christ's promise of abundant life. What we say about creation establishes a context and trajectory for theology as a whole.

---

[21] Elizabeth Johnson, *Consider Jesus: Waves of Renewal in Christology* (New York: Crossroad, 1990), 168.

[22] Norman Wirzba, *The Paradise of God: Renewing Religion in an Ecological Age* (Oxford: Oxford University Press, 2007), 13.

Two Seeds for a Theology of Flourishing

Losing Creation, Reimagining Creation

Despite the symbol of creation's potential to recenter Christian theology and praxis on flourishing, we must acknowledge that in most cases the doctrine of creation lingers at the margins of theological discourse despite the important contributions of ecological theologians. One can imagine many reasons why this is the case. Perhaps creation remains marginal because attention to creation as an object of concern unwittingly truncates its significance as a grounding doctrine of Christian faith. As Daniel Horan suggests, "The result [of creation's displacement as a theological locus] has been a post factum effort to address the symptoms of climate change and environmental degradation without substantively asking whether the way we articulate our doctrinal commitments is sufficient in the first place or if they are in need of reexamination."[23] If this is the case, then giving priority to heavenly salvation reifies the sense that the cosmos is a sort of scrim against which the drama of sin and grace unfolds, reinforcing the view that Christianity is a religion of individual salvation beyond this world, not flourishing within it. As Paul Santmire puts it, within such a paradigm, creation operates as a means to "being-beyond-the-earth," wherein "the ascent to the heights may in fact represent an attempt to separate oneself from the earth, in order to enter into a totally landless ethereal glory."[24] When yoked to a

---

[23] Daniel P. Horan, OFM, *All God's Creatures: A Theology of Creation* (Lanham, MD: Lexington Books/Fortress Academic, 2018), xi.

[24] H. Paul Santmire, *The Travail of Nature: The Ambiguous Ecological Promise of Christian Theology* (Minneapolis: Fortress Press, 1985), 25. Wirzba writes that the idea that bodies are something to be left behind "has been a disaster for Christian traditions, because it has so often led to a private faith and an abstract love that has little purpose beyond the transport of individual disembodied souls to a distant heaven." Norman Wirzba, *From Nature to Creation: A Christian Vision for Understanding and Loving Our World* (Grand Rapids, MI: Baker Academic, 2015), 21.

14   *A Theology of Flourishing*

paradigm of hierarchical dualism that places "soul over body, man over woman, and God over the world," the "trivialization of nature" thus becomes embedded in the status quo of the Christian imagination, relegating creation to the background according to the masculine principle that places humans over the earth, mind over matter, and so on.[25] Theology is left to proceed without thinking too much about the meaning and significance of one of its primary doctrines.

Adding to the issue, when creation does receive attention as more than an object of concern, it is often associated only with the question of cosmic origins as they are understood by the sciences, typically in conjunction with discussions of the relationship between science and religion.[26] While these are important matters, reducing the doctrine of creation to questions of origins

---

[25] On hierarchical dualism, see Elizabeth A. Johnson, *Women, Earth, and Creator Spirit* (New York: Paulist Press, 1993), 17–20. For Johnson's fuller treatment of how theology has rendered creation a backdrop for human salvation, see Elizabeth A. Johnson, "Turn to the Heavens and the Earth: Retrieval of the Cosmos in Theology," *Proceedings of the Catholic Theological Society of America* 51 (1996): 1–14.

[26] Despite my great interest in the topic, to maintain focus on flourishing this book intentionally sidesteps philosophical questions about the meaning of creation in the sciences and theology, including the ever-important discussion of the relationship between *creatio ex nihilo* and *creatio continua*. For one outstanding theological treatment of this question, see Brian Robinette, *The Difference Nothing Makes: Creation, Christ, Contemplation* (Notre Dame, IN: University of Notre Dame Press, 2023). The theological writings of William Stoeger also offer important contributions to this conversation. See, for example, William R. Stoeger, "Describing God's Action in the World in Light of Scientific Knowledge of Reality," in *Chaos and Complexity: Scientific Perspectives on Divine Action*, ed. Robert John Russell, Nancey Murphy, and Arthur R. Peacocke (Vatican Observatory and Berkeley: Center for Theology and Natural Sciences, 1995), 239–62; and "Conceiving Divine Action in a Dynamic Universe," in *Scientific Perspectives on Divine Action: Twenty Years of Challenge and Progress*, ed. Robert John Russell, Nancey Murphy, and William R. Stoeger (Notre Dame, IN: University of Notre Dame Press, 2008), 225–47.

Two Seeds for a Theology of Flourishing   15

further truncates its critical potential, rendering it an answer to a specific question rather than a comprehensive context for theology as a whole. Wirzba explains:

> While talk about the origination of the universe is itself important . . . the beginning is really a prelude to the more practically significant talk of determining the order of creation as a whole and seeing in that ordering the placement of humans within the creation before God. In other words, the teaching of creation, besides being a teaching of how the world began, is about the characterization of human identity and vocation within the world. In it we see who we are and what we are to become. A developed account of creation will thus invariably alert us to the value and character of what is and, in doing so, inform us about the nature of our interdependence with the creator and the creation and our responsibility for this interdependence.[27]

Linking the concerns I have raised about perceiving creation as a backdrop for human salvation with the reduction of creation to questions of origins reveals how theological history has gradually and probably unwittingly truncated the positive meaning of the doctrine in direct parallel with the emergence of heavenly salvation as the normative metaphor for redemption in Christ. This conclusion seems especially clear when creation, as a faith-based account of cosmic origins, functions in ecclesial discourse as a prelude to "the fall." Such a rendering produces the view that, while things were made good—they were good "once upon a time"—they are no longer so. Creation comes to be defined in contradistinction to a now-fallen

---

[27] Wirzba, *The Paradise of God*, 13.

world; that was then, this is now. This development further marginalizes creation as a theological category, as the original graced order serves only as a prelude to the present drama, and new life for creation is projected beyond this world to a promised heavenly future. In other words, the glorification of creation in union with God is eclipsed by a vision of salvation apart from this world, reinforcing a soteriological imaginary that is far removed from concerns about the fullness of life in the here and now. Practically speaking, all this makes it easier to understand how Christians can feel assured of salvation while remaining complicit in systems that enable poverty, oppression, and ecological degradation. Enabled by the marginalization and impoverishment of the symbol of creation, salvation apart from this world seems predisposed toward indifference to the cares of the world.

In this context, just as Johnson reimagined the symbol of God in light of the ongoing hold of patriarchy and oppression of women, reimagining creation in light of the interlocking realities of social injustice and ecological degradation leads us to hear long-suppressed echoes that proclaim a God of life, who, in immeasurable love, created this world to flourish. Again, this is not to suggest that Christianity should stop talking about sin and salvation. Rather, reimagining and recentering creation resituates the idea of salvation vis-à-vis flourishing, such that sin and salvation cannot be conceived apart from the exigencies of finite, material reality. Guided by the witnesses of Jantzen, Johnson, and others, a theology of flourishing probes scripture and tradition anew, seeking glimmers of grace in a world too often called fallen, and deploys these resources in hope for a new world— what Johnson describes as "a more just social order within the wider struggle for life as a whole, for healthy ecosystems where all living creatures can flourish."[28]

---

[28] Johnson, "Turn to the Heavens and the Earth," 11.

A First Bud:
A Preliminary Understanding of Flourishing

As the foregoing analysis of Jantzen and Johnson shows, ecofeminist thinkers offer vital perspectives on flourishing that provide a foundation for a theology rooted in Christ's promise of abundant life. Because I envision flourishing as something that is discerned in relationship to God and creation in and through the concreteness of creaturely life, I must be careful to avoid over-defining flourishing. Still, it seems prudent to conclude this first chapter by sketching the understanding of flourishing that guides my exploration of scripture, theology, and praxis, and that grounds my constructive proposal of a theology of flourishing in its own right.

Jantzen proffers a helpful etymological starting point, associating flourishing with creation through the image of flowers in bloom:

> The word "flourish" is etymologically linked with flowers, with blossoming. It is related to the Middle English *florir* and the Latin *florere*, which mean "to flower." As a noun form, a "flourish" is the mass of flowers on a fruit tree, or the bloom of luxuriant, verdant growth. In the more common verb form, to flourish is to blossom, to thrive, to throw out leaves and shoots, growing vigorously and luxuriantly. In the human sphere it denotes abundance, overflowing with vigour and energy and productiveness, prosperity, success, and good health. The concept of flourishing is a strongly positive concept; one who flourishes is going from strength to strength.[29]

This etymological whirlwind tour corresponds well with existing theological reflections on the meaning of flourishing. In

---

[29] Jantzen, *Becoming Divine*, 159–60.

the absence of a singular definition of the term, I lift up these reflections as strokes in an impressionistic portrait of abundant life. Writing from the perspective of disability, Mary Grey describes flourishing as "true peace, food in plenty, celebration, bodily integrity—all within a context of renewed and restored relation. Something definitely to be celebrated as a this-worldly reality—not endlessly deferred to eternal bliss."[30] Reflecting on the experience of poor women of color, M. Shawn Copeland writes that "the various theologies for human liberation push us in self-giving love to work for [the realization of humanity] and its flourishing in disregarded subjects—exploited, despised poor women of color. Only in and through solidarity with them, the very least of this world, shall humanity come to fruition."[31] Linking flourishing directly to God's will—what I have described and will describe as God's intentions for creation—Johnson asks, "What is God's will? As revealed in Jesus, God's will is our well-being. God wants the wholeness, the healing, and the salvation of every creature and of all of us taken together. The reign of God, then, involves justice and peace among everyone, healing and wholeness everywhere, fullness of life enjoyed by all."[32]

Taken together, these authors offer valuable resources for reflecting on the meaning of flourishing in principle and in practice. Connecting salvation and creaturely self-actualization, flourishing is the first fruits of a just, peaceful, compassionate, and hospitable socio-ecological order that respects the integrity of every creature in its beloved particularity. Second, flourishing is relational, integrating self, society, community, and ecosystem into a holistic vision of abundance. Thus, in contrast to individualistic

---

[30] Mary Grey, "*Natality* and *Flourishing* in Contexts of Disability and Impairment," in *Grace Jantzen: Redeeming the Present,* ed. Elaine Graham, 197–211 (New York: Routledge, 2010), 199.

[31] M. Shawn Copeland, *Enfleshing Freedom: Body, Race, and Being* (Minneapolis: Fortress Press, 2010), 92.

[32] Johnson, *Consider Jesus*, 52.

Two Seeds for a Theology of Flourishing 19

notions of salvation, flourishing happens in community and demands solidarity. When one flourishes, all flourish; when one suffers, all suffer (cf. 1 Cor 12:26). Third, as Copeland suggests, flourishing is only authentic when it extends to the "disregarded subjects" of our world, human or otherwise. In practice, this means that a theology of flourishing is inherently ordered toward the abolition of systems and institutions that perpetuate injustice and oppression and oriented toward proclaiming a social, ecclesial, and ecological order guided by the intentions God has revealed and continues to reveal to us in Christ, in the Spirit, and in our flesh. In sum, flourishing is an embodied process of creaturely self-actualization that occurs when members of socio-ecological communities, in relationship with God and one another, are liberated to discern what it means to experience abundant life in their unique, embodied particularity and empowered to actualize this abundance on the way toward the eschatological union of all things with God and each other. Flourishing is also a practice. As creatures flourish, their glorious liveliness breaks out of itself, inspiring others to love all things in faithful cooperation with God's life-giving love on behalf of the fullness of life for all creation.

This chapter's engagement with Jantzen and Johnson established the fundamental commitments and basic trajectory that undergird my proposal of a theology of flourishing. Rooted in the vision of creaturely self-actualization in relationship with God and the world that this chapter articulated, the second chapter lays out the methodological and hermeneutical framework that guides my approach and situates this approach within the landscape of discussions of flourishing in and beyond theology.

2

Approaching a Theology
of Flourishing

Method and Context

Critically analyzing the doctrines of creation and salvation in view of both the perdurance of socio-ecological injustice and Christ's proclamation of abundant life, the first chapter proposed that a theology that takes *flourishing* as its starting point and center of gravity might attune Christian consciousness to God's life-giving intentions for creation and foster a praxis of revolutionary love that is oriented toward the fullness of life for all creation. But how might we approach the task of retelling the story of creation and salvation with flourishing in mind? What lens on tradition—or what set of interpretive principles—might guide such a project?

To chart a path toward such a *ressourcement*, this chapter presents the overall method that guides my proposal of a theology of flourishing and situates this proposal amid extant treatments of flourishing from a diverse range of disciplines. This methodological foundation establishes the hermeneutical lens that I apply to scripture and texts from the theological tradition as I trace the thread of flourishing through Christian history in the chapters

21

22   *A Theology of Flourishing*

to come, on the way toward the construction of a theology of flourishing in its own right.

The Method That Guides This Study: A Hermeneutics of the Fullness of Life

As the preceding chapter suggested, a theology of flourishing takes the self-actualization of creatures—their growth into the fullness of what God intends them to be—as the preeminent hermeneutical criterion for theological claims. This hermeneutical approach necessarily affords primacy to experience, as the conditions of creaturely life shape what it means for creatures to flourish in relationship to God and other creatures in their concrete socio-ecological contexts.

The theological writings of Jesuit astronomer and astrophysicist William Stoeger develop a similar view. Throughout his theological works, Stoeger associates the validity of theological claims, what he terms theological knowledge, with "the *life-giving character* living according to this knowledge manifests: 'By their fruits you shall know them.'"[1] Building on this principle in terms that evoke John 10:10, he writes:

> The basic criterion is always, "by their fruits you shall know them." This demands careful and ongoing elaboration. Invitations and experiences which are recognized to be life-giving, integrating, freeing, expansive and putting us into concrete, reverent contact with reality, not just immediately but over a period of time, are considered genuine and legitimate. Those that isolate, enslave, deaden, kill or detach us from the material world and its pain and

---

[1] William R. Stoeger, "Our Experience of Knowing in Science and in Spirituality," in *The Laws of Nature, the Range of Human Knowledge, and Divine Action* (Tarnow, Poland: Biblos, 1996), 10.

Approaching a Theology of Flourishing 23

suffering, its possibilities and its wonders, are to be rejected as dangerous and illusory.[2]

This discussion of human experience in the world and in relationship to God offers rich resources for constructing a hermeneutics of the tradition that is centered on the fullness of life. In practice, Stoeger suggests, doctrinal and theological claims that enrich creaturely life, fostering freedom to experience the fullness of life within reality, are authentic and consistent with God's life-giving will. Those that isolate, degrade, or remove us from deep contact with material reality—including the experience of suffering—are "dangerous" and must, he says, be "rejected." The validity of theological claims rests on the fruit they bear in the life of individual persons and in the way that these persons come to live in the world.

Whereas Stoeger offers a basic hermeneutical principle, Mercy Oduyoye explicitly relates the fullness of life to social and ecological realities. Oduyoye thus hones this hermeneutic's ability to interpret the tradition with a view toward the flourishing of all things, individually and collectively, within a holistic socio-ecological paradigm. In ways that parallel Stoeger, Oduyoye writes that reflection on the sources of the Christian tradition must "identify what enhances, transforms or promotes in such a way as to build community and make for life-giving and life-enhancing relationships."[3] In effect, interpretations of tradition that generate communities of flourishing find validation in their ability to actualize Christ's proclamation of abundant life. This, she writes, renders theology both socially and "ecologically sensitive, as all have to live, aware of the right of the other to

---

[2] William R. Stoeger, "Reflections on the Interaction of My Knowledge of Cosmology and My Christian Belief," *CTNS Bulletin* 21, no. 2 (Spring 2001): 14.

[3] Mercy Amba Oduyoye, *Introducing African Women's Theology* (Cleveland, OH: Pilgrim's Press, 2001), 16.

a qualitative existence."[4] Oduyoye summarizes this vision with the words "wholeness," which she defines as "all that makes for the fullness of life, and makes people celebrate life," and *alafia*, or "complete integral well-being."[5] Together, these observations operationalize the proclamation of abundant life in John 10:10 for theology and praxis, honing the methodology that guides the proposed theology of flourishing.

Because it takes seriously the embodied particularity of creatures—how they experience or do not experience fullness of life in their beloved uniqueness—a theology of flourishing also gives hermeneutical priority to experiences of oppression, marginalization, or degradation of any kind. A hermeneutical application of the preferential option for the poor, this principle necessitates the interrogation and often the rejection of interpretations of Christian tradition that legitimate or contribute to the socio-ecclesial subordination of women and the exclusion of LGBTQ+ persons, structural racism, the relegation of people with disabilities to the margins of society, colonization and imperialism, the extinction of species, and the degradation of the biosphere. This interrogation must be accompanied by a concomitant practice of radical hospitality that hears and trusts in the stories of those who suffer and experience oppression, individually and collectively, knowing that the Creator who loves all things to fulfillment hears their cries, as God heard the cries of Hagar in the wilderness and Israel enslaved in Egypt. A passage by Elizabeth Johnson on the flourishing of poor women of color gives force to the point, further emphasizing that no one flourishes unless all flourish:

> For me the goal of feminist religious discourse pivots in its fullness around the flourishing of poor women of color in violent situations. Not incidentally, securing the well-being

---

[4] Oduyoye, 17.
[5] Oduyoye, 32.

Approaching a Theology of Flourishing 25

of these socially least of women would entail a new configuration of theory and praxis and the genuine transformation of all societies, including the churches, to open up more human ways of living for all people, with each other and with the earth. The rising of the women is the rising of the race—precisely because women with their network of relationships are at the lowest ebb, marginalized, and yet sustaining every society. The incoming tide lifts all the boats in the harbor. Only when the poorest, black, raped, and brutalized women in a South African township—the epitome of victims of sexism, racism, and classism, and at the same time startling examples of women's resiliency, courage, love, and dignity—when such women with their dependent children and their sisters around the world may live peacefully in the enjoyment of their human dignity, only then will feminist theology arrive at its goal.[6]

As Johnson suggests, giving hermeneutical priority to women in situations of oppression is a precondition for understanding and realizing what flourishing is all about. At the same time, in keeping with Jantzen's observations, giving hermeneutical priority to experiences of suffering and oppression also raises the question of how it can be the case that oppression continues in and through a tradition that proclaims the fullness of life and the salvation of the world. This question, in turn, necessitates humble recognition of the ways Christians, and Christianity as a whole, have been complicit in violence and injustice. In Stoeger's analysis such recognition is a seedbed for discernment, necessitating that theologians and churches come to terms with the fact that "mixed in with the tradition can be systematic blindnesses, misdiscernments and socially and politically induced

---

[6] Elizabeth Johnson, *She Who Is: The Mystery of God in Feminist Theological Discourse* (New York: Crossroad, 1991), 11.

distortions" that taint the foundations of the Christian faith.[7] In all this a hermeneutics of the fullness of life sees the concrete, embodied experience of the "least of these" as an indispensable criterion for reading the tradition and assessing the validity of Christian truth claims.

An important corollary emerges here, as the evaluation of Christian theology in view of the fullness of life implies that theological claims that steal, kill, and destroy—that deal death instead of life—are, as Oduyoye says, "repudiated as being against God's will for humanity and the rest of creation."[8] In other words, if Stoeger's comment on blindnesses and misdiscernments holds true—if Christianity has perpetrated or perpetuated, whether consciously or unwittingly, actions or thought structures that enable oppression and violence against persons or the earth—then the interpretations that gave rise to such violence must be rejected. For indeed, as Johnson asks, "if something consistently results in the denigration of human beings, in what sense can it be religiously true?"[9] Seen in this light, theologies and practices that exclude, demean, or destroy are inconsistent with Christ's proclamation of the fullness of life and so serve as a call to protest and transformation. Recognizing this point reinforces the need for radical hospitality and openness to new possibilities, especially among those who hold power in church and society—a bold capacity to let go of what does not foster flourishing and ask the Holy Spirit to reveal new possibilities, even if these possibilities run counter to long-established ways of proceeding.

Finally, radical attunement to the needs of the world and action on behalf of the self-actualization of creatures in relationship to God and one another means that theoretical principles

---

[7] Stoeger, "Reflections on the Interaction of My Knowledge of Cosmology and My Christian Belief," 14.

[8] Oduyoye, *Introducing African Women's Theology*, 19.

[9] Johnson, *She Who Is*, 30.

Approaching a Theology of Flourishing 27

are not sufficient in themselves. For a theology of flourishing, interpretations of the tradition are also subject to the criterion of praxis. Oduyoye articulates the point well: "From the affirmations of faith . . . flow the praxis that gives birth to liberating and life-enhancing visions and further actions and reflections."[10] The unity of theory and praxis, reflection and action, is intrinsic to a theology that sees Christ's proclamation of the fullness of life as the preeminent expression of God's life-giving will. Drawing these methodological threads together, Stoeger concludes that the "long-term success and fruitfulness" of theological claims depends on their "capacity for giving life and wholeness to individuals and to communities."[11] As a baseline hermeneutical norm, this summary statement guides the coming engagement with scripture and theology and grounds my proposal of a theology that fosters the fullness of life for all creation.

Situating a Theology of Flourishing: Preliminary Commitments and Limitations

In addition to the methodological, theological, and praxiological considerations discussed thus far, a growing body of interdisciplinary research—including research emerging from the disciplines of theology and religious studies—attests to the need for a fully realized theology of flourishing.[12] Much of this

---

[10] Oduyoye, *Introducing African Women's Theology,* 17.

[11] William Stoeger, "Relating the Natural Sciences to Theology: Levels of Creative Mutual Interaction," in *God's Action in Nature's World: Essays in Honour of Robert John Russell,* ed. Ted Peters and Nathan Hallanger (Burlington, VT: Ashgate, 2006), 36.

[12] See, for example, Andrew Briggs and Michael J. Reiss, *Human Flourishing: Scientific Insight and Spiritual Wisdom in Uncertain Times* (Oxford: Oxford University Press, 2021); Helen Cameron, John Reader, and Victoria Slater, *Theological Reflection for Human Flourishing: Pastoral Practice and Public Theology* (London: SCM Press, 2012); Adam B. Cohen, ed., *Religion and Human Flourishing* (Waco, TX: Baylor University Press, 2020); Chris J. Cuomo, *Feminism and*

research also provides helpful resources for establishing flourishing as a theological category in its own right. In *Flourishing: Why We Need Religion in a Globalized World*, Miroslav Volf writes that flourishing "stands for the life that is lived well, the life that goes well, and the life that feels good—all three together, inextricably intertwined. . . . It evokes an image of a living thing, thriving in its proper environment: a tree 'planted by streams of water, which yields its fruit in its season' and whose leaves 'do not wither' (Psalm 1:3)."[13] Volf's development of this definition in the context of globalization helpfully illustrates how centering flourishing in theology might lead us to reimagine what it means to be Christian in view of Christ's promise of abundant life. He writes:

Ecological Communities: An Ethic of Flourishing (New York: Routledge, 1998); Carol Taylor and Roberto Dell'oro, eds., *Health and Human Flourishing: Religion, Medicine, and Moral Anthropology* (Georgetown: Georgetown University Press, 2006); Margaret B. Adam, "The Purpose of Creatures: A Christian Account of Human and Farmed Animal Flourishing," *Sewanee Theological Review* 62, no. 4 (2021): 733–66; Jakob Hero, "Toward a Queer Theology of Flourishing: Transsexual Embodiment, Subjectivity, and Moral Agency," in *The Bloomsbury Reader in Religion, Sexuality, and Gender* (London: Bloomsbury, 2017), 219–30; Angela Kallhoff, "Plants in Ethics: Why Flourishing Deserves Moral Respect," *Environmental Values* 23, no. 6 (2014): 685–700; John Kleinig and Nicholas G. Evans, "Human Flourishing, Human Dignity, and Human Rights," *Law and Philosophy* 32, no. 5 (2013): 539–64; Nadia Marais, "'Adorn the Cross with Roses'?: Justice and Human Dignity, Beauty and Human Flourishing," *Acta Theologica* 29 (2020): 77–92; Katia Moles, "A Culture of Flourishing: A Feminist Ethical Framework for Incorporating Child Sexual Abuse Prevention in Catholic Institutions," *Journal of Feminist Studies in Religion* 36, no. 2 (2020): 63–83; Douglas B. Rasmussen, "Individual Rights and Human Flourishing," *Public Affairs Quarterly* 3, no. 1 (1989): 89–103; Hava Tirosh-Samuelson, "Human Flourishing and History: A Religious Imaginary for the Anthropocene," *Journal of the Philosophy of History* 14, no. 3 (2020): 382–418; Tyler J. VanderWeele, "On the Promotion of Human Flourishing," *Proceedings of the National Academy of Sciences of the United States of America* 114, no. 31 (2017): 8148–56.

[13] Miroslav Volf, *Flourishing: Why We Need Religion in a Globalized World* (New Haven, CT: Yale University Press, 2015), ix.

Lives flourishing and loved and lives languishing and despised—bread, water, and friendship given to the most vulnerable and these valuables withheld from them—would both have to figure in assessing globalization. . . . As a Christian, who believes that Jesus Christ is the measure of true humanity, the incarnation of love for God and others, my normative assessment of globalization boils down to this: it is good to the extent that it helps me and others participate in the character and mission of Jesus Christ, and it is deficient to the extent that it doesn't.[14]

I also concur with Jonathan Rowson's caution, articulated in another theological study of flourishing, about conflating flourishing and pleasure, success, or happiness, and I share his view that flourishing has a "path quality," which manifests in "the lifelong process of becoming."[15] I likewise value Helen Rhee's discussion of the external and internal dimensions of human flourishing. She writes, "Human flourishing always encompasses both external and internal dimensions of life; the 'external' or communal dimension includes material circumstances, social systems and relations, and physical conditions of a person whereas the 'internal' or individual dimension involves the very soul and spiritual and affective aspect of a person."[16] Any account of flourishing must be holistic.

While these conclusions correspond with key aspects of my argument, my study charts a different path from many existing studies of flourishing for four key reasons. First, as illustrated by

---

[14] Volf, 16.

[15] Jonathan Rowson, "*Status Viatoris* and the Path Quality of Religion: Human Flourishing as a Sacred Process of Becoming," in *Religion and Human Flourishing*, ed. Adam B. Cohen, 33–42 (Waco, TX: Baylor University Press, 2020), 34.

[16] Helen Rhee, "Philanthropy and Human Flourishing in Patristic Theology," *Religions* 9 (2018): 1.

30   *A Theology of Flourishing*

the examples above, most studies focus explicitly if not exclusively on *human* flourishing.[17] Analysis of humanity's relationship to creation sometimes appears, but humans generally remain at the center. For example, while I respect Volf's use of ecological metaphors and appreciate his observation that environmental degradation must stand alongside social injustice and political violence in contemporary Christian discourse, his account of flourishing is thoroughly human-centered, focused principally on economic and political concerns.[18]

This orientation is somewhat understandable, since Volf's analysis of flourishing arises within a study of religion and globalization. At the same time, given the pressing needs of our socio-ecological moment, a fully realized theology of flourishing must bridge the ecological and anthropological, the social and environmental, providing a holistic framework for discerning what flourishing means in light of myriad forms of injustice and degradation. In focusing on humanity, anthropocentric accounts of flourishing sideline the flourishing of other-than-human creatures and the holistic co-implication of human persons, communities, and other species in earthly life. In practice, focusing on human flourishing thus inhibits our ability to account for the ways that human social systems and ecosystems are intertwined—from the extraction and consumption of resources to the universal need for drinkable water and breathable air in a world marred by global inequality and threatened by climate change. Moreover, as subsequent chapters show, I contend that the witness of scripture and tradition demand that any treatment of flourishing be both ecological and social, uniting human and other-than-human flourishing under the reign of a God who is

---

[17] Two major projects fit this description: the Templeton Foundation's What Is Human Flourishing? and the Human Flourishing Program at Harvard's Institute for Quantitative Social Science.

[18] Volf acknowledges that ecological issues receive only marginal attention. Volf, *Flourishing*, xi.

Approaching a Theology of Flourishing

"powerful and compassionate, is coming close and wills to save, to establish justice and peace for *all*."[19]

Second, many human-centered studies appropriate and develop the Aristotelian ideal of *eudaimonia* as a basis for understanding flourishing. Such approaches hold promise, especially in ethics, for thinking about flourishing in terms of happiness, self-realization, and "integral human fulfillment."[20] Yet if, as Mary Grey argues, "flourishing means all that is life-giving for people, earth, and earth creatures together," *eudaimonia*'s anthropocentric orientation limits its potential to ground a holistic, socio-ecological theology of flourishing.[21] Moreover, from a methodological standpoint, I hesitate to deploy a Greek philosophical principle, no matter its influence, as a basis for constructing a Christian theology of flourishing until *after* engaging the basic understanding of flourishing that is revealed in scripture, theology, and spirituality.

Third, many studies aim to articulate the characteristics and properties of flourishing—how it takes shape in the concrete. Although it is important to articulate what flourishing is (and isn't), in alignment with Rowson's discussion of the "path quality" of flourishing, this book presents flourishing as something of an "emergent property" that takes root, sprouts, and grows in a creature's relationship to God and others, conditioned by the particulars of creaturely life. Thus, while it is valuable to articulate conditions that characterize flourishing, I hesitate—especially as a white male scholar—to attempt to define flourishing in anything

---

[19] Elizabeth Johnson, *Consider Jesus: Waves of Renewal in Christology* (New York: Crossroad, 1990), 53. Emphasis mine.

[20] Carl-Henric Grenholm, "Happiness, Welfare, and Capabilities," in *The Practices of Happiness: Political Economy, Religion, and Wellbeing*, ed. John R. Atherton, Elaine L. Graham, and Ian Steedman (New York: Routledge, 2011), 47.

[21] Mary Grey, "*Natality* and *Flourishing* in Contexts of Disability and Impairment," in *Grace Jantzen: Redeeming the Present*, ed. Elaine Graham, 197–211 (New York: Routledge, 2010), 198.

approaching a universal sense. In other words, because flourishing is discerned in the embodied particularity of a creature's life, its shape and character cannot be prescribed. Although we know it when we see and experience it, there is no one-size-fits-all definition of flourishing. This project thus aims to provide a modest framework that places flourishing at the center of the Christian imaginary in a way that can be adapted and applied in a variety of theological and pastoral contexts, using diverse methods to address diverse concerns.

Fourth, as the previous chapter demonstrated, while talk of flourishing often appears in liberation theologies broadly, and in feminist and queer theologies in particular, these disciplines rarely offer a fully realized account of flourishing as a theological category in its own right. Integrating scripture, theology, and spirituality—with a particular emphasis on the contributions of liberationist, feminist, queer, and ecological theologians—this book takes a first step toward filling this gap.

Having established the methodological principles that guide the proposed theology of flourishing and situated it within the field, the journey through the Christian tradition begins. Applying the hermeneutics of the fullness of life developed in this chapter, the next chapter undertakes a close reading of key creation texts from the Hebrew Bible, seeking a renewed understanding of creation and salvation that can ground a theology oriented toward the self-actualization of all creatures, so that all may enjoy the fullness of life for which they are made.

Part II

EXPLORATIONS

*Tracing the Thread of Flourishing
through Scripture and History*

3

Abundant Life
in the Order of Creation

Hebrew Bible Foundations for a
Theology of Flourishing

The Hebrew Bible abounds with reflections on the meaning of creation as God's beloved handiwork. When interpreted through the lens of flourishing, with a hermeneutics of the fullness of life, its texts depict a God who, from "the beginning," intends for every creature and creation as a whole to flourish, individually and collectively, in their embodied, beloved particularity. This interpretation highlights how, rather than acting through an assertion of power over and above creation, God collaborates with creation to draw forth its own potential for self-actualization, providing all things with what they need to experience the fullness for which they are made. As a result, these texts provide an indispensable foundation for the proposed theology of flourishing.

This interpretation also runs counter to the view that the Hebrew Bible establishes a gendered hierarchy that authorizes the domination and exploitation of the earth and other-than-human creatures, subjugates women, and marginalizes LGBTQ+

36   *A Theology of Flourishing*

persons. While the text can be and has been interpreted in these ways, this chapter rejects such interpretations, undertaking a close reading of four key creation texts—Genesis 1 and 2—3, Psalms 19 and 104, and the Wisdom literature[1]—to illustrate how the thread of flourishing flows through the Hebrew Bible. Following this through line reveals that, at the most basic level, the Hebrew Bible attests to a God who, as Creator, desires the fullness of life for every creature and creation as a whole. In practice, such an interpretation has the potential to ground deep attentiveness to God's life-giving intentions as a basis for protest against injustice and a praxis of love that nurtures the flourishing of all.

Framing the Interpretations:
Biblical Creation Texts as "Cultural Cosmologies"

As the previous chapter suggested, taking the symbol of creation as a grounding basis for a theology of flourishing requires us to understand creation as more than just an object of concern or a teaching about cosmic origins.[2] Without disregarding the

------

[1] Biblical Wisdom literature includes a range of texts centered on the cultivation of virtue. This literature includes Proverbs, Wisdom, and Sirach, which deal directly with Wisdom as a character and path toward virtue, and Psalms, Job, Song of Songs, and Ecclesiastes, which reflect on Wisdom in poetic and narrative form.

[2] In addition to the concerns raised in Chapter 1, reducing the doctrine of creation to the question of cosmic origins contributes to the view that science and religion are inherently opposed to one another. To my mind, Ian Barbour's account of the parallel structure of biblical literalism and scientific materialism offers an outstanding explanation of this purported conflict. As Barbour observes, by holding to a univocal understanding of truth, biblical literalists and scientific materialists *both* assume a philosophical position that exceeds the evidentiary basis for their view. Further, as a pre-scientific text, the Hebrew Bible cannot offer scientific explanations of origins; neither can an empirical method of inquiry disprove the existence of an immaterial entity like God. For a detailed treatment of this problematic, see Ian Barbour, *Religion and Science: Historical and Contemporary Issues* (San Francisco: HarperSanFrancisco, 1997).

Abundant Life in the Order of Creation   37

importance of care for creation or the dialogue between science and religion, the importance of creation for a theology of flourishing emerges most clearly when we treat it as a theological locus in its own right. Biblical creation narratives, then, function as what the Jesuit astronomer and theological writer William Stoeger terms cultural cosmologies. For Stoeger, unlike scientific cosmologies, which offer empirically verified mathematical models of physical reality, cultural cosmologies offer holistic, values-laden perspectives on reality that are rooted in distinct cultural and religious views.[3] Think of the difference between the Big Bang theory, a mathematical model of the physical origins the universe, and the *Enuma Elish* (the Babylonian creation myth)—or Genesis itself.

Situating biblical creation texts alongside scientific cosmologies and viewing them as experientially grounded interpretations of reality that are based in a particular community's relationship with the God in whom its members place their trust focuses interpretation on the particularity of what texts say about God, creation, and the God-world relationship. This orientation also strengthens the foundations for utilizing biblical creation texts as a basis for fostering care for creation. For, just as the God these texts reveal intends that all creatures may flourish, so too should human creatures who profess faith in God foster each other's flourishing, in keeping with the orientation of all things toward the fullness of life.

Genesis 1

Since Lynn White's 1967 essay "The Historical Roots of the Ecological Crisis," Genesis has received significant criticism for its apparent establishment of an anthropocentric hierarchy that authorizes humans to exploit creation on the order of extractive

---

[3] William R. Stoeger, "Biblical Creation Literature," 1–3. Unpublished presentation.

38   *A Theology of Flourishing*

capitalism, taking whatever they need from the world to advance their interests and aims. Guided by the insight that "what people do about their ecology depends on what they think about themselves in relation to things around them," White argues that biblical creation narratives lead to the view that "God planned all of this [creation] for man's benefit and rule: no item in the physical creation had any purpose save to serve man's purposes." On this basis, White concludes that, "especially in its Western form, Christianity is the most anthropocentric religion the world has seen."[4]

It is important to recognize the possibility of such interpretations, as well as the real impacts such interpretations have had on human-earth relations in and beyond the Christian world. Scholars such as Richard Bauckham, however, observe that, although White's reading of Genesis corresponds with an influential strand in the history of interpretation, it may be better attributed to interpreters such as Francis Bacon than to Genesis itself.[5] There is something of a chicken-egg problem here. One might ask whether Genesis really justifies Bacon's view that the earth has been given over to humans and can be freely exploited in the name of scientific progress, or whether, as Bauckham argues, Bacon used the text to justify an exploitative, technocratic vision of creation in contrast to the text's

---

[4] Lynn White, "The Historical Roots of Our Ecologic Crisis," *Science* 155, no. 3767 (1967): 1205.

[5] Richard Bauckham, *The Bible and Ecology: Rediscovering the Community of Creation* (Waco, TX: Baylor University Press, 2010), 6. For a full treatment of this history, including an analysis of Bacon's calls for humanity to reclaim dominion through scientific advancements, see Richard Bauckham, *God and the Crisis of Freedom: Biblical and Contemporary Perspectives* (Louisville, KY: Westminster John Knox, 2002), esp. chap. 7. Richard Samuel Deese integrates gender into an analysis of Bacon's views in "The Gospel of Eve: Francis Bacon, Genesis, and the *Telos* of Modern Science," *Journal for the Study of Religion, Nature, and Culture* 11, no. 4 (2017): 435–54.

Abundant Life in the Order of Creation   *39*

own presentation of God's aims.[6] Taking cues from Bauckham, I argue that a careful rereading of Genesis 1 reveals a Creator who is fascinated—even obsessed—with life and who desires the flourishing of all creation.

Genesis 1 opens with God looking over *tohu wabohu*, a watery void that represents primordial chaos—a common trope in Ancient Near Eastern creation myths. Next, a "wind from God," *ruah Elohim*, sweeps across the waters. Notably, this passage on the first page of the Bible exemplifies the regular association of breath and life in the ancient Hebrew imagination. Here, *ruah* prepares the watery chaos for the work of creation that follows, representing the soon-to-be-realized possibility of creaturely existence.

After creating light and establishing the skies and earth, on the third day God populates the land with living things. First, using a taxonomy rooted in agricultural knowledge, the author offers an etiology of two kinds of plants: "plants yielding seed, and fruit trees of every kind . . . that bear fruit with the seed in it" (1:11). This detail is striking, as it reflects an ancient form of ecological knowledge that describes how plants and their seeds function within life systems. But God's method of creation is even more striking. Contrary to the assumption that God placed things on the earth in fixed and final form, such that creation amounts to a demonstration of divine power from outside the material realm, God in Genesis 1 manifests what commentator Terence Fretheim describes as "a highly relational way of proceeding."[7] With the words, "Let the earth put forth vegetation" (1:11), God *invites*

---

[6] White makes passing mention of the "Baconian creed," but he ultimately does not hold Bacon accountable for this interpretive trajectory; he maintains that Christianity is to blame. See White, "The Historical Roots of Our Ecologic Crisis," 1203.

[7] Terence E. Fretheim, *God and World in the Old Testament: A Relational Theology of Creation* (Nashville, TN: Abingdon Press, 2005), 271.

40   *A Theology of Flourishing*

earth to bring forth life, speaking in what Walter Brueggemann describes as "a mood of authorization."[8] In Hebrew, this statement, like most of the divine declarations that follow, utilizes the jussive case. In contrast to direct imperatives, jussive constructions have the sense of suggestion, or invitation, whereby the addressee retains agency: think "let it be that" rather than "do this." As a result, Fretheim notes, in this text "creation takes place not from outside the created order but from within."[9] Moreover, as William Brown observes, this account of creation thus attests to an intrinsic link between the life-giving function of ecosystems and divine agency. He writes, "These creative environments are deeply connected to divine creativity: through the rhetoric of divine command, God works collaboratively with earth and the waters to fashion life."[10] In other words, the God of Genesis 1 does not substitute divine power for earth's own creativity. God *invites* earth to bring forth, empowering it to produce myriad plants and fruits by its own agency. This process repeats on the days that follow: God prepares water for fish, the sky for birds, and land for living creatures.[11] In every case the initiative *for* creation lies with God, but agency *in* creation remains with creatures. As such, Brueggemann notes, God's purpose in creating is "to make possible an ordered, reliable place of peaceableness and viability . . . a place of fruitfulness, abundance, productivity, extravagance."[12] Creation is a process of collaboration between God and material reality that is fundamentally oriented toward

---

[8] Walter Brueggemann, *Theology of the Old Testament: Theology, Dispute, Advocacy* (Minneapolis: Fortress Press, 1997), 529.

[9] Fretheim, *God and World in the Old Testament*, 38. On the jussive, Fretheim notes, "Grammatically, the use of the jussive 'let' means that God's speaking does not function as an imperative; it leaves room for creaturely response."

[10] William P. Brown, *A Handbook to Old Testament Exegesis* (Louisville, KY: Westminster John Knox Press, 2017), 237.

[11] As Bauckham and Brown both observe, environments and habitats are created on days 1–3, and their inhabitants are created on days 4–6.

[12] Brueggemann, *Theology of the Old Testament*, 529.

Abundant Life in the Order of Creation 41

life and in which God enables and empowers creatures to flourish while respecting their autonomy and integrity.

The sign of this divine respect for creaturely life as creaturely life shines through in the blessing that every species—from sea creatures to birds and beasts of the land—receives from God. The blessing commands creatures to "be fruitful and multiply" and to fill their ecological niches such that "[each] creature's own activity as a constitutive element in the process of creation is seen in harmony with God's action."[13] Further, at the end of each phase of creation, God looks at what God has made and declares that it is good. Each part of creation has its own integrity, its own goodness, its own standing, in both form and function—its capacity to manifest and actualize God's work of life. In this way the integrity of creaturely life flows from and expresses God's intentions such that the goodness of each part of creation manifests in its concrete contribution to the whole. As Michael Welker states, "The creature is drawn into and bound up into the process of creation by developing and relativizing itself and thereby fruitfully bringing itself into these associations of relations of interdependence, without which the creature would not exist."[14] God's recognition of the goodness of creation relates intrinsically to each creature's life-giving contributions, fulfilling the terms of God's blessing in relationships of life, flourishing, and communion. This point grounds a theological vision of flourishing wherein each creature is made to experience and contribute to the fullness of life in its unique context, according to its beloved, God-given particularity.

On the sixth day humans enter the scene. In an effort to counteract the anthropocentric assumptions readers often bring

---

[13] Michael Welker, *Creation and Reality* (Minneapolis: Fortress Press, 1999), 13. Similarly, Fretheim describes God's blessing as "a word of empowerment, of divine power-sharing with the creature, which is then capable of fulfilling the named responsibilities." Fretheim, *God and World in the Old Testament*, 50.

[14] Welker, *Creation and Reality*, 13.

to the text, it is important to observe that the story does not grant humans their own day of creation. Rather, they are made on the same day as other land creatures: the cattle (domesticated animals), creeping things, and wild animals. Yet there are also important differences that separate and, in some ways, elevate humanity within the order of creation. First and foremost, humans are given "dominion"—not domination—over animal life. Notably, while this dominion applies explicitly to fish, birds, and land animals, it does not apply to habitats—an important point of consideration in view of clear-cutting and forestry practices that cause deep ecological harm. Second, humans are the only creatures created "in the image of God" (1:27).[15] Creation in God's image corresponds with the conferral of dominion and the addition of the word *subdue* to God's blessing of humans. Whereas other creatures are told to multiply and fill their ecosystems, humans are told to multiply, fill, and *subdue* the earth. It is not difficult to find here a foundation for what Pope Francis in *Laudato Si'* names "tyrannical," "misguided," and "excessive anthropocentrism," especially if a person already operates with an anthropocentric mentality cast in the mold of Baconian progress (no. 68). Yet such a perspective is clearly opposed to the holistic vision of flourishing evoked earlier in the text. Given this tension, does Genesis 1 really aim to authorize the human destruction of God's creation? There are three reasons to suspect the answer to this question is "no," such that the text may be seen as proclaiming a vision of the self-actualization of all creatures in communion with God and each other.

---

[15] For a review of interpretations and commentary on the image of God in relation to creation, see J. Richard Middleton, "The Image of God in Ecological Perspective," in *The Oxford Handbook of the Bible and Ecology*, ed. Hilary Marlow and Mark Harris (Oxford: Oxford University Press, 2022), 284–98. See also Fretheim, *God and World in the Old Testament*, 48–53; and William P. Brown, *The Seven Pillars of Creation: The Bible, Science, and the Ecology of Wonder* (Oxford: Oxford University Press, 2010), 41–44.

Abundant Life in the Order of Creation 43

First, the creation and blessing of humanity must be interpreted in relationship to the creation, blessing, and goodness of other creatures. Interpretations of humanity's standing in creation cannot simply dispense with the fact that God created and blessed every living thing on earth and declared it good. As such, the conferral of dominion and the command to subdue are normed by the goodness of other creatures, a goodness that finds expression in their own fruitfulness according to God's intentions, irrespective of the standing of humans. Together, these factors nuance the meaning of *dominion,* providing textual buffers against any construal of dominion that violates the autonomy, integrity, and divinely declared goodness of other species.

Second, despite dominion, humans are not intended to eat other animals—at least not according to Genesis 1:29. There, God states, "See, I have given you every plant yielding seed that is upon the face of all the earth, and every tree with seed in its fruit; you shall have them for food." Notably, here, God does not direct humans to eat meat; we are created herbivores. Some may claim that the absence of a mention of meat does not mean that humans are not intended to eat other animals. But evidence to the contrary appears eight chapters later, at the conclusion of the flood narrative. In Genesis 9:3–4, God states:

> "The fear and dread of you shall rest on every animal of the earth, and on every bird of the air, on everything that creeps on the ground, and on all the fish of the sea; into your hand they are delivered. Every moving thing that lives shall be food for you; and just as I gave you the green plants, I give you everything. Only, you shall not eat flesh with its life, that is, its blood."

As David Clough observes, given the prescription of a plant-based diet in Genesis 1, Genesis 9 amounts to a "concession by God to the human inability to live within the original constraints envisaged in Genesis 1 and 2."[16] Whereas humans were first permitted to eat plants, they now can eat meat that is cooked (as long as it isn't rare!).

More important for thinking about flourishing, however, is God's observation that other creatures will fear humans because of their now-predatory status. From a narrative standpoint, God's concession provides an etiology and justification for the practice of eating meat. Yet this etiology must be read against the shift in the character of the relationship between humans and other species. Presumably, in the original order of creation humans and other animals lived in harmony in a world without violence—an order that returns in Isaiah's eschatological vision of the lion and lamb. In this sense, even as the priestly author offers this explanation for the practice of eating meat, he does so against the backdrop of a nonviolent world. God's intention was, simply yet profoundly, that all creatures may flourish peacefully *together*, free from fear. That God establishes a covenant of radical *nonviolence* with "every living creature of all flesh" in 9:15 gives force to this point and provides a key norm for a theology of flourishing—for where there is violence, there can be no fullness of life. Thus, despite granting humans permission to consume animals, God's covenant with "all flesh" suggests that God remains mindful of the integrity and goodness of every creature and still intends for each to flourish according to the order of original blessing.

Third, despite the elevated status and responsibility granted humans in the text, humans do not receive their own declaration of goodness. From an anthropocentric perspective, this may lead some to conclude that God's final declaration that all things are "very good" suggests that humans are a jewel in the

---

[16] David L. Clough, *On Animals,* vol. 1: *Systematic Theology* (London: Bloomsbury, 2011), 121. On this theme, compare Robert Gnuse, "The Covenant with Noah in Genesis 9," *Biblical Theology Bulletin* 52, no. 2 (2021): 68–76. This does not, however, address the matter of animal sacrifice, which remains acceptable in the Hebrew Bible imaginary.

Abundant Life in the Order of Creation 45

crown of creation. But nothing in the text suggests that this is the case. Rather, after God declares the land animals good and creates humans, the text states, "God saw everything that he had made, and indeed, it was very good" (1:31). No special callout to humans appears here; humans are not characterized as a keystone species, much less a shining gem. God looks at the *whole* creation—what the Septuagint translates as *ta pánta*, in direct parallel with New Testament literature on the redemption of *all things*—and declares it "very good." The whole is, indeed, greater than the sum of its parts. In many ways, too, this is the basic rule of ecology. While each creature in an ecosystem is breathtaking in its own right (humans included, as we are parts of the ecosystems we inhabit and never stand apart from or above them), ecosystems are fascinating because of the ways that they function as complex wholes, with every creature playing a vital part in making life flourish in a particular context. As Brown observes, this life-giving participation can be seen as a basis for the divine declaration of goodness. He writes: "Creation deemed good by God is creation set toward the furtherance of life. . . . Robust, resilient, fecund life is part and practice of creation's 'goodness.'"[17]

Moreover, as Ellen Davis notes, God's declaration of goodness is a matter of beholding, or perception. Only after *perceiving* the whole order of creation does God declare it very good; the declaration is, then, a response to what God beholds.[18] In the fourth century, long before the dawn of contemporary ecology, Basil of Caesarea expressed a similar view:

> "*And God saw that it was good.*" God does not judge of the beauty of His work by the charm of the eyes, and He does not form the same idea of beauty that we do. What He esteems beautiful is that which presents in its perfection all

---

[17] Brown, *The Seven Pillars of Creation*, 45.

[18] Ellen F. Davis, *Scripture, Culture, and Agriculture: An Agrarian Reading of the Bible* (Cambridge: Cambridge University Press, 2009), 46.

46 *A Theology of Flourishing*

the fitness of art. . . . It is thus that Scripture depicts to us the Supreme Artist, praising each one of His works; soon, when His work is complete, He will accord well deserved praise to the whole together.[19]

In beholding creation, with each creature flourishing as intended, God declares the magnificence of the cosmos and all that dwells therein.

All this reshapes the context in which we understand dominion. In a monarchical context like the Ancient Near East, to have dominion is to be charged with carrying out the ruler's will. As such, to understand the meaning of dominion, we must first know the ruler's intentions. Here, God's intentions determine the meaning of dominion.[20] In light of the preceding analysis, we can conclude that, indeed, the dominion granted humans "must be understood in terms of care-giving, not exploitation," as God is the author of life and ultimate caregiver of creation.[21] Dominion

---

[19] Saint Basil of Caesarea and Saint Gregory of Nyssa, *Hexaëmeron with On the Making of Man* (Brookline, MA: Paterikon Publications, 2017), 62. Thinking socio-ecologically, Basil observes that the water is good both because of its beauty and because of the economic functions it serves. He writes that water "facilitates the inter-communication of mariners. By this means it gives us the boon of general information, supplies the merchant his wealth, and easily provides for the necessities of life, allowing the rich to export their superfluities, and blessing the poor with the supply of what they lack." Basil, *Hexaëmeron*, 73–74.

[20] James Limburg, "Who Cares for the Earth? Psalm Eight and the Environment," *Word and World Supplement 1* (1992): 43–52. Bauckham analyzes the relationship between dominion and stewardship in *Bible and Ecology*, 1–12.

[21] Bruce C. Birch, Water Brueggemann, Terence E. Fretheim, and David L. Petersen, *A Theological Introduction to the Old Testament* (Nashville, TN: Abingdon Press, 1999), 44. The authors base this conclusion on an intertextual analysis of *radah* in Psalm 72 and Ezekiel 34. William Brown echoes this intertextual reading, using Ezekiel 34:4 to illustrate a prophetic condemnation of "dominion that is specifically violent and cruel." William P. Brown, *The Ethos of the Cosmos: The Genesis of Moral Imagination in the Bible* (Grand Rapids, MI: Eerdmans, 1999), 238.

Abundant Life in the Order of Creation 47

is, then, primarily about *responsibility* to lovingly manage and maintain creation so that all things can flourish in harmony with the divine intentions God inscribed into creation with the words, "let there be," and "let there bring forth." Seen in this way, if dominion is more about responsibility within creation than power over it, the placement of humans at the end of the narrative should not be seen as an exaltation in status but as the placement of a "capstone" that maintains the life-giving order that God made. As Theodore Hiebert puts it, "If God brings a flourishing world into being, it is the human's primary work to ensure that the world continues to flourish as God created it and wishes it to flourish."[22] The meanings of *radah* (rule) and *kabash* (subdue) also take their meanings from this interpretation, with humans ruling and subduing in ways that nurture earth's productivity in harmony with its God-given autonomy and integrity—perhaps through practices of cultivation.[23] Even the *imago Dei* may be understood in this way, reflecting humanity's status as stewards. We humans are not creatures authorized to steal, kill, or destroy in contradiction to God's will-to-life, flourishing, and communion. We are creatures charged to carry out God's will for the good of all, in keeping with the relationship between divine initiative and creation's agency to which the narrative of creation attests.

In sum, as Bauckham concludes, "The human dominion, like God's, is a matter not of use but of care."[24] This posture orients humans to be beholders of creation, who, like God, discern and appreciate the goodness of life systems and who respond to creation's needs when its integrity is threatened. Here, I might even suggest that anthropocentrism is unwarranted, not because the text does not manifest anthropocentric bias—it does—but

---

[22] Theodore Hiebert, "Genesis," in *The Oxford Handbook of the Bible and Ecology*, ed. Hilary Marlow and Mark Harris (Oxford: Oxford University Press, 2022), 85.

[23] Bauckham, *The Bible and Ecology*, 17.

[24] Bauckham, 19.

48

because the vision of creation presented in the text challenges humans to give up anthropocentric claims to superiority in service of God's aims, such that the very things that set us apart from other creatures become a basis for deep love and care. In its autonomy and integrity as a beloved partner of God, celebrated and declared "very good," all creation is made to flourish.

Genesis 2—3

The preceding analysis of Genesis 1 establishes context for everything that follows. Thus, analysis of subsequent passages will be appropriately intertextual, interpreting other texts of the Hebrew Bible through the lens of the creational vision of Genesis 1 to assess their unique contributions to a theology of flourishing.

Despite its origins in another literary tradition (the Jahwist tradition), reading Genesis 2 against the backdrop of Genesis 1, with an eye toward flourishing, elicits recognition of important thematic parallels, of which the most significant is God's intention that all creatures may flourish in the fullness of life. In Genesis 2, this will-to-life manifests in the image of a thriving garden—a space of relational co-flourishing. Indeed, as Wirzba observes, the image of a garden "hooks up with the rest of the natural world (the whole wild world of microorganisms, pests and predators, pollinators, weather cycles, and their evolutionary histories) and so grounds human experience in the realities of soil, water, and light."[25] Yet at the start of the story no rain had fallen, and "there was no one to till the ground" (2:5). This prelude sets the terms of the story, again establishing a profoundly relational framework for understanding creation. Whereas in Genesis 1 God invites and empowers habitats to produce life,

---

[25] Norman Wirzba, *The Paradise of God: Renewing Religion in an Ecological Age* (Oxford: Oxford University Press, 2007), 113.

Abundant Life in the Order of Creation 49

here creation appears as a collaborative process involving God, humanity, soil, rain, and the act of cultivation.[26]

The collaborative character of creation appears yet again in the creation of the earthling, *ha'adam*.[27] In the creation of the earthling, *ruah* appears once more, not as wind that brings order to chaos but as breath that animates dirt, giving life to the creature God makes—a composite of earth and breath, a union of the creaturely and divine.[28] In common translation, this earthling is charged with "tilling and keeping" the garden, though commentators observe that the Hebrew verbs may be more naturally translated as "serve" and "protect," or "preserve."[29] No matter the translation, interpretations of this vocation consistently reflect an orientation toward abundant life, realized through collaboration among God, humans, and earth. As Pope Francis writes in *Laudato Si'*: "'Tilling' refers to cultivating, ploughing or working, while 'keeping' means caring, protecting, overseeing and preserving. This implies a relationship of mutual responsibility between human beings and nature" (no. 67). In a similar way Wirzba reflects, "Adam, by learning the skills of gardening, is

---

[26] Welker, *Creation and Reality*, 9–10. See also Birch et al., *A Theological Introduction to the Old Testament*, 50–51.

[27] I have chosen to use the term *earthling* as a riff on the Hebrew word for "earth," the basis for Adam's name.

[28] Yet as Hiebert explains, God's act of imparting the breath of life to the earth creature must not be understood as a dualistic fusion of body and spirit. For this reason Hiebert cautions strongly against translating *ruah* as "spirit" at all. "From their usage by the Yahwist and other biblical authors, we can see that nišmat ḥayyîm, and rûaḥ, its synonym, do not describe an independent, incorporeal part of a person that may be split off from the body and translated 'soul' or 'spirit.' This is the same physical breath that God gives to all animate beings at birth. It sustains their lives on earth, and it returns to God at death (Gen 2:7; 7:22; cf. Ps 104:29–30). The Yahwist does not view the human through the lenses of Cartesian dualism that splits the world between spirit and matter and body and soul." Hiebert, "Genesis," 83.

[29] For example, Fretheim renders *'abad* and *samar* "serve and protect." Fretheim, *God and World in the Old Testament*, 53. I have followed Brown's translation, "serve and preserve." Brown, *The Seven Pillars of Creation*, 81.

learning to participate in God's life-giving, life-sustaining, life-celebrating ways with the world."[30] Fretheim likewise argues that in Genesis 2 "human activity stands in the *service* of the nonhuman world, moving it toward its fullest possible potential."[31] To "till and keep," or "serve and preserve," is to partner with God and the earth in the work of life.

In all this, Genesis 2 also employs a motif of order, but the character of this order is more ecological—concerned with "earthy matters" in the garden—than cosmic. Indeed, the flourishing garden manifests the order of creation: the earthling acts as the garden's caretaker, tilling and planting to maintain the system of abundant life established by God. With *'adam*, other creatures contribute to the ecosystem in ways unspoken by the text: bees and winds pollinate, animal byproducts fertilize, rains water, and so on. All participate in the work of flourishing. All likewise partake of the fruits of this work and, as in Genesis 1, do not feed on each other—a point apparent but easily missed in God's declaration that humans may eat from any of the trees in the garden except the tree of the knowledge of good and evil. This arboreal admonition also takes on deeper importance when seen in light of the ecological order of the garden. Despite their important role, the story indicates that humans must also know their place in the garden, not transgressing the divine order by eating that which they are not entitled to eat. Gracious humility before other creatures is key to the flourishing of all things.

In this way, too, the order of flourishing that governs God's garden provides the backdrop against which sin enters the world, disrupting the fulfillment of God's life-giving intentions. This ordering—flourishing first, sin second—gives further support to Jantzen's call to situate sin and salvation under the umbrella of

---

[30] Norman Wirzba, "The Art of Creaturely Life: A Question Of Human Propriety," *Pro Ecclesia* 22, no. 1 (2013): 27.

[31] Fretheim, *God and World in the Old Testament*, 53.

Abundant Life in the Order of Creation 51

flourishing. Moreover, this reorientation changes the context in which we interpret the eating of the forbidden fruit. For, within a framework of flourishing, this act of disobedience is not so much about disobedience to God's will in a legalistic sense, as if the main problem is that the first humans did something they were told not to do. More deeply, their disobedience *manifests in the concrete a disregard for the life-giving potential of creation as God established it.* Far beyond "not doing what they were told," eating the forbidden fruit manifests a hubristic hope to transcend their place in creation and exploit the world in ways that contradict God's purposes. Thus, just as "the embrace of limits . . . is crucial because it makes possible an honest estimation of ourselves as embodied, communal creatures belonging to, living within, and nurtured by a vast membership of creatures ranging from bacteria to bees to beekeepers," the rejection of limits demonstrates an attitude of defiance toward our place in the garden and our God-given vocation to serve and preserve what God has made.[32] This model of disobedience provides a new foundation for understanding what sin is and how sin functions as an obstruction to the life-giving order of creation God established.

That the threefold punishment that follows humanity's disobedience results in a trifecta of degradations of the socio-ecological order makes sense given this ordering of the relationship between flourishing and sin. Just as the first act of disobedience is mediated through a concrete action within a relational order, its results play out "in a breakdown of relationships at multiple levels, including devastating effects upon God's good world."[33] The first punishment introduces a breakdown in the ecological order. God curses the serpent for tempting the first humans into disobedience. This curse has two dimensions. The first explains why serpents slither about rather than walking upright (the text

---

[32] Wirzba, "The Art of Creaturely Life," 23.

[33] Birch et al., *A Theological Introduction to the Old Testament*, 44.

52   *A Theology of Flourishing*

suggests that this was originally a walking, talking snake). The second anticipates the breakdown in human-animal relationships that occurs in Genesis 9, with God placing "enmity" between the serpent and the woman for all generations. Ecologically, this curse thus establishes an adversarial relationship between humans and serpents, a development that contradicts the peaceable original order of creation.

The punishment of the woman first entails an increase in pain during childbirth. This unhappy development indicates that childbirth was less painful before the punishment than after it. In socio-ecological perspective, however, the greater punishment follows, in the subjugation of the woman to the man. God states, "Your desire shall be for your husband, and he shall rule over you" (3:16).

As Bruce Vawter observes, this statement originated within an already patriarchal social order that accepted the subjection of women.[34] As such, whether it is meant to be descriptive or prescriptive, the punishment narrative offers both an etiology and a divine justification for the subordination of women to men. Yet, crucially, *this is not what God intended.*

Contra Thomas Aquinas's claim that woman was in a state of subjection even before sin, the fact that patriarchy results from punishment implies that the original order of creation was not patriarchal because the woman would not need to be punished with subjection if she were already in a subjugated position.[35] Fascinatingly, the authors and redactors of Genesis implicitly recognize this fact. Yet this recognition makes sense if we assume that the original order of creation was oriented toward the flourishing of all creatures in union with God and one another. What

---

[34] Bruce Vawter, *On Genesis: A New Reading* (New York: Doubleday, 1977), 85.

[35] Thomas Aquinas, *Summa Theologica*, trans. Fathers of the English Dominican Province (Cincinnati: Benziger Brothers, 1947), I.1.92.a2.

Abundant Life in the Order of Creation   53

follows humanity's act of disobedience thus fractures creation, blocking God's intentions.

Correlatively, as Phyllis Trible observes, when seen in this light, God's judgment against the woman should in fact function as a protest against patriarchy and heterosexism. She writes:

> [The judgments] protest; they do not condone. . . . This statement is not license for male supremacy, but rather it is condemnation of that very pattern. Subjugation and supremacy are perversions of creation. Through disobedience the woman has become slave. Her initiative and her freedom vanish. The man is corrupted also, for he has become master, ruling over the one who is his God-given equal. The subordination of female to male signifies their shared sin.[36]

This observation reveals a great deal about God's intentions for the world. Even as this text tacitly justifies a system of oppression, flourishing provides the foundational context for understanding the meaning and implications of sin: sin is a corruption of creation.

The third judgment—the punishment of the man—enacts a direct rupture in the garden's order of flourishing. No longer will plants produce freely; due to the disobedience of *ha'adam*, the ground is cursed, with concrete impacts on the intended fruitfulness of the soil. God declares, "Thorns and thistles it shall bring forth for you" (3:17), and humanity is consigned to a life of toil, eating "by the sweat of your face" and consuming

---

[36] Phyllis Trible, "Eve and Adam: Genesis 2—3 Reread," in *Eve and Adam: Readings on Genesis and Gender*, ed. Kristen E. Kvam, Linda S. Shearing, 'and Valarie H. Ziegler, 431–38 (Bloomington: Indiana University Press, 1999), 436. See also "Not a Jot, Not a Tittle: Genesis 2—3 after Twenty Years," 439–44 in the same volume.

"plants of the field" rather than the fruits of the earth. Here, as before, the original order of life is fractured by sin, as toil replaces tilling in a world that flourishes less easily than it did before.

Traditional prelapsarian and postlapsarian frameworks find in this text a "fall." Genesis 2, however, clearly demonstrates how flourishing, equality, and peace function as dimensions of a background theory for sin, wherein sin appears as a disruption of God's intentions for creation. Through a material transgression—an act of exploitation that violates God's order of life in the interest of human desires—creation becomes a place of domination. Here, then, the "wages of sin is death" (Rom 6:23). But in view of God's will that all creatures may experience abundant life, this death manifests not so much in the end of mortal existence as in the death of the order of flourishing God intended. Even as this necrophilic emphasis emerges, flourishing abides in the narrative background, reminding us that, before sin, there was abundant life—and this life is the Creator's principal aim.

Interlude:
Flashes of Flourishing, Disobedience, and Sin within Covenantal History

Although a full account is impossible, a brief look at two paradigmatic texts reveals how the preceding analysis of creation, flourishing, and sin shapes the Hebrew Bible's covenantal imagination. The establishment of the covenant with Abram in Genesis 15 is rooted in a metaphor of flourishing, as YHWH promises Abram descendants as countless as the stars in the sky (15:5). We might imagine this promise as a development of the original blessing of creation: "Be fruitful and multiply." This image provides a backdrop for the narratives of Israel's covenantal

Abundant Life in the Order of Creation   55

obedience and disobedience, with the question of Israel's flourishing punctuating prophetic and historical texts. In this way, as Fretheim argues, the whole sweep of covenantal history can be imagined as mediating a struggle between chaos and the divinely established order, with the promise of flourishing providing a background theory for the covenantal imagination.[37] Seen in this light, obedience to Torah provides a means for realizing the fullness promised by YHWH in creation and covenant.

This theme continues in the Exodus narrative and in a special way in the call of Moses through the burning bush (Ex 2:23—3:15). There, God responds to Israel's suffering in Egypt—its inability to flourish under the yoke of oppression—with a promise of liberation that restores Israel's ability to prosper in keeping with the promise to Abraham. As I have written elsewhere, although YHWH—the name God gives Moses—is unpronounceable, it comprises a string of breathy consonants. Asking what Moses heard when God spoke this name brings to mind the sound of air, breath, *ruah*—the creational force that stilled the waters of chaos and animated dirt in Genesis 1—2.[38] In ways consistent with the promise to Abraham, we might imagine that YHWH identifies as *life itself*, the promise of flourishing. Even more, this God who wills life, gives life, and is life acts to free those who cannot self-actualize under unjust conditions so that they may experience the fullness of life. Indeed, "God is at work to bring wholeness to those who are broken and dehumanized in the sociopolitical order, to bring hope to those broken of body and not just of spirit."[39] And even in so striking a theophany, God respects creation's autonomy and integrity, not destroying the bush to

---

[37] Fretheim, *God and World in the Old Testament*, 115–16.

[38] Paul J. Schutz, "Fire of Justice, Breath of Life: Exodus 3 as Foundational Narrative for Ecopolitical Theology," *Heythrop Journal* 63, no. 6 (2002): 1178–93.

[39] Birch et al., *A Theological Introduction to the Old Testament,* 119.

56
A Theology of Flourishing

make divine power known but collaborating with creation to proclaim and actualize God's intentions.

Psalms 19 and 104

Whereas Genesis provides the grounding vision of creation that guides a theology of flourishing, the psalms deploy this vision in prayerful, poetic reflections on the created order. In this way the psalms provide resources for reflecting on flourishing as God's principal intention. Although a huge array of psalms could be used to illustrate this point, the cosmological and theological visions of two psalms—19 and 104—make uniquely valuable contributions to a theology oriented toward the fullness of life for all creation.

Psalm 19

Psalm 19 opens,

> The heavens are telling the glory of God;
>> and the firmament proclaims his handiwork.
> Day unto day pours forth speech,
>> and night to night declares knowledge.
> There is no speech, nor are there words;
>> their voice is not heard;
> yet their voice goes out through all the earth,
>> and their words to the end of the world.
> (Ps 19:1–4)

These opening lines offer fascinating reflections on the relationship between creation and the human knowledge of God, cast in what Brueggemann describes as "awed doxology . . . the appropriate response to the miracle of creation that enacts Yahweh's

Abundant Life in the Order of Creation 57

will to life."[40] Yet, although these reflections originate with a human author, the psalm makes creation the agent of doxology, imagining the heavens and earth proclaiming God's glory and attesting to God's works. The psalm then deploys a metaphor of speech to advance this vision, as day and night soundlessly attest to God's presence and action in creation. Yet, if there is no sound, how does creation speak?

Following the logic established in Genesis, one can imagine that the heavens and earth proclaim God's glory simply by being what they are. In their own beauty, in their own activity—governing night and day, bringing forth vegetation—the heavens and earth reveal God. The psalm's vision is expansive here, as their voice resounds "through all the earth," everywhere and for every creature, including humans. Psalm 19 thus imagines creation as having the agency to attest to God's works, leaving humans—like the psalmist—to perceive creation's praise.

The following verses use the movement of the sun to deepen this vision, focusing in particular on the ordered movement of sun through the skies. Like a bridegroom on his wedding day, the sun emerges from its "tent" and "runs its course with joy" (19:5). In the seventh verse, creational metaphors abruptly fall away (v. 10's reference to the sweetness of honey notwithstanding), and the psalm shifts to an exaltation of Torah, "the law of the LORD" (19:7). Although some scholars have argued that there is no relationship between the parts of the psalm—that it simply consists of two disparate texts—the fact that a redactor linked these texts together still calls interpreters to ask why this is the case.[41]

In light of the importance of the theme of order throughout the Hebrew Bible, I contend that the psalmist intends to suggest

---

[40] Brueggemann, *Theology of the Old Testament*, 529.

[41] Robert Alter, *The Book of Psalms: A Translation with Commentary* (New York: Norton, 2007), 62.

that just as the rhythms of creation reveal the life-giving order God established, so Torah orders human existence and gives life. As one commentator observes, "The 'instruction of the Lord' is built into the very structure of the universe. It is as fundamental and reliable and close-at-hand as the progression of day and night (v. 2), the rising and setting of the sun (v. 6)."[42] In this way creation functions in Psalm 19 as a primordial revealer of God's intentions, connecting the order of nature with the order human life and reinforcing the idea that the flourishing of creation provides a critical backdrop for reflecting on God's ways, including the possibility of disobedience or unfaithfulness to what God intends. Moreover, just as discerning God's intentions for creation leads to the possibility of human participation in the work of life, perceiving creation's proclamation of praise orients humans to discern a way toward the fullness of life in keeping with God's ways, while also deepening humanity's sense of creation's integrity and agency. This sensibility—what I have elsewhere called a "creation imagination"—is vital for understanding the significance of creation vis-à-vis flourishing.[43]

Psalm 104

Psalm 104 reiterates many of the themes considered above. Yet this psalm, which Brown names "the most extensive creation psalm in the Bible," manifests an ecological sensibility that is unmatched within the biblical literature.[44] This sensibility deepens the insights into God's way of creating and intentions for creation articulated in the texts considered above, with a distinctive

---

[42] J. Clinton McCann, Jr., *A Theological Introduction to the Book of Psalms: The Psalms as Torah* (Nashville, TN: Abingdon Press, 1993), 28.

[43] Paul J. Schutz, "From Creatureliness to a Creation Imagination," *The Other Journal* 28 (2018).

[44] Brown, *The Seven Pillars of Creation*, 141.

Abundant Life in the Order of Creation 59

emphasis on the dynamics of divine providence and flourishing in creation. Beginning in the tenth verse, the psalm offers a cascading series of reflections on the relationship between aspects of creation and their purposes. These reflections are not just quantitative (for example, "water allows plants to grow"). Each possesses a rich qualitative aspect that links the purpose of each facet of creation to the flourishing of life, in direct parallel with Genesis 1. Flowing springs provide drink to wild animals (104:10–11); the trees provide habitats for birds (104:12); grass grows to feed cattle; and earth's fruits nourish humans (104:14).

And there is more to the story. The psalm explicitly links creaturely responses to the gifts they receive from God through creation with the quality of their lives. As they experience God's providence, the creational foundation of flourishing, they rejoice. For example, birds do not just live in the trees; "they sing among the branches." Water does not just nourish the earth; "the earth is *satisfied* with the fruit of [God's] work" (104:13). From earth's flora, we humans make wine to gladden our hearts and bread to give us strength (104:15). This socio-ecological revue evokes deep interconnectedness among plants and animal species, and the exchange of creation's gifts elicits joy and praise in birdsong, earth's satisfaction, and humanity's joy.[45]

Then, after reflecting further on animal habitats, which Brown observes as evoking what ecologists term niche construction, the psalm proffers a profound reflection on the function of the moon and the sun, which, in rising and setting, govern the actions of all earth's creatures.[46] The psalm states:

---

[45] On the topic of animals in the imagination in Psalm 104, see Ken Stone, "All These Look to You: Reading Psalm 104 with Animals in the Anthropocene Epoch," *Interpretation: A Journal of Bible and Theology* 73, no. 3 (2019): 236–47. On animals' praise, see Elizabeth A. Johnson, "Animals' Praise of God," 259–71, in the same issue.

[46] Brown, *The Seven Pillars of Creation*, 154–56.

> You make darkness, and it is night,
>> when all the animals of the forest come
>>> creeping out.
> The young lions roar for their prey,
>> seeking their food from God.
> When the sun rises, they withdraw
>> and lie down in their dens.
> People go out to their work
>> and to their labor until the evening.
>> (Ps 104:2–23)

Here, as in Genesis 1:14, where the "lights in the dome of the sky" serve as "signs and for seasons and for days and years," night and day govern the comings and goings of all types of creatures. Seeking sustenance from God, lions join forest creatures in a nightly prowl. At sunrise, they return home to their dens, and humans leave their homes to spend the day at work, until sunset calls them back in what Robert Alter describes as "a beautifully imagined diurnal cycle of seeking sustenance."[47] In addition to the governing power of the sun and moon, that all creatures are subject to their rhythms is striking, evoking "a certain parity of existence between human being and wild animal."[48] Indeed, humans do not determine nature's rhythms; these rhythms are inscribed into creation, and like lions and forest animals, we humans are subject to the order of creation, oriented as it is toward the sustenance of all.

A joyous exclamation of praise follows these reflections:

> O LORD, how manifold are your works!
>> In wisdom you have made them all;
>>> the earth is full of your creatures. (Ps 104:24)

---

[47] Alter, *The Book of Psalms,* 366.
[48] Brown, *The Seven Pillars of Creation,* 156–57.

Abundant Life in the Order of Creation   *61*

Here, the psalmist—overcome by the sight—marvels at creation and praises Wisdom at work in the world, in terms that will recur in the description of Wisdom's role in Proverbs 3. Imagining this moment in view of contemporary science, Brown writes, "Armed with a microscope, the psalmist would have also marveled over the more minute forms of biological life, down to the unicellular, all vibrant and thriving, all bounded and interdependent."[49] The species of earth and the order of creation are a source of awe, and, in beholding the fulfillment of God's blessing—"be fruitful and multiply, and fill"—Brueggemann concludes, "Israel is dazzled."[50]

Having so surveyed creation, the Psalmist concludes in prayer:

> May the glory of the LORD endure forever;
>   may the LORD rejoice in his works. (Ps 104:31)

God's rejoicing in creation here appears in parallel to the enduring revelation of God's glory in creation. As in Psalm 19, God is glorified through God's works, which the heavens proclaim and earth declares. Following this logic we might also conclude that if God glories in creation, then creation's degradation—whether socially or ecologically—would surely not be cause for divine rejoicing. As Brown puts it: "If Leviathan falls, then so do we all. If creation's wondrous variety is diminished, then the psalmist's worst fear is realized: creation left to wither away."[51] All in all, this text reaffirms the integrity of creaturely life in ways that carry tremendous potential to foster love and care for all things as co-participants in the life system we call creation. And so, the text concludes by again sounding notes of praise anchored in the experience of beholding what God has made—both individual

---

[49] Brown, 151.
[50] Brueggemann, *Theology of the Old Testament,* 530.
[51] Brown, *The Seven Pillars of Creation,* 159.

62   *A Theology of Flourishing*

creatures and the life-giving relationships of interdependence that link them, guided as they are by the rhythms of night and day, held in being by the *ruah Elohim* that orders and enlivens all things. "Bless the LORD, O my soul. Praise the LORD!" (104:35), the psalmist concludes. Hallelujah, indeed!

Proverbs and Wisdom

Flourishing's function as a foundational principle of creation and background theory for covenant comes to concrete expression as a guiding framework for creaturely life in the Wisdom literature. In the Wisdom books, creation remains central. "Wisdom thinks resolutely within the framework of a theology of creation," as Walther Zimmerli observes.[52] The expansive scope of the Wisdom texts makes it impossible for this brief section to "trace [Wisdom's] course from the beginning of creation" (Wis 6:22). Still, the perspectives on creation and salvation found in key discourses on Wisdom have great significance for a theology of flourishing, as discerning and following the way of Wisdom in creation leads to the fullness of life. This orientation manifests in two key ways: in the relationship between Wisdom and creation, and in seeing Wisdom as a perceptual framework—a lens on creation—that orients human life and society toward God's intention that all creatures may flourish in the fullness of life.

The Wisdom literature depicts Lady Wisdom, a feminine expression of divinity, as the one who orders and renews creation and as the order of creation itself. For example, in terms that will later be ascribed to Christ, Wisdom 7 describes Lady Wisdom as "a breath of the power of God and a pure emanation of the

---

[52] Walther Zimmerli, "The Place and Limit of Wisdom in the Framework of the Old Testament Theology," *Scottish Journal of Theology* 17, no. 2 (1964): 148.

Abundant Life in the Order of Creation 63

glory of the Almighty" (Wis 7:25).[53] Given the link between *ruah* and life in the Hebrew Bible, as well as God's creation by word in Genesis 1, this use of "breath" makes concrete the connection between Wisdom and the created order. This connection finds further support in the verses that follow, culminating in 8:1, which declares, "She reaches mightily from one end of the earth to the other, and she orders things well."

The Book of Proverbs builds on this point. There, Wisdom is described as the force by which God "founded the earth" (3:19), the "first of his acts of long ago" (8:22). After this introduction, she speaks in the first person of being brought forth before the depths and springs, mountains and hills, fields, skies, and seas (8:24–29). Beside God "like a master worker" (8:30), playing and delighting in the world God made, Wisdom pervades every corner of creation and every dimension of human life, all as part of her creational work. As Brown states, "The wisdom by which God established creation, the wisdom reflected in nature, is the same wisdom found in the bustling marketplace, city gates, and street corners. In Proverbs, cosmic Wisdom makes her home in the day-to-day world of human intercourse."[54] Having built her house on seven pillars (9:1), Wisdom binds the natural world and human society into a bustling system of life, offering a concrete basis for discerning and attuning ourselves to God's life-giving intentions in all things. By becoming attuned to Wisdom's work in every nook and cranny of creation, theology may find a further basis for perceiving creation as an order of graced goodness and abundant life. Indeed, Wisdom's own declaration, "whoever

---

[53] For one treatment of the relationship among Wisdom, Christ, and creation, see Denis Edwards, *Ecology at the Heart of Faith* (Maryknoll, NY: Orbis Books, 2006), 52–58. See also Carole R. Fontaine, "Proverbs," in *The Old Testament and Apocrypha: Fortress Commentary on the Bible*, ed. Gale A. Yee, Hugh R. Page Jr., and Matthew J. M. Coomber (Minneapolis: Fortress Press, 2014), 610.

[54] Brown, *The Seven Pillars of Creation*, 163.

64   *A Theology of Flourishing*

finds me finds life" (8:35), leads Leo Perdue to conclude that life is "the core value" of the Wisdom texts and Fretheim to argue that Wisdom operates "for the sake of life."[55]

Put simply, life is the fruit of Wisdom's work. In beholding this work—in following her ways—humans come to see themselves as co-participants with all things in an encompassing order that is fundamentally oriented toward the fulfillment of that life in union with God. Individually and communally, Wisdom reorients Christian thought and praxis toward denouncing forces of death and working on behalf of the fullness of life for all creation. This vision is indeed world changing, fostering a kind of self-actualization that, as Johnson puts it, "enables individuals to arrive at their destiny, and in the end enables the whole world and its history to be rightly ordered in justice and peace."[56] As a concrete expression of *ruah* of divine power that enlivens all things, walking in the way of Wisdom facilitates the fulfillment of God's intentions: that all things may come to the fullness of life for which they were made.

Key Insights for the Path Ahead

Taken together, the creation texts of the Hebrew Bible—from Genesis through Exodus to the Psalms and Wisdom literature—present life, abundance, and flourishing as God's principal intentions for creation. These are indeed texts of natality, proclaiming the magnificent story of a world being born. Within this world, creatures of all types—from amoebas and elms to humans, water, and air—subsist in life-giving relationships that attest to

---

[55] Leo G. Perdue, *Wisdom Literature: A Theological History* (Louisville, KY: Westminster John Knox Press, 2007), 51; Fretheim, *God and World in the Old Testament*, 207.

[56] Elizabeth Johnson, *She Who Is: The Mystery of God in Feminist Theological Discourse* (New York: Crossroad, 1991), 90.

Abundant Life in the Order of Creation   65

the presence and action of their Creator. This is indeed a world where, as Basil puts it, "beasts bear witness to the faith."[57] These texts thus offer invaluable resources for discerning God's intentions for this world, providing the foundational understanding of creation that grounds the proposed theology of flourishing. Moreover, while it is possible to derive a domineering view of human-earth relations from these texts, this view must be rejected on the basis that it stands in fundamental contradiction to God's life-giving aims. It is sinful, not "normal," to find a justification for any form of injustice or exploitation in the Genesis text.

Even so, if "creation is not so much a concept to be mastered as a conviction to be lived," this analysis also poses important theological and practical challenges, which later chapters will consider.[58] How should theologians and communities of faith engage insights from contemporary ecology, biology, and physics? How do emerging scientific insights about the nature of reality bear on ethics, natural law, and so on? In a different vein, if the world is made to flourish, how should Christians respond to the brokenness of the created order evoked in the punishment discourse of Genesis 2? Should Christians accept this brokenness as "just the way things are now" and thus as somehow acceptable to God? Or, in step with Trible's observation that, even amid a long history of patriarchal interpretation, "grace makes possible a new beginning," should the divine intentions revealed in these texts challenge Christians to ask anew what flourishing means and guide them to live as agents of flourishing in a fractured world?[59] Later chapters will suggest answers to these questions. For now, we continue to lay foundations for a theology of flourishing by

---

[57] Basil, *Hexaëmeron*, 149.

[58] D. Brent Laytham, "'So as Not to Be Estranged': Creation Spirituality and Wendell Berry," *The Covenant Quarterly* 66, no. 1 (February 2008): 38.

[59] Trible, "Eve and Adam," 465.

examining the New Testament literature, giving special attention to how the revolutionary love that is revealed in the incarnation functions as a foundation for flourishing, in keeping with the divine intentions revealed in creation.

4

Revolutionary Love for "All Things"

*New Testament Foundations
for a Theology of Flourishing*

Seen through the prism of Hebrew Bible creation texts, the proclamation of abundant life in John 10:10 illuminates an intrinsic resonance between the memories of Jesus that are articulated in the Gospels and the religious imaginary in which Jesus was formed as a first-century Jew living under Roman rule. In this way the New Testament invites us to recognize that his proclamation of life did not arise *ex nihilo*, as if from an unconditioned divine consciousness that transcended the time and place in which Jesus lived. Son of God though he was, his understanding of life—as well as his understandings of justice, peace, mercy, and love—were informed and conditioned by the faith tradition he lived out and the cultural circumstances in which he dwelled. Although we may not be able to specify precisely how, the blessings of creation in Genesis, the proclamations of praise and wonder in the psalms, and the discourses on Wisdom's wondrous work in creation surely informed Jesus's religious identity and understanding and shaped his prophetic mission.

The correspondence between the emphasis on life in the Hebrew Bible and Christ's proclamation of abundant life leads

67

68 *A Theology of Flourishing*

naturally to an analysis of New Testament texts, connecting God's life-giving intentions for creation with the revolutionary love of Christ. This correspondence also demands that we reject any Marcionite-like claims to discontinuity between the Hebrew Bible and the New Testament, which wrongly suggest that God's original intentions for creation differ from what Christ reveals. Interpreting the New Testament in relation to God's intentions for creation—giving attention to the importance of the materiality of creation and seeing the Christ as a manifestation of divine Wisdom—offers tools for employing Christ's vision of justice, mercy, peace, and above all, love as foundations for a theology and praxis oriented toward the flourishing of all creation.

As Bernard Anderson wrote long ago, "God's work in Christ is the restoration of the original intention of the creation and, therefore, a foretaste of the final consummation when all things will be made new."[1] To demonstrate this point, this chapter first synthesizes the cosmic Christologies of the prologue to the Gospel of John and Colossians 1 into a foundation for a holistic, socio-ecological interpretation of the New Testament. The chapter then follows a through line that links the discourses on revolutionary love in 1 Corinthians and Matthew with the call to a praxis of embodied care in the Johannine corpus to provide further foundations for a theology of flourishing oriented toward the fullness of life for *ta pánta*—all things.

Christological Context: Creation, Incarnation, and Flesh in John 1 and Colossians 1

Numerous theologians—including Denis Edwards, Elizabeth Johnson, and Ilia Delio—have argued for deeper recognition of

---

[1] Bernard W. Anderson, "The Earth Is the Lord's: An Essay on the Biblical Doctrine of Creation," *Interpretation* 9, no. 1 (January 1955): 19.

Revolutionary Love for "All Things"   69

the connection between Christ and creation, a necessary foundation for a holistic, socio-ecological understanding of flourishing.[2] Whether by proposing a Cosmic Christ or a paradigm of deep incarnation and resurrection, these thinkers draw on New Testament texts to link creation and incarnation through Christ's *sarx*, or flesh.

For example, in *Ecology at the Heart of Faith* Edwards elucidates how early Christian communities interpreted the Christ-event through the lens of Wisdom. Given the connection between Wisdom and creation, these interpretations imputed a cosmic dimension to Christ's existence. Just as Wisdom "was beside him [God], like a master worker" (Prv 8:30) in the creation of the cosmos, so Christ was seen as the one through whom all things exist (1 Cor 8:6).[3] This link likewise paved the way for an expanded understanding of incarnation that—in keeping with the use of "in the beginning" at the start of John's Gospel and the parallel use of *dabar-logos*-word and *hokmah-sophia*-wisdom across the testaments—connects the fundamental claim of Johannine Christology, "the Word became flesh and lived among us" (Jn 1:14), to the whole cosmos.[4] Thus, as Bauckham concludes,

---

[2] See Denis Edwards, *Jesus the Wisdom of God: An Ecological Theology* (Maryknoll, NY: Orbis Books, 1995); Elizabeth Johnson, *Ask the Beasts: Darwin and the God of Love* (London: Bloomsbury, 2015); and Ilia Delio, *Christ in Evolution* (Maryknoll, NY: Orbis Books, 2008).

[3] Denis Edwards, *Ecology at the Heart of Faith* (Maryknoll, NY: Orbis Books, 2006), 53.

[4] Edwards, 55. Raymond Brown notes this connection in the appendix to his 1966 *Anchor Bible* Commentary, as well. See Raymond E. Brown, PSS, *The Gospel according to John (i–xii): The Anchor Bible* (New York: Doubleday, 1966), 521–23. For an extended historical and scriptural treatment of Wisdom and Christology, see James D. G. Dunn, *Christology in the Making: A New Testament Inquiry into the Origins of the Doctrine of the Incarnation* (Philadelphia: Westminster Press, 1980), 163–212. For a similar treatment of Word, see 213–50 in the same volume. For a reading of John's Gospel through the lens of Wisdom traditions, see Mary L. Coloe, *John 1–10: Wisdom Commentary* (Collegeville, MN: Liturgical Press, 2021).

70   *A Theology of Flourishing*

"John situates his story of Jesus on Earth in the widest possible temporal and spatial context."[5]

A theology of flourishing moves beyond merely linking Christ to creation in parallel with Wisdom, also observing the connection John makes between Christ's incarnation and life. Just as Lady Wisdom declared that "those who find me find life," John's Gospel proclaims, "What has come into being in him was life, and the life was the light of all people" (1:3b–4). In addition to anticipating the proclamation of abundant life in John 10:10, this passage further connects the incarnation with God's life-giving intentions for all creatures. Assessing the theological implications of this view, Raymond Brown writes that, in the incarnation, "the whole of God's message, in the full sense of 'Word,' inextricably bound itself to the sphere of the flesh. [John] shows this by stressing that Jesus communicated His greatest gift, life, through the things of this world."[6] By becoming flesh, in and through material reality, Christ enlivens the world.

Along with the Gospel of John, Edwards observes how the hymn in Colossians 1:15–20 presents Christ "as both the *source* of creation and its *goal*."[7] Brown concurs with this reading, once again casting the connection in terms of the through line from Wisdom to Christ. He writes, "The closest and most commonly accepted background for the description in 1:15–16a is the OT picture of personified female Wisdom, the image of God's goodness (Wisdom 7:26) who worked with God in establishing all other things (Prov. 3:19)—that Wisdom was created by

---

[5] Richard Bauckham, *The Bible and Ecology: Rediscovering the Community of Creation* (Waco, TX: Baylor University Press, 2010), 162.

[6] Raymond E. Brown, PSS, "The Theology of the Incarnation in John," in *New Testament Essays* (London: Geoffrey Chapman, 1965), 99.

[7] Edwards, *Jesus the Wisdom of God*, 56.

Revolutionary Love for "All Things" 71

God at the beginning (Prov. 8:22; Sirach 24:9)."[8] The key to this interpretation is the repetition of the phrase "*ta pánta*"—all things. The Colossians hymn repeats this expression four times, with reference to the act of creation and the purpose of all things (1:16); Christ's pre-existence and function in holding all things together (1:17, again like Wisdom); and the redemption of all things "by making peace through the blood of the cross" (1:20). Commenting on this use of "peace," Bauckham notes that the word does not describe "merely the absence of conflict, but the wholeness, harmony, and well-being of the whole creation that transpires when the creatures are in right relationship with each other."[9] The peace that Christ brings is not a passing condition but a holistic socio-ecological order, a reordering of creation toward God's life-giving intentions for all things, in direct parallel with the vision of creation articulated in the Hebrew Bible.

From Vision to Praxis:
Creation, Life, and Love in the Pauline Corpus

Analysis of key texts from the Pauline corpus shows how the thread of flourishing shaped the understanding of the earliest Christian communities. In Paul's call for "faith working through love" on behalf of "new creation," and in the revolutionary implications of his famous image of the body with many parts, we find a commitment to working in faith on behalf of abundant life for all, especially the "least of these." By means of exegesis and consideration of intertextual resonances, this analysis reveals a consistent focus on the necessary connection between the

---

[8] Raymond E. Brown, *An Introduction to the New Testament* (New Haven, CT: Yale University Press, 1997), 603–4.

[9] Bauckham, *The Bible and Ecology*, 157.

72　　　　　　　　　　　　　　　　　　*A Theology of Flourishing*

profession of faith in Christ and embodied practices of love—what we might, as a unity, call "life in Christ."

Faith Working through Love on Behalf of New Creation: Galatians and 2 Corinthians

Given its angry tone, Paul's Letter to the Galatians may appear to be a strange source for discussing the connection among faith, love, and the fullness of life.[10] In the letter, Paul aims to confront a major conflict that has arisen in the church he established. He writes that the Galatians have turned to "a different gospel" (1:6) that is being proclaimed by preachers who have also undermined his authority. As John Gager explains, the crux of the issue is circumcision and the relation of Gentile converts to the Law of Moses. "In a word, anti-Pauline apostles *within the Jesus-movement* had persuaded members—some? Most? All? Paul does not say—of his congregation to accept circumcision and to follow at least some elements of the Mosaic law."[11] Paul rejects this view, arguing that righteousness comes not through keeping the works of the law but through faith in Jesus.[12]

---

[10] For example, 3:1 declares, "You foolish Galatians!"

[11] John G. Gager, *Reinventing Paul* (Oxford: Oxford University Press, 2000), 79.

[12] Here, it is critical to reject any supersessionist interpretation of this passage. As Gager argues at length, Paul does not reject the law. Rather, "The key phrase, 'works of the law' (*erga tou nomou*), refers specifically to the ambiguous status of Gentiles under the law and should not be rendered as 'the law' or 'Torah.'" Gager, *Reinventing Paul*, 79. Moreover, Paul's highly stylized rhetorical response comes in the midst of a conflict over whether circumcision and adherence to some parts of the law are required for Gentile followers of Jesus. His commentary says nothing about the status or experience of Jewish Christians. As Gager notes, "Paul himself never uses the term [Christianity] in any form. Is it too much to insist that since he failed to use the term he may not have had any notion of a new religion as the term Christianity implies?" See Gager, 23–25.

Revolutionary Love for "All Things" 73

Amid this rebuke of the Galatians, Paul exclaims: "For through the law I died to the law, so that I might live to God. I have been crucified with Christ, and it is no longer I who live, but it is Christ who lives in me" (2:19–20a). Here, the theme of life returns once more, now cast as the first fruits of faith in Christ. Through faith in Christ, Paul states, his former understanding of the law as a basis for righteousness found fulfillment, and he became aware of Christ alive within him.

What does it mean to say that Christ lives "in" a person? Some might argue that this is about "being saved" on the way toward full union with God after death. That may well be part of the picture. But Paul also indicates that "life in Christ" elicits changes in the life of the one who has faith. The conclusion of 2:20 states, "And the life I now live in the flesh [*en sarkì*] I live by the faith of the Son of God, who loved me and gave himself for me." Here, in direct contrast to a dualistic understanding of flesh and spirit or a notion of life in Christ as spiritual enlightenment that takes a person beyond this world, Paul speaks of life *en sarkì*, such that Christ is envisioned as working out God's intentions through Paul's own self-actualization.

In Paul's terms—which significantly pre-date but appear consistent with usages of life in the Johannine corpus—Paul emphasizes how faith draws Christians into the fullness of life and makes them agents of that life through their being "in Christ." As the subsequent analysis of 1 John bears out, this consistency demonstrates a focus in early Christian writings on the relationship among life, faith, and embodiment. The idea of salvation beyond the world only garners secondary attention. Upon experiencing God's life-giving presence and action in the flesh, Christians respond not by declaring assurance of heavenly salvation but by living lives that proclaim, "It is no longer I who live, but it is Christ who lives in me." Further, contrary to the idea that Galatians presents a *sola fide* vision of salvation, the idea of faith lived out in the flesh pervades

74 *A Theology of Flourishing*

the text. This approach culminates in Paul's statement that "in Christ Jesus, neither circumcision nor uncircumcision counts for anything; the only thing that counts is *faith working through love*" (Gal 5:6). Loving as Christ loved—in this world, in the flesh—serves as the fundamental expression of faith in Jesus.

Similarly, the Second Letter to the Corinthians speaks of "new creation" in Christ (2 Cor 5:14–21). Although the statement that Christ died for all (*hypèr pántōn*) should be understood primarily in anthropological terms, David Horrell finds "scope enough in the Pauline texts to encourage the development of his thought in [a cosmic] direction, as is already evident in the cosmic Christology of Colossians."[13] Paul uses this claim to imagine the incorporation of people, and perhaps all creatures, into the life of Christ, bringing about "a fundamental reorientation to the other, and to the needs and interests of the other above the self."[14]

Then follows a famous phrase, typically translated, "So whoever is in Christ is a new creation" (2 Cor 5:17, NABRE). As Horrell points out, however, the Greek text lacks clear verbs, which must be provided by the translator (who, I would make explicit, is acting as interpreter given the indeterminate grammar).[15] While many—in keeping with the translation above—argue that the "new creation" to which the passage refers happens in the life of the follower of Jesus, in light of the cosmic and eschatological vision of other Pauline writings, Horrell suggests that this phrase may also be seen as heralding the eschatological arrival of a new creation.[16] If this is so, the grammatical indeterminacy allows for other translations, such as the NRSV's rendering, "So if anyone is in Christ, there is a new creation: everything old has passed

---

[13] David G. Horrell, "Ecojustice in the Bible? Pauline Contributions to an Ecological Theology," in *Bible and Justice: Ancient Texts, Modern Challenges*, ed. Matthew J. M. Coomber, 158–77 (London: Equinox, 2011), 165.

[14] Horrell, 165.

[15] On the history of translation, see Horrell, 166, and citations therein.

[16] Horrell, 167.

Revolutionary Love for "All Things" 75

away; see, everything has become new!" This translation shifts focus from the conversion of the individual follower of Jesus to the actualization of God's will that comes about *in creation as a whole* through conversion.[17] In other words, to supply "there is" rather than "that person is" before "new creation" is to claim, in ways that reflect the consistent use of "all things" in Colossians, that new creation comes about wherever Christ is present. Lives lived in and for Christ thus effect the realization of the promise inaugurated in Christ's redemptive work, here dubbed "new creation." As Horrell concludes, then, "2 Cor 5:19a—'God was in Christ reconciling the cosmos to himself'—can stand as a concise expression of the heart of this theology," which finds practical expression in radical love that fosters the fullness of life for all things.[18]

1 Corinthians: Revolutionary Love on Behalf of Socio-ecological Transformation

Galatians and 2 Corinthians demonstrate how, in the Pauline imagination, faith in Christ is oriented toward practices of love that bring about "new creation"—the fulfillment of God's life-giving will. Demonstrating Paul's rhetorical prowess, the discourse on the body in 1 Corinthians 12–13 deepens insight into how he imagined faith in Christ being put into practice on behalf of the flourishing of all, especially the "least of these."

As Wayne Meeks and John Fitzgerald explain, Corinth was a city largely settled by freed slaves from Italy. This situation allowed for "a kind of social mobility rare in ancient towns," and thus makes it unsurprising "that questions of status are prominent in Paul's letter."[19] Making this point clear, Dale Martin argues

---

[17] Horrell, 168.

[18] Horrell, 172.

[19] Wayne A. Meeks and John T. Fitzgerald, eds., *The Writings of St. Paul: Annotated Texts, Reception and Criticism*, 2nd ed. (New York: Norton, 2007), 21.

that questions of social status split the Corinthian church into two factions. The first faction is the "strong," whose purported superiority was made manifest in their wisdom, eloquence, and glossolalia, speaking in tongues. The others, whom the letter names the "weak," occupied a lower social status and were, it seems, oppressed by the "strong."[20] As such, the dynamics of oppression and liberation occasion Paul's writing. Given the priority that a hermeneutics of the fullness of life gives to experiences of oppression and injustice, we must recognize these dynamics at play in the Corinthian church.

In the midst of such division Paul deploys numerous metaphors to exhort the community toward social and religious harmony, including the metaphor of the body and its many members. As Martin shows, the speech in which this metaphor appears employs rhetorical techniques from Greco-Roman *homonia* (concord) speeches to urge the Corinthians to act in unity for the good of all. The metaphor of the body thus functions to help the Corinthian community see itself as a single entity united by a common faith in Christ. Within this body, all contribute: as "ears" or "eyes," as "hands" or "feet" (12:14–17). And as with a human body, no part can say to another, "I have no need of you" (12:21), because all contribute to the proper functioning of the whole.

The speech's emphasis on the integrity of the body and each of its members corresponds well with the divine declaration of goodness in Genesis 1:31: the whole is greater than the sum of its parts. Moreover, the image of a body working in unison for the common good aligns well with a vision of flourishing rooted in embodied practices of love that serve the needs of all. Yet as Martin explains, there is another, more subversive dimension

---

[20] Dale B. Martin, *The Corinthian Body* (New Haven, CT: Yale University Press, 1995), xv–xvi. Chapters 1–4 of the epistle make extensive rhetorical use of "weak" and "strong." See, for example, 1 Cor 4:10: "We are fools for the sake of Christ, but you are sensible people in Christ. We are weak, but you are strong. You are honored, but we are dishonored."

Revolutionary Love for "All Things" 77

to this discourse. Paul's use of *homonia* rhetoric, he writes, "is surprising and quite at odds with the dominant goal of *homonia* speeches, which is to solidify the social hierarchy by averting lower-class challenges to the so-called natural status structures that prevail in society. . . . In 1 Corinthians he [Paul] turns it against its usual role as a prop for upper-class ideology."[21] That is, whereas typical *homonia* speeches exhort unity to preserve the status quo, Paul employs *homonia* rhetoric to *overturn* the dominant social hierarchy, aiming to raise up the "weak" and bring down the "strong" in keeping with both the Magnificat (Lk 1:46–55) and the Matthean vision of love.[22] As 1 Corinthians 12:22–26 puts it:

> On the contrary, the members of the body that seem to be weaker are indispensable, and those members of the body that we think less honorable we clothe with greater honor, and our less respectable members are treated with greater respect; whereas our more respectable members do not need this. But God has so arranged the body, giving the greater honor to the inferior member, that there may be no dissension within the body, but the members may have the same care for one another. If one member suffers, all suffer together with it; if one member is honored, all rejoice together with it.

This is revolutionary language. Far beyond an attempt to preserve the status quo, Paul calls for a radical reorientation of society on the basis of God's intentions—here, the way God "arranged the body." His call challenges the Corinthians to pursue God's intentions that all creatures may flourish entails interrogating and overturning long-held social and religious assumptions in

---

[21] Martin, 47.
[22] Martin, 59–60.

78   *A Theology of Flourishing*

the name of love. This love, which seeks solidarity in the fullness of life, once more requires attentiveness, contemplation, and action, so that all may "have the same care for one another" (12:25). To this practice of care, Paul's speech adds attentiveness to how sociopolitical and ecclesial systems enable or obstruct self-actualization—grounding another indispensable aspect of a theology of flourishing. Reading the metaphor of the body in view of the struggle between the strong and weak in Corinth thus demands that contemporary applications of this passage consider whether social and ecclesial structures, including those that affect the natural world, operate as instruments of division and oppression—rendering humans indifferent to myriad forms of socio-ecological injustice, as in Corinth—or whether they foster mutual care that enables self-actualization so that God's life-giving intentions may be realized.

Given this analysis, it is unsurprising that Paul's exhortation culminates in a discourse on love, which he famously dubs "a still more excellent way" (12:31). Paul's statements here are structured according to a formula: "If I . . . but do not have love . . . I am . . . ." Each statement relativizes what is likely the basis for a claim to authority or superiority among the "strong" of Corinth and reframes it in terms of love. For example, 13:1 states, "If I speak in the tongues of humans and of angels but do not have love, I am a noisy gong or a clanging cymbal." Speaking in tongues may be wondrous, but it serves no purpose if the one speaking lacks love. So, too, with "prophetic powers" (13:2) and even—in an interesting resonance with the Matthean parable of the rich young man—the act of giving up one's possessions.

Love relativizes all things, putting them in their proper place. This culminating discourse thus reaffirms and develops the subversive, revolutionary character of love in the New Testament, which acts not out of deference to law and tradition but seeks "a more excellent way." This love may sometimes be transgressive, defying sociopolitical and religious conventions on the basis of

Revolutionary Love for "All Things" 79

carefully discerned attentiveness to the Spirit's life-giving purposes. Above all, love appears in embodied practices of care, so that all may experience the material conditions that allow for abundant life to break forth as the fruit of Christ's redemptive action in, with, and for all things.

The Gospel of Matthew: Revolutionary Love and the Flourishing of the "Least of These"

To say that Christ's saving action extends to all creation through embodied practices of love is only a starting point. What does this love look like in practice, and how does love foster the fullness of life for all things in New Testament terms? Moving from preaching to narrating the life of Christ, the Gospel of Matthew offers important resources for answering this question.

Commenting on Matthew 22:39, Brevard Childs names "the heart of the law . . . love of God and love of neighbor."[23] Indeed, if, as Dale Allison shows, Jesus's statement on the unity of the love of God and love of neighbor in Matthew 22:37–39 radicalizes the *Shema* (Dt 6:4–9) and Leviticus 19:18, then we may rightly conclude that "Jesus reduces everything to love, which is the fulfilling of the law."[24] Here again, Jesus is not so much introducing

---

[23] Brevard Childs, *Biblical Theology of the Old and New Testaments: Theological Reflection on the Christian Bible* (Minneapolis: Fortress Press, 1992), 275.

[24] Dale Allison, *Matthew: A Shorter Commentary* (London: T & T Clark, 2004), 322. The *Shema* reads, "Hear, O Israel: The Lord is our God, the Lord alone. You shall love the Lord your God with all your heart and with all your soul and with all your might. Keep these words that I am commanding you today in your heart. Recite them to your children and talk about them when you are at home and when you are away, when you lie down and when you rise. Bind them as a sign on your hand, fix them as an emblem on your forehead, and write them on the doorposts of your house and on your gates." Leviticus 19:18 reads, "You shall not take vengeance or bear a grudge against any of your people, but you shall love your neighbor as yourself: I am the Lord." Warren Carter observes anti-imperial implications in this passage that parallel

80

A Theology of Flourishing

something new as he is reinterpreting and radicalizing what Rabbi Akiba named "the encompassing principle of the Torah," speaking in a prophetic idiom from within Judaism.[25] Therefore, as Allison concludes, Jesus's statement that love fulfills the Law and the Prophets (Mt 22:40) does not negate but "confirms the Torah's truth."[26]

What does such love look like in practice, and how does love relate to flourishing? In Luke 10, Jesus's statement on the unity of the love of God and love of neighbor introduces the parable of the Good Samaritan—a story about the radicalization of love to which I will return. In Matthew, however, the story of the rich young man (Mt 19:16–22) is instructive. In ways that anticipate the double love command, the young man in the story asks Jesus what he must do to inherit eternal life. In response, Jesus quotes the prohibitions against murder, adultery, and theft from the Ten Commandments and adds Leviticus's command to love one's neighbor as oneself (19:18). The young man tells Jesus that he has kept these commandments and, rather admirably, asks what else he might lack. Here as before, Jesus's response radicalizes the command to love, casting it in terms of human economic life. He states, "Go, sell your possessions, and give the money to the poor, and you will have treasure in heaven; then come, follow me" (Mt 19:21). This, it seems, is what it means for the unity of love of God and love of neighbor to fulfill the law. To love God is to give all one has for the good of those most in need and to follow Christ in what Ulrich Luz describes as "a

---

certain themes from my analysis of 1 Corinthians. See Warren Carter, "Love as Societal Vision and Counter-Imperial Practice in Matthew 22:34–40," in *Biblical Interpretation in Early Christian Gospels*, vol. 2, ed. Thomas R. Hatina (London: T & T Clark, 2008), 30–44.

[25] For a summary of Rabbinic treatments of these passages, see Allison, *Matthew*, 382–90.

[26] Allison, 72.

Revolutionary Love for "All Things" 81

radical expression of the love command that for Jesus knows no boundary."[27] At the same time, to divest of one's possessions is to liberate oneself toward new forms of self-actualization, becoming what one truly is, so that one may follow Christ in a more radical way. Perhaps this is another way to understand Paul's phrase, "Christ lives in me."

Yet the relationship among commandment, love, and life in Matthew possesses an even more revolutionary character, which emerges clearly in the narratives of Jesus picking grain and healing on the Sabbath in violation of the letter of the law.[28] In both stories Jesus's response to challenges from religious authorities makes the point. In the story of picking grain, he responds to the Pharisees' challenge, "See, your disciples are doing what is unlawful to do on the Sabbath" (Mt 12:2), with a phrase from Hosea: "I desire mercy, not sacrifice" (Hos 6:6). Likewise, when on the Sabbath Jesus heals the man with the withered hand (Mt 12:9–14), he calls the Pharisees to reflect on what achieves the greater good: strict observance of the law or the restoration of the man's health. As Johnson notes, this pattern illustrates Jesus's interpretation of the tradition to which he belonged and provides a basis for an understanding of love that does whatever it can, even breaking religious conventions, to foster the flourishing of those in need. She writes:

> In every single case when the law was set aside, it was because the well-being of someone was at stake. In face of the

---

[27] Ulrich Luz, *Matthew 8–20: A Commentary*, trans. James E. Crouch (Minneapolis: Augsburg Fortress, 2001), 513.

[28] For an exhaustive review of literature on this pericope, see John P. Meier, "The Historical Jesus and the Plucking of the Grain on the Sabbath," *The Catholic Biblical Quarterly* 66 (2004): 561–81. My interpretation is rooted in the consensus view that the Pharisees view the action of picking grain on the Sabbath as opposed to the Law.

82   *A Theology of Flourishing*

> sick, the suffering, and the hungry, the sabbath observances
> were given second priority. That is how he interprets the
> Torah. . . . In other words love is at the heart of the reign
> of God. . . . Such love grounds the law, puts it in correct
> perspective, and fulfills it.[29]

These stories impart a subversive character to Christian love. Christian love fulfills the law by transgressing the law, such that healing, forgiveness, wholeness, and life—constitutive aspects of flourishing—hold priority over the social and religious status quo. Allison makes this point well, observing how in these stories "God's generous actions break the rule of reciprocity and cost/benefit analysis" to promote flourishing within the embodied conditions of our existence.[30]

No Matthean pericope illustrates the orientation of love toward embodied well-being and wholeness more clearly than the parable of the Last Judgment in Matthew 25:31–46. In this story the Son of Man judges "the nations," separating those who fulfilled his will (the "sheep") from those who did not (the "goats"). In light of the preceding analysis, what is most significant about this passage is the criterion by which judgment is issued. The Son of Man states:

> "I was hungry and you gave me food, I was thirsty and
> you gave me something to drink, I was a stranger and you
> welcomed me, I was naked and you gave me clothing, I
> was sick and you took care of me, I was in prison and you
> visited me." (Mt 25:35–36)

The inverse is also true (Mt 25:42–43). To their surprise, the proverbial sheep and goats are told that embodied practices of care

---

[29] Elizabeth Johnson, *Consider Jesus: Waves of Renewal in Christology* (New York: Crossroad, 1990), 56.

[30] Allison, *Matthew*, 322.

Revolutionary Love for "All Things"

for the "least of these"—a category I interpret as all those in need, in keeping with the recent consensus—are the medium by which their love for Christ was expressed, or not expressed.[31] In Allison's reading, this parable provides a critical insight into the Matthean conception of love, namely, that "the believer prepares for the *Parousia* by living the imperative to love one's neighbors, especially the marginal. The chief moral imperative (7:12, 19:19, 22:39) is the law by which all are judged on the far side of history."[32] As in theologies of liberation, a theology of flourishing finds in this passage clear evidence that serving for the needs of others is an *a priori* condition for entry into "eternal life" (Mt 25:46) and is, as Gutiérrez observes, "incompatible with an alleged Matthean 'spiritualism.'"[33] As Jantzen would have it, here, this-worldly flourishing provides the context for heavenly salvation, as the promise of heavenly fulfillment is contingent upon lived expressions of love whereby people work to foster the material conditions necessary for the "least of these" to flourish. In honoring the least among us, we honor Christ—even when we do not know it.

---

[31] John R. Donahue describes the meaning of the "least of these" as the "most debated" question in scholarship on Matthew 25. At stake is whether this phrase refers to all those in need or Christian disciples alone. According to the scholarly consensus, Matthew likely had a limited understanding of this phrase, and probably intended it to refer to missionary disciples. However, as Ulrich Luz notes, today the majority of scholars support a more universal interpretation of this phrase as referring to those in need. In my view the combination of what Luz terms the "ignorance motif" (the "sheep" did not know that they had served Christ, so their service was not likely to have been rendered toward disciples alone) and the eschatological character of the parable legitimize a universal interpretation. John R. Donahue, SJ, raises the question in *The Gospel in Parable* (Minneapolis: Fortress Press, 1988), 120. For a full treatment of the scholarly debate, see Ulrich Luz, *Matthew 21–28: A Commentary*, trans. James E. Crouch (Minneapolis: Augsburg Fortress, 2005).

[32] Allison, *Matthew*, 459.

[33] Gustavo Gutiérrez, *A Theology of Liberation: History, Politics, and Salvation*, rev. ed., trans. Sister Caridad Inda and John Eagleson (Maryknoll, NY: Orbis Books, 1988), 119.

84   *A Theology of Flourishing*

The Gospel of Matthew upholds and radicalizes the idea that love of God and the observance of God's ways means giving of what one has for the flourishing of all, especially the "least of these." This orientation implies that the posture of a Christian in the world entails a deep attunement to and contemplation of the needs of others in view of one's own needs, in service of the promotion of abundant life. The unique, embodied realities of others thus shape what it means to love God and so challenge Christians to love even when it requires us to transgress the boundaries of accepted practice or the status quo.

1 John:
Incarnation, Love, and Enfleshed Care for All Things

The foregoing analysis focused on the Pauline and Matthean traditions' emphases on embodied practices of love and care as expressions of faith in the Word made flesh. Well known for its emphasis on love, the First Letter of John—which dates from decades after Paul's death—further emphasizes the importance of *flesh*, or embodiment, in Christ's work, grounding another central dimension of a theology of flourishing. The letter begins:

> We declare to you what was from the beginning, what we have heard, what we have seen with our eyes, what we have looked at and touched with our hands, concerning the word of life—this life was revealed, and we have seen it and testify to it and declare to you the eternal life that was with the Father and was revealed to us—what we have seen and heard we also declare to you so that you also may have fellowship with us, and truly our fellowship is with the Father and with his Son Jesus Christ. (1 Jn 1:1–3)

Like the Greek texts of Genesis and John 1, this passage opens with mention of "the beginning," establishing continuity

Revolutionary Love for "All Things" 85

between this text and John's Gospel and reinforcing the link among creation and incarnation in the Johannine imagination. In addition, sense language pervades this passage: the author refers to what we have heard, seen, looked at, and touched. All this concerns the *lógou tis zois*, the "word of life," which "was with the Father and was revealed to us."[34] Here as before, life—divine, eternal life revealed in creation and fulfilled in the love of Christ—stands at the center of the discourse. Jesus, the word who was with God in the beginning, took flesh. And life came through this flesh, as his body was seen, as his words were heard, as his hands touched those he healed and loved. Seen in this light, Christ's proclamation of abundant life, again, is anchored in materiality. It may stretch toward fulfillment in heavenly union with God, but the abundant life the Johannine community experienced and to which its scriptures attest cannot be conceived apart from materiality, flesh, *sarx*.

Scholarly analyses of this passage give force to the point and suggest a vital link between creation, flesh, flourishing, and salvation in the New Testament. Articulating the consensus view, Brown shows that 1 John intends to address a division within the Johannine community.[35] This division centered on an early Docetism or Cerinthianism, which exaggerated the preexistence of the Word described in the prologue to John's Gospel to such an extent that some downplayed or even denied the reality of Christ's flesh. Practically, this conflict resulted in an understanding of the redemption accomplished by Christ that denigrated

---

[34] For an in-depth analysis of the use of sense language, see Raymond E. Brown, *The Epistles of John: The Anchor Bible* (New York: Doubleday, 1982), 161–63.

[35] Brown's commentaries established the norm for subsequent interpretations of the Johannine corpus, including two influential commentaries that inform my interpretation. See Georg Strecker, *The Johannine Epistles* (Minneapolis: Fortress Press, 1996); and Judith M. Lieu, *I, II, & III John: A Commentary* (Louisville, KY: Westminster John Knox Press, 2012).

86   *A Theology of Flourishing*

the flesh, spiritualized redemption, and supported the view that a person can "know Christ" (on the order of Gnosticism) without loving others.[36] This tension pervades 1 John, bursting to clarity in key verses such as 4:2–3a, which, using the same phrase found in Paul's discourse on life in Christ, states, "every spirit that confesses that Jesus Christ has come in the flesh [*en sarki*] is from God, and every spirit that does not confess Jesus is not from God."[37]

Recognizing this tension in the Johannine community's view of salvation, Brown and Georg Strecker find a notion of "realized salvation" that obviates the need for practices of love in the opposing party's emphasis on spiritual knowledge. As Brown explains:

> Realized salvation would have been part of their theory that after a person believed and became a child of God, subsequent behavior had no salvific import. . . . The author of 1 John challenges this approach, not by denying realized eschatology, but by insisting that one must not neglect future judgment because that too is part of the gospel which was heard from the beginning. He admits that Christians already possess eternal life; yet that life is not a static possession and must be manifest in the way one "walks."[38]

In contrast to assurances of salvation divorced from praxis, we see here an implicit invocation of the Johannine command to love others as Christ loved us—to be perfect in love, "because as he is, so are we in this world" (1 Jn 4:17). Notably, this way of loving happens "in this world," such that concerns for the reality

---

[36] Scholars have long discussed the influence of Gnosticism on the Gospel of John. For a summary, see James G. Dunn, *Unity and Diversity in the New Testament* (Philadelphia: The Westminster Press, 1977), 296–305.

[37] Strecker, *The Johannine Epistles*, 16.

[38] Brown, *Epistles of John*, 99. Cf. Strecker, *Johannine Epistles*, 41–43.

Revolutionary Love for "All Things" 87

of Christ's flesh and the enfleshed life of the community meet in the call for concrete practices of love. This love is both a means toward and concrete expression of the abundant life proclaimed by Christ, in direct contrast to forces that kill, steal, or destroy.

The connection between word and deed thus emerges as a second area of concern for the author of 1 John, one with clear ties to the promise of abundant life. Illustrating this point, Strecker observes in 1 John numerous "antithetical parallelisms" that may represent what the opposing party claimed amid the community's debates about Christ's bodily existence.[39] Like Paul's statements on love in 1 Corinthians 13, these statements have two parts: a negative opening phrase that begins, "Whoever says . . ." (for example, 2:4, 6a) and a positive statement that begins "Whoever does . . . " (for example, 2:5, 6b). These parallelisms concretize the tension between word and deed in direct parallel with Jantzen's concerns about the concrete implications of traditional notions of salvation (word) and the possibilities offered by a shift toward flourishing (action). To consider just one example, 1 John 2:4 states, "Whoever says, 'I have come to know him,' but does not obey his commandments is a liar." Emphasis here falls on a claim to knowledge, or spiritual enlightenment, and stands in stark contrast to the subsequent mention of obedience to Christ's commandments. 1 John 2:5 offers an action-oriented counterpoint: "But whoever obeys his word, truly in this person the love of God has reached perfection." This verse sets knowledge in tension with obedience that is perfected through embodied practices of the commandment to "love one another" (Jn 13:34).[40] Interpreting 1 John in the context of the Gospel of John elucidates the centrality of love as action amid the community's conflict, on the model of Christ himself. As Brown observes, salvation through special knowledge of God is nowhere

---

[39] Strecker, *Johannine Epistles*, 47.

[40] See Brown, *Epistles of John*, 79–86, esp. 83–86.

in view. Rather, "[Jesus's] concern is the knowing and loving and serving God in this life—the things we can do. He leaves to His Father the mysterious allotment of gifts in the next life. The Son became incarnate to teach men how to live a life in this world and not primarily to unveil the secrets of the next."[41] Word and deed are inseparable in a theology of flourishing.

All in all, the Johannine account of the incarnation attests to an intrinsic unity between materiality and the "word of life" that grounds the community's understanding and practice of love. As a result, Sandra Schneiders concludes, the revelation of love as a world-changing praxis is the very purpose of the incarnation. She writes, "Jesus sums up the purpose of the incarnation: 'I have come that they may have ζωή, and have it abundantly' (10:10). The term refers not to some quality or even power possessed by the human being, but to the *whole person as divinely alive*."[42] Following this interpretation, Christianity has no place for the denigration of flesh or quests to escape materiality. Quite the contrary, the incarnation reveals that the meaning of eternal life lies in the deepest possible entry into materiality through embodied practices of love, toward "the fruition and fulfillment of life's gift, in God."[43]

To follow the word of life is, then, to enter fully into this world as agents of abundant life, as "'Life' is realized in the love of brothers and sisters that is demanded of Christians."[44] Such a

---

[41] Brown, "Theology of the Incarnation," 99.

[42] Sandra Schneiders, "The Resurrection (of the Body) in the Fourth Gospel: A Key to Johannine Spirituality," in *Life in Abundance: Studies of John's Gospel in Tribute to Raymond E. Brown*, ed. John R. Donahue (Collegeville, MN: Liturgical Press, 2005), 170–71. Emphasis mine.

[43] Nicholas Lash, *Believing Three Ways in One God: A Reading of the Apostles' Creed* (Notre Dame, IN: University of Notre Dame Press, 1994), 119.

[44] Strecker, *Johannine Epistles*, 17. For a contemporary treatment of Johannine ethics, including the application of John's Gospel to contemporary issues in social and ecological ethics, see Dorothy A. Lee, "Creation, Ethics, and the Gospel of John," in *Johannine Ethics: The Moral World of the Gospel and Epistles of John*, ed. Sherri Brown and Christopher W. Skinner, 241–59 (Minneapolis: Fortress Press, 2017).

Revolutionary Love for "All Things" 89

logic offers an important theological and practical development of Christ's connection to the cosmos, which resituates heavenly salvation under the umbrella of love's power to transform this world in keeping with God's life-giving aims. Giving force to this point, Brown concludes an essay on the theology of the incarnation with an explicit critique of the phrase "salvation of souls" and a call for deeper entry into the world through practices of love and care for all. He writes:

> Hence we cannot settle for the salvation of souls. This life is too important a part of human existence to be written off as merely a trial. If this were not true, the Word would not have become flesh and God would not have loved the world. The salvation of the soul is a transition from a rich life based on acceptance of God through Jesus and service in His name. The next world does not constitute a refuge from this world, but involves a continuation of the Christian life begun here below. That is why John assures us that he who believes already possesses eternal life and has passed from death to life (5:24). . . . God's will must come about on this earth as well as in heaven.[45]

The recognition of Christ's connection to material reality provides a model for how those who profess faith in the Word made flesh are to live in this world, in the flesh, as co-partners in the work of flourishing for *ta pánta*, all things.

Key Insights for the Path Ahead

With this exploration of love, life, embodiment, and flourishing complete, we come full circle to the incarnation, the grounding basis of Christ's redeeming work. As creation groans

---

[45] Brown, "The Theology of the Incarnation," 100–101.

90 *A Theology of Flourishing*

for fulfillment, "and not only the creation, but we ourselves" (Rom 8:22–23), we find hope in the life, death, and resurrection of Christ, seeing the world as Christ saw it—in its beauty and pain. In faith we invite Christ to live in us so that we may mediate his love, acting as agents of flourishing on behalf of all creatures, especially the "least of these."

Applying this paradigm entails expanding and disrupting traditional boundaries of the body, asking "who is my neighbor?" in ways that connect us humans with all creation by virtue of the link between the Word made Flesh and the flesh of all things that participate socially and ecologically in the expansive body of creation. Guiding this vision, John 10:10 functions as a positive and negative norm that orients followers of Jesus toward contemplation, discernment, and action in service of "life as a sacred individual and collective reality that should be loved, respected, and preserved."[46] Positively, given the link between Christ's flesh and the body of the cosmos, this verse proclaims that the abundant life promised by Christ is meant for all. Negatively, it provides a foundation for critical discernment on contemporary social, political, economic, and ecclesial systems that kill, steal, and destroy—obstructing the possibility of flourishing and thus calling Christians to protest.

This conclusion parallels Bauckham's interpretation of the cosmic meaning of the Colossians hymn. Just as Christ quells "powers" and "principalities," whether in this world or beyond it,

> in our contemporary context, we might appropriately apply [the pacification of the powers] to the forces at work in the current destruction of nature: the global economic system, consumerism with the addiction to excess that it promotes, the seemingly unavoidable "short-termism" of

---

[46] Ivone Gebara, *Longing for Running Water: Ecofeminism and Liberation* (Minneapolis: Fortress Press, 1999), 129.

Revolutionary Love for "All Things" 91

even the most democratic political systems. Such realities of our world may seem out of human control, subjecting us to their fateful direction rather than implementing some collective will. Their hostility to God's purpose is more than the sum of human intentions to despoil and destroy God's world. In such a context, we may understand Christ's pacification of such powers as taking effect through us, as we confront them and seek peace between humans and the rest of creation despite their seeming supremacy.[47]

In all these ways the New Testament calls Christian theology and praxis to confront the thieves of the world—the agents of death, theft, and destruction—with a radical commitment to "faith working through love" in service of the flourishing of all creatures. Later chapters consider further how the revolutionary love of Christ informs a theology of flourishing writ large. In the meantime, to continue building foundations for such a theology, the next chapter considers how the themes discussed in the Hebrew Bible and the New Testament inform the vision of flourishing in three early Christian thinkers: Irenaeus, Athanasius, and Gregory of Nyssa.

---

[47] Bauckham, *The Bible and Ecology*, 159–60.

5

Creation, Deification, and Flourishing in Early Christian Thought

Irenaeus, Athanasius, and Gregory of Nyssa

Hebrew Bible and New Testament texts attest to a God of life, who desires the flourishing of all creatures, individually and communally, each according to its unique, beloved kind. Such flourishing is grounded in God's own love, expressed in creation and, on the example of Christ himself, worked out in the life of faith through embodied practices of care that promote the self-actualization and well-being of all things in keeping with God's life-giving intentions. This vision bridges horizons, integrating hope for heavenly salvation with the fullness of life in this world, calling Christians to oppose injustice and live as agents of flourishing in the here and now.

Although by the time of Augustine emphasis began to fall on the dynamics of sin, grace, and salvation, the thread of flourishing continued to weave itself through Christian thought and praxis (this is true even in Augustine), albeit often as a suppressed other to a theological paradigm centered on personal salvation from

93

sin.[1] This thread is most discernible in the theological fabric of the Greek East—and in particular in the doctrine of deification, a process by which humans become more Christlike, more Godlike, through participation in God's own life in Christ and the Spirit. Yet careful qualification is needed here. Despite the doctrine's potential to contribute a framework for understanding the actualization of the human person in relation to self, others, and God, most patristic notions of deification are—as Jantzen observes—cast in a profoundly intellectualist mold that locates the fulfillment of deification in the *nous*, or intellect, rising above the body. Moreover, these accounts tend to be rooted in a dualistic, patriarchal rendering of the relationship between mind and body, male and female, spirit and matter.[2] Given the emphasis it places on the positive character of embodiment and materiality vis-à-vis this-worldly flourishing, a theology of flourishing must read against the grain of these biases to clarify these authors' potential contributions to a theology of flourishing. Further, it is important to note that, while I undertake a close reading of these authors' texts, I am reading them with contemporary concerns in mind. That said, I have sought to avoid imposing contemporary "issues" on their writings. I aim instead to discover how a hermeneutics of the fullness of life might enable theologians to unearth in these thinkers a long-suppressed strand of the tradition.

---

[1] For a brief introduction to Augustine's theology of creation, see Denis Edwards, *Christian Understandings of Creation: The Historical Trajectory* (Minneapolis: Fortress Press, 2017), 65–86.

[2] Grace M. Jantzen, *Power, Gender, and Christian Mysticism* (Cambridge: Cambridge University Press, 1995), 50–54; 139–42. One of Jantzen's examples of this concern involves Gregory of Nyssa, whom this chapter engages. In *The Life of Macrina*, Gregory questions his sister Macrina's womanhood on the basis that she "surpassed her nature." Although he may be suggesting that Macrina surpasses nature as a whole, the gendered language corresponds closely with the influence of Greco-Roman hierarchical dualism on Gregory's thought. I hope my analysis will allow us to read Gregory against his historical context, finding in him a vision of the spiritual life oriented toward liberation and flourishing.

Creation, Deification, and Flourishing in Early Christian Thought   95

These qualifications in place, by examining selected writings of three early Christian authors—Irenaeus of Lyons, Athanasius of Alexandria, and Gregory of Nyssa—this chapter traces the thread of flourishing toward a qualified appropriation of the doctrine of deification, pursuing what Francine Cardman names "a road not taken in the West."[3] Beyond simply presenting their thought, however, this analysis interprets their writings through the prism of creation, noting how the doctrine informs their views of God, world, and deification and their understandings of how deification operates in the concrete—bringing Christians to the fullness of life and inviting them into the divine work of flourishing in service of all things.

Irenaeus of Lyons

Against Heresies, Irenaeus's classic refutation of Gnosticism, offers invaluable resources for constructing a theology of flourishing.[4] As New Testament authors linked Wisdom and Word in the person of Christ, Irenaeus links the depictions of Lady Wisdom in Proverbs to the Spirit's work in creation, offering a vision

---

[3] Francine Cardman, "Irenaeus: As It Was in the Beginning," in *The T & T Clark Handbook of Theological Anthropology*, ed. Mary Ann Hinsdale, IHM, and Stephen Okey, 137–46 (London: T & T Clark, 2021), 137. Introductions to the idea of deification in the Greek East include Stephen Finlan and Vladimir Kharlamov, eds., *Theosis: Deification in Christian Theology*, vol. 1 (Cambridge, UK: James Clarke, 2006); Vladimir Kharlamov, ed., *Theosis II: Deification in Christian Theology*, vol. 2 (Cambridge, UK: James Clarke, 2012); and Norman Russell, *The Doctrine of Deification in the Greek Patristic Tradition* (Oxford: Oxford, 2005).

[4] For background on Irenaeus's life and the context for his work, see Edwards, *Christian Understandings of Creation*, 21–25. For a fuller introduction to Irenaeus, see Dennis Minns, OP, *Irenaeus: An Introduction* (London: Bloomsbury, 2010). Mary Ann Donovan offers an in-depth historical analysis of the context and content of *Against Heresies* in *One Right Reading? A Guide to Irenaeus* (Collegeville, MN: Liturgical Press, 1997).

of the world suffused with divine presence.[5] This presence of God in creation is fulfilled in Christ, the incarnate Word, "who in the last times was made a man among men, that He might join the end to the beginning, that is, men to God."[6] Here, Irenaeus demonstrates a clear anthropocentrism that is typical of his time. Yet he situates his account of incarnation and divine-human communion, the foundations of deification, within the context of creation, noting that the Word of God intended from the beginning to "be present with His own creation, saving it, and becoming capable of being perceived by it."[7] Christ saves all creation, not only humans. And it is through creation that the Word makes God known to humanity, in what Julie Canlis describes as "a radical reconception of the God–world relation, based on a doctrine of creation in which God's transcendence suggests an extreme of divine involvement in the world."[8] Such self-involvement follows the logic of the divine love expressed

---

[5] Irenaeus, *Against Heresies*, trans. Alexander Roberts and William Rambaut, *Ante-Nicene Fathers*, vol. 1, ed. Alexander Roberts, James Donaldson, and A. Cleveland Coxe (Buffalo, NY: Christian Literature Publishing, 1885), IV.20.3. Revised and edited by Kevin Knight for newadvent.org.

[6] Irenaeus, IV.20.4. Although I have preserved the original translation of these texts, I acknowledge the use of masculine language here and throughout other sources I engage. Latin translations of Irenaeus's text (we don't have the Greek) use *homo* rather than *vir*, in parallel with the universal connotation of *Mann* in German or *anthropos* in Greek (Irenaeus's word), rather than *andros*.

[7] Irenaeus, IV.20.4. For an extended historical treatment of Irenaeus's understanding of creation, see Matthew Steenberg, *Irenaeus: The Cosmic Christ and the Saga of Redemption* (Boston: Brill, 2008).

[8] Julie Canlis, "Being Made Human: The Significance of Creation for Irenaeus' Doctrine of Participation," *Scottish Journal of Theology* 58, no. 4 (November 2005): 441. Scholars continue to analyze the links between Irenaeus and biblical authors. See Todd D. Still and David E. Wilhite, eds., *Irenaeus and Paul* (London: Bloomsbury, 2020). For an extended treatment of Irenaeus's engagement with Paul's writings on creation with attention to contemporary applications, see J. J. Johnson Leese, *Christ, Creation, and the Cosmic Goal of Redemption: A Study of Pauline Creation Theology as Read by Irenaeus and Applied to Ecotheology* (London: Bloomsbury, 2018). For a brief study of the connection between vision and life in Irenaeus and John, see Sophia Theodoratos, "See,

Creation, Deification, and Flourishing in Early Christian Thought 97

in creation, such that "there are, for Irenaeus, not two distinct economies—creation followed by salvation—but only one all-embracing economy, creation and salvation, together."[9]

Again like the New Testament authors, Irenaeus clearly links the service of God in this world to the hope of heavenly union with God after death, as the action of the Word "[causes] us to serve Him in holiness and righteousness all our days . . . in order that man, having embraced the Spirit of God, might pass into the glory of the Father."[10] By embracing the Spirit's work in creation and in us, we humans share in God's creative work through service and so enter into God's own glory. Here, Irenaeus anticipates the doctrine of deification. When we humans accept God's work within us, we enter more fully into the image of God in which we are created and partner with God through faith in the divinizing work that brings all creation to fulfillment.

In these ways, *Against Heresies* demonstrates remarkable consistency with the biblical foundations for a theology of flourishing. Yet this consistency is only a starting point. The link to flourishing bursts to light in the following sections, which focus explicitly on the fullness of life. Speaking of those who are "within the light," Irenaeus states that the brilliance of God's splendor "vivifies them; those therefore, who see God, receive life." He then notes that, while God remains incomprehensible *in se*, God made Godself "visible, and comprehensible . . . *that He might vivify* those who receive and behold Him through faith."[11] Here, Irenaeus makes a radical claim that implicitly parallels the emphasis on the fleshly reality of Christ in 1 John. Against those who would deny the importance of the flesh in the order of salvation, he argues that the very purpose of God's

---

That You May Have Life: From St. John to St. Irenaeus," *Phronema* 37, no. 1 (2022): 49–71.

[9] John Behr, "Nature, Wounded and Healed in Early Patristic Thought," *Toronto Journal of Theology* 29, no. 1 (2013): 88.

[10] Irenaeus, *Against Heresies*, IV.20.4.

[11] Irenaeus, IV.20.5.

98   *A Theology of Flourishing*

self-communication is to vivify, to give life, by becoming visible and comprehensible—by entering into materiality. And as we have already seen, to have this life is to know God and to live in service of the others.

These passages provide vital context for the climactic and oft-quoted declaration, "For the glory of God is a living man; and the life of man consists in beholding God."[12] This phrase clearly testifies to the same life-giving intentions expressed in biblical creation texts: to behold God is to enter into the life-giving fullness that God *is* and to experience "the full flowering of God's love."[13] Furthermore, this entry into the fullness of life glorifies God. This claim is powerful on its own, but it acquires greater power in light of what precedes and follows it. The vivifying power of God that pervades creation comes to fullness in the flourishing human person, and this creative power breaks out beyond an individual person back into the world, uniting all things to the holiness and righteousness of God through the love, service, and self-actualization of those who are enlightened by the Spirit. As Wirzba writes, "The love of God sets creatures free to fully become themselves."[14]

Without a doubt, Irenaeus is focused here on the human person, but the following passage circles back to creation, reiterating that all things participate in God's gift of life and are brought to fulfillment through it. He writes, "For if the manifestation of God which is made by means of the creation, affords life to *all living in the earth*, much more does that revelation of the Father which comes through the Word, give life to those who see

---

[12] Irenaeus, IV.20.7.

[13] Norman Wirzba, *The Way of Love: Recovering the Heart of Christianity* (New York: HarperOne, 2016), 53. For a commentary on the implications of Irenaeus's maxim for spirituality, see Mary Ann Donovan, SC, "Irenaeus: At the Heart of Life, Glory," in *Spiritualities of the Heart: Approaches to Personal Wholeness in Christian Tradition*, ed. Annice Callahan, RSCJ (New York: Paulist Press, 1990), 11–22.

[14] Wirzba, *The Way of Love*, 54.

Creation, Deification, and Flourishing in Early Christian Thought **99**

God."[15] Faith in God through the Word thereby enlivens those who behold God, beginning "a dynamic realization of the human condition involving the full development of all our potentialities inscribed in us already in the creation project."[16] Despite his focus on the fullness of human life in God, Irenaeus clearly sees this fullness as extending the life-giving work that God began in creation. Here again, God's blessing "be fertile and multiply" orients creation toward a fullness yet to come. And, as in Paul, the trajectory toward fullness begins in the flesh, as human persons are deified in union with God and, as a result, oriented toward the good of all. Flourishing is a matter of the here and now.

Two subsequent excerpts from *Against Heresies* give further support to this reading of the origins of creaturely flourishing in the life-giving order of God's creation. First, Irenaeus writes:

> [God's] wisdom [is shown] in His having made created things parts of one harmonious and consistent whole; and those things which, through His super-eminent kindness, receive growth and a long period of existence, do reflect the glory of the uncreated One, of that God who bestows what is good ungrudgingly. . . . By this arrangement, therefore, and these harmonies, and a sequence of this nature, man, a created and organized being, is rendered after the image and likeness of the uncreated God—the Father planning everything well and giving His commands, the Son carrying these into execution and performing the work of creating, and the Spirit nourishing and increasing [what is made], but man making progress day by day, and

---

[15] Irenaeus, *Against Heresies*, IV.20.7. Emphasis mine.

[16] Brendan Leahy, "'Hiding behind the Works': The Holy Spirit in the Trinitarian Rhythm of Human Fulfilment in the Theology of Irenaeus," in *Holy Spirit in the Fathers of the Church: The Proceedings of the Seventh International Patristic Conference, Maynooth, 2008*, ed. D. Vincent Twomey and Janet E. Rutherford, 11–31 (Dublin: Four Courts Press, 2010), 27.

100   *A Theology of Flourishing*

ascending towards the perfect, that is, approximating to the uncreated One.[17]

Here, as before, Irenaeus follows a logic that begins from a vision of creation wherein all things "reflect the glory of the uncreated One." Within this logic, the deification of the human person is cast in parallel with nature's own movement toward fulfillment in God, such that the fullness of life made manifest in natural systems provides a metaphor for understanding human fulfillment in the vision of God—here cast as "approximating to the uncreated One."

Second, when Irenaeus speaks of the incarnation, he writes that only through love did Christ "*become what we are, that He might bring us to be even what He is Himself.*"[18] At face value, this statement offers a textbook definition of deification: by becoming what we humans are, Christ provided a way for us to become what he is. Yet here, we must interpret the "what he is" in the context of Irenaeus's broader understanding of creation and life in Christ. Just as the incarnation extends the logic of divine love that creation manifests, and just as the fullness of human life parallels the life-giving power of creation, so the deification of humanity expresses the logic of creation. In this way, too, the incarnation shows "humankind what the realized image ought to look like, how it ought to be actualized, and what it implies for obedience and the human-divine relationship," as Matthew Steenberg writes.[19] Deification is not separation from creation but the actualization and perfection of creaturely existence *within* creation.

Applied in the concrete, to be like Christ is to be an embodied beacon of the fullness of life that Christ is—to live as persons

---

[17] Irenaeus, *Against Heresies*, IV.38.3.

[18] Irenaeus, Preface to V.

[19] M. C. Steenberg, *Of God and Man: Theology as Anthropology from Irenaeus to Athanasius* (London: Bloomsbury, 2009), 47.

Creation, Deification, and Flourishing in Early Christian Thought 101

who co-participate in the life-giving work of flourishing for all creation, precisely as it is held in being and loved to fulfillment by God. All of this occurs in materiality, in flesh, with what Richard Norris describes as an "insistence on the intrinsic goodness and redeemability of the generate order."[20] Furthermore, as Steenberg notes, Irenaeus attributes great value to "earthiness," and "the fact that the human individual is in some sense living earth is, for Irenaeus, the most emphatic evidence of God's true power."[21] Correlatively, nowhere in the foregoing passages does Irenaeus use "spirit" to refer to a noncorporeal aspect of humanity. All is encoded in what he terms *plasma*, earthiness. Indeed, as Edwards notes, Irenaeus "resists all disembodied theologies" and speaks of materiality not as fallen but as a positive expression and locus of God's own life.[22] Countering his Gnostic opponents, Irenaeus thus sees earth and bodies as loci of divine presence, grounding an indispensable dimension of the vision with which a theology of flourishing proceeds—a dimension to which the incarnation itself attests. Salvation is, indeed, a matter of flesh.

Against Heresies counters the Gnostic view that flesh cannot take on divine life with a positive appraisal of materiality and embodiment. As Behr notes, "The economy culminates not in a mystical union of the soul with God, but with the perfecting of the mud in the image and likeness of God."[23] In this way all

---

[20] Richard A. Norris, DD, *God and World in Early Christian Theology: A Study in Justin Martyr, Irenaeus, Tertullian and Origen* (London: Adam and Charles Black, 1965). For an insightful analysis of the relationship between Irenaeus's theology of God and his theological anthropology, see Vicky Petrakis, "The *Plasma* as Salvation History in St. Irenaeus of Lyons," *Phronema* 34, no. 2 (2019): 103–23. For an assessment of the influence of *plasma* on later theological perspectives on the body, see Laure Solignac, "Corps, âme, esprit: L'Homme selon Saint Irénée et Saint Bonaventure, en passant par Saint Augustin," *Théophilyon* 22, no. 2 (2017): 347–71.

[21] Steenberg, *Irenaeus*, 118–19.

[22] Edwards, *Christian Understandings of Creation*, 29.

[23] Behr, "Nature, Wounded and Healed in Early Patristic Thought," 97.

102   *A Theology of Flourishing*

creation is encompassed in God's deifying work, such that "the liberation of creation from bondage to corruption is the fulfillment of the Father's creative and restorative purposes in the work of the Son, and . . . completes the work of the incarnation as the Creator's outreach to the embrace of all creation."[24] In the case of humans, this outreach is the work of the Holy Spirit, through whom humans are prepared "for incorruption, being little by little accustomed to receive and bear God."[25] All in all, countering the Gnostic denial of the goodness of material reality—even to the point of denying the incarnation itself—Irenaeus argues that, as it was in the creation of all things through the Word made flesh, so it is now—as by the Spirit creaturely life is oriented toward a fullness that glorifies God in the flesh, in anticipation of creation's ultimate glorification in union with God.

Athanasius of Alexandria

Khaled Anatolios observes that although fourth-century bishop and theologian Athanasius never acknowledges his influence, it is widely accepted that Irenaeus had a significant impact on Athanasius, a second indispensable contributor to the doctrine of deification.[26] Indeed, Athanasius's well-known claim, "For He was made man that we might be made God; and He manifested

---

[24] Paul Blowers, "The Groaning and Longing of Creation: Variant Patterns of Patristic Interpretation of *Romans* 8:19–23," in *Studia Patristica* (Leuven: Peeters, 2013), 45–54.

[25] Irenaeus, *Against Heresies*, V.8.1. This pneumatological dimension stands at the center of the theology I propose in Chapter 8.

[26] Khaled Anatolios, "The Influence of Irenaeus on Athanasius," *Studia Patristica*, vol. 36, ed. M. F. Wiles and E. J. Yarnold, 463–76 (Leuven: Peeters, 2001). For background on Athanasius's life and the context for his work, see Edwards, *Christian Understandings of Creation*, 45–46. Anatolios has contributed two important introductions to Athanasius's life and thought: *Athanasius: The Coherence of His Thought* (Oxford: Taylor and Francis, 1998), and *Athanasius* (Oxford: Taylor and Francis, 2004). For a comparison of the soteriologies of Irenaeus and Athanasius, see Eugen Maftei, "Irénée de Lyon et Athanase

Creation, Deification, and Flourishing in Early Christian Thought 103

Himself by a body that we might receive the idea of the unseen Father; and He endured the insolence of men that we might inherit immortality," offers a pithy summary of the relationship between the incarnation and the fulfillment of divine-human communion.[27]

Also from Irenaeus, Athanasius inherits what Anatolios names "an emphatic insistence on . . . the 'immediacy of relation between God and world.'"[28] This immediacy situates Christ's incarnation within the order of creation. As Athanasius puts it, "But the reason why the Word, the Word of God, has united Himself with created things is truly wonderful, and teaches us that the present order of things is none otherwise than is fitting." On this basis, he concludes that, despite its finitude, creation reveals the goodness of God, who does not "grudge even existence, but desires all to exist, as objects for His loving-kindness."[29] Seen in this way, the incarnation participates in the "fittingness" of the created order, revealing the fullness of God's life-giving intentions within material reality.

In alignment with Hebrew Bible creation texts, this theme of order pervades Athanasius's writings, providing a valuable resource for a relational understanding of creation, in which "all the elements of creation work together in a kind of kinship."[30] This way of seeing the created order provides useful resources for thinking of flourishing vis-à-vis the dynamics of complex socioecosystems. For example, in ways that echo Paul's body

---

d'Alexandrie: Ressemblances et différences ente leur sotériologies," in *Studia Patristica XCIII*, ed. Markus Vinzent, 275–302 (Leuven: Peeters, 2017).

[27] Athanasius, *On the Incarnation of the Word*, trans. Archibald Robertson, *Nicene and Post-Nicene Fathers, Second Series,* vol. 4, ed. Philip Schaff and Henry Wace (Buffalo, NY: Christian Literature Publishing, 1892), 54.3. Revised and edited by Kevin Knight for newadvent.org.

[28] Anatolios, "The Influence of Irenaeus on Athanasius," 464.

[29] Athanasius, *Contra Gentiles*, trans. Archibald Robertson, Schaff and Wace, *Nicene and Post-Nicene Fathers, Second Series,* vol. 4, III.43.

[30] Edwards, *Christian Understandings of Creation*, 48.

104 *A Theology of Flourishing*

metaphor, *Contra Gentiles* uses the image of a many-stringed lyre to illustrate how different parts of creation function together, producing an animating harmony that enlivens all things:

> For just as though some musician, having tuned a lyre, and by his art adjusted the high notes to the low, and the intermediate notes to the rest, were to produce a single tune as the result, so also the Wisdom of God, handling the Universe as a lyre, and adjusting things in the air to things on the earth, and things in the heaven to things in the air, and combining parts into wholes and moving them all by His beck and will, produces well and fittingly, as the result, the unity of the universe and of its order, Himself remaining unmoved with the Father while He moves all things by His organising action, as seems good for each to His own Father.[31]

Images of the order of creation reflecting and revealing God's saving work pervade Athanasius's writings. Images from human society achieve the same end: workers perform their labors, sailors sail, carpenters build, doctors provide treatment to the sick, and so on. All this reflects the order of creation, wherein each creature contributes to the optimal function of the whole. Making this perspective clear in a passage that reflects contemporary understandings of ecosystems and the cosmos, Athanasius states, "In like manner then we must conceive of the whole of Creation, even though the example be inadequate, yet with an enlarged idea. For with the single impulse of a nod as it were of the Word of God, all things simultaneously fall into order, and each discharge their proper functions, and a single order is made up by them all together."[32] Within this order, deified humans

---

[31] Athanasius, *Contra Gentiles*, III.42.
[32] Athanasius, III.43.

Creation, Deification, and Flourishing in Early Christian Thought 105

operate as conduits of God's transformative grace, not by fleeing creatureliness for heaven but by actualizing God's intentions for creation by entering fully into creaturely life.

As Edwards states, "Deification, then, is not a transcending of the human, but the true fulfillment of the human."[33] In all this, alongside his many contributions to the doctrine of deification, Athanasius's vision of the integrity of creation advances the biblical and Irenaean understanding of a created order that is oriented toward the fullness of life as revelatory of God's intentions. Within this framework, humans partake of divine life, being "made God" through the incarnation, and charged to collaborate with God in what Edwards names the "ethical aspect of deification, our growth in holiness," which I term co-participation in activating God's life-giving intentions for all.[34]

Gregory of Nyssa

Although cast in allegorical form, Gregory of Nyssa's *The Life of Moses* echoes many of the theological and christological themes that surface in the writings of Irenaeus and Athanasius, contributing a third early Christian resource to a theology of flourishing. For Gregory, the quest for the vision of God begins from a desire for the good and finds fulfillment in beholding the mystery of God. But because God is infinite and divine goodness "has no limit, the participant's desire itself necessarily has no stopping place but stretches out with the limitless."[35] With this foundation in place, Gregory casts the story of Moses as an epic of deification that culminates in an admittedly intellectual vision of God.

---

[33] Denis Edwards, *Partaking of God: Trinity, Evolution and Ecology* (Collegeville, MN: Liturgical Press, 2014), 44.

[34] Edwards, 44.

[35] Gregory of Nyssa, *The Life of Moses*, trans. Abraham J. Malherbe and Everett Ferguson (New York: HarperOne, 2006), 5.

106　　　　　　　　　　　　　　　　*A Theology of Flourishing*

Seen through the lens of a theology of flourishing, however, several moments in the text jump immediately to the fore.

First, his interpretation of the burning-bush theophany explicitly emphasizes the role of *materiality* in the manifestation of God. He writes, "Lest one think that the radiance did not come from a material substance, this light did not shine from some luminary among the stars but came from an earthly bush and surpassed the heavenly luminaries in brilliance."[36] Over against the idea that divine revelation comes from outside creation, Gregory emphasizes that God makes Godself known through "an earthly bush" that outshines the heavens. Here, it bears repeating—though Gregory does not make the point—that God respects creation's autonomy and integrity, even in making Godself known. Furthermore, while Gregory indicates that, in the theophany, Moses comes to understand that all things truly subsist not by what can be appreciated by the senses but by the transcendent essence of God, this observation does not, as intellectualist bias might have it, lead him to conclude that material reality is merely a means to an end. Rather, Gregory writes that, by virtue of what Moses experienced, "so now does everyone who, like him, divests himself of the earthly covering and looks to the light shining from the bramble bush" gain access to "the true light and the truth itself."[37] Such enlightenment comes through beholding nature as Moses beheld it.

Second, Gregory does not interpret the fruits of this encounter in a spiritualistic manner. Rather, he writes that one who encounters God as Moses did "becomes able to help others to salvation, to destroy the tyranny which holds power wickedly, and to deliver to freedom everyone held in evil servitude."[38] Writing nearly seventeen-hundred-years before the

---

[36] Gregory of Nyssa, 37.

[37] Gregory of Nyssa, 39.

[38] Gregory of Nyssa, 39.

Creation, Deification, and Flourishing in Early Christian Thought 107

emergence of liberation theologies, Gregory interprets this episode not as a tale of spiritual fulfillment beyond the world but as the story of a world-changing encounter with a God who sees, responds, and liberates. Gregory finds in this encounter the basis for a radical proclamation of God's reign. *Epektasis*, or spiritual growth, is inseparable from social concern in *The Life of Moses*. Spiritual growth does not orient a person away from the world in a hyper-mystical state of political indifference. On the contrary, Gregory's mysticism penetrates the world, orienting those who behold God toward the needs of others, charging them with the work of confronting tyranny and servitude. Those who encounter God's transformative presence and begin the journey of *epektasis* return to the world as agents of life, flourishing, and communion, working to abolish systems that exploit and enslave so that all may flourish. By definition, such work entails the cultivation of material and social conditions that make flourishing possible within the socio-ecological circumstances of creaturely life.

Gregory's reading of the miracle of manna in the desert gives force to this point. Rather than spiritualizing the reception of manna and the prohibition against storing manna until morning (Ex 16:19), he interprets the manna event in terms of the Israelite community's care for one another, according to need. He writes:

> With this marvel was seen also another: Those who went out to gather the food were all, as one might expect, of different ages and capacities, yet despite their differences one did not gather more or less than another. Instead, the amount gathered was measured by the need of each, so that the stronger did not have a surplus nor was the weaker deprived of his fair share.[39]

---

[39] Gregory of Nyssa, 16.

108   *A Theology of Flourishing*

Here, alongside the "marvel" of God's providence, is a recognition that providence is mediated in community. All take only what they need, so as to ensure care for the needs of all, in harmony with Matthew's account of the final judgment, Paul's body metaphor, and the Johannine love command. Gregory's reading of Israel's battles continues in this vein. Alone, Moses cannot keep his arms raised long enough to ensure Israel's victory, but the power of community and mutual care make victory possible.[40] For Gregory, life flourishes in relationship—especially in times of hardship—and God's providence is mediated by collective practices of care that cultivate conditions that make flourishing possible.

Third and finally, Moses's journey with Israel culminates in his mountaintop experience, wherein he enters into darkness, and his *nous*, or intellect, "gains access to the invisible and the incomprehensible, and there it sees God."[41] Illustrating the concerns raised by Jantzen, the Greek philosophical categories in which Gregory was formed are clearly in play here, as the intellect transcends the senses and offers insights that are not attainable within material reality. Yet the orientation toward justice that emerges in his account of Moses's ascent counterbalances this concern to some extent. As such, Gregory's understanding of deification retains relevance for a this-worldly account of flourishing. Moreover, while he characterizes Moses's enlightenment in intellectualist terms, he is quick to note that the true vision of God rests not in beholding God in the *nous* but in "never [being] satisfied in the desire to see him."[42] No matter how far the *nous* may reach, it will never attain fully to God and so is bound to seeking God in material reality. While some may read this passage as a warrant for seeing spiritual enlightenment on a higher

---

[40] Gregory of Nyssa, 17–18.

[41] Gregory of Nyssa, 81.

[42] Gregory of Nyssa, 106.

Creation, Deification, and Flourishing in Early Christian Thought **109**

plane than what the world can provide, I interpret the perpetual unsatisfaction that one experiences in seeking God as implying a constant return to the needs of the world. As a result, "each step toward God is both a fulfillment and a new beginning. Moses has reached the summit only in the sense that he recognizes the unlimited, ungraspable reality of God, and the dynamism of the soul in relation to God, which has been operative all along and will continue to carry Moses ever deeper into the divine life."[43]

Even as Gregory's account of the spiritual life finds fulfillment in the darkness of unknowing, it never leads beyond the world. Rather, in the spirit of Moses's own *metanoia*, the spiritual journey involves a cyclical rhythm of beholding God, being unsatisfied with one's vision of God, and returning to the world to seek God anew. John McGuckin concurs with this reading, interpreting Gregory's vision of deification as a kind of liberation from conditions that, as in the parable of the Rich Young Man, obstruct the human capacity to experience authentic self-actualization in relationship to God:

> The deification, he suggests, is not a posthumous transcending of human nature, but a passing beyond the limits of human nature, in that glorified nature. The restricting limitations that were once imposed on human nature by long ages of its common experience as a "nature that was separated from God" will be lifted . . . by the admission of the creature into the radiant fullness of the very purpose of creaturely human being, which is intimate communion with the endless mystery of the Life-Giving Presence.[44]

---

[43] Patrick F. O'Connell, "The Double Journey in Saint Gregory of Nyssa: *The Life of Moses*," *Greek Orthodox Theological Review* 28, no. 4 (1983): 318–19.

[44] John A. McGuckin, "The Strategic Adaptation of Deification in the Cappadocians," in *Partakers in the Divine Nature: the History and Development of Deification in the Christian Traditions* (2008), 109.

110   *A Theology of Flourishing*

There is, then, no escape in Gregory's account of deification. There is only beholding and seeking anew through a desire "to follow God wherever he might lead."[45] This seeking happens in the world, in community and creation. For, just as Moses encountered God in the burning bush and the Israelites survived their journey to the Promised Land, so all those who *see* God *seek* God and participate in God's life-giving work, providing manna to those in need.

Gregory himself recognizes all this. God's "passing by signifies his guiding the one who follows," showing the way to the good.[46] All Christians are likewise called to follow and guide, which are, notably, embodied, communal practices in themselves. Within this dynamic all people discover their God-given purpose, just as Moses did. Gregory writes: "What then are we taught through what has been said? To have but one purpose in life: to be called servants of God by virtue of the lives we live."[47] Here again, the mystical and spiritual return to the world, as the fruits of the vision of God manifest through acts of service to God in the lives of deified persons. Gregory thus concludes that the goal of "the sublime way of life" lies not in salvation beyond the world but in "being called a servant of God."[48]

Though he utilizes the metaphor of a mountain for the spiritual life, Gregory's account of Moses's journey toward God does not degrade this world—as in Santmire's paradigm of being-beyond-the-earth—but operates on the basis of a fundamental continuity between creaturely life and heavenly fulfillment. Therefore, in seeing creation as a medium of God's self-revelation, Gregory—like Irenaeus and Athanasius—illustrates how the spiritual and material coincide in creaturely life, leading creatures to experience the fullness of life in friendship with God—and

---

[45] Gregory of Nyssa, *Life of Moses*, 106.
[46] Gregory of Nyssa, 110.
[47] Gregory of Nyssa, 129.
[48] Gregory of Nyssa, 130–31.

Creation, Deification, and Flourishing in Early Christian Thought **111**

to share that life with others. Such is the essence of deification, or perfection, for Gregory, who ends *The Life of Moses* with a reflection on friendship with God that relegates hope for heavenly reward to secondary status in favor of flourishing in friendship with God in the here and now:

> This is true perfection: *not to avoid a wicked life because like slaves we servilely fear punishment, nor to do good because we hope for rewards,* as if cashing in on the virtuous life by some business-like and contractual arrangement. On the contrary, *disregarding all those things for which we hope and which have been reserved by promise*, we regard falling from God's friendship as the only thing dreadful and we consider becoming God's friend the only thing worthy of honor and desire. *This, as I have said, is the perfection of life.*[49]

Key Insights for the Path Ahead

Together, the accounts of deification in Irenaeus, Athanasius, and Gregory of Nyssa present the order of creation as the foundation for incarnation and situate the Christian spiritual life within—never over or above—material reality. In so doing, they manifest a comprehensive consistency with the witness of biblical texts on creation, embodiment, life, and love. While oriented toward fulfillment in God, deification remains inextricably tied to the conditions of creaturely life. Finitude, embodiment, materiality, suffering, and injustice shape the diverse contexts in which deification occurs, thus conditioning its meaning across time and space. In all this, creation—from bushes aflame to Christ's own flesh—mediates divine presence and communicates God's call. The vision of God serves as the foundation for participation in the fullness of life, an invitation to flourish and a command to

---

[49] Gregory of Nyssa, 132. Emphasis mine.

foster the self-actualization of all God's creatures through collective friendship with God.

This inquiry into early Christian precedents for a theology of flourishing establishes a trajectory that the next two chapters pursue. Chapter 6 traces the thread of flourishing through the medieval period, considering how this thread weaves its way through the writings of Hildegard von Bingen, Julian of Norwich, Duns Scotus, and Nicholas of Cusa. Turning to the twentieth century, Chapter 7 follows this line through the writings of Jesuit theologian Karl Rahner and his students Johann Baptist Metz and Ignacio Ellacuría, solidifying the foundation for the theology of flourishing that I propose in Chapter 8.

6

Creation, Life, and Love in and beyond the Medieval Period

Hildegard of Bingen, John Duns Scotus, Julian of Norwich, and Nicholas of Cusa

Early Christian writings unite the themes of creation, incarnation, life, justice, and the vision of God under the umbrella of deification. Within this paradigm the human journey toward God is a journey into flourishing, both as the individual person undergoes self-actualization that glorifies God and as this self-actualization attunes persons to the needs of the world, fostering practices that liberate others from tyranny, injustice, and exploitation. This, in turn, makes the fullness of life proclaimed by Christ possible on an ever-widening scale.

Building on this foundation, this chapter engages four thinkers who lived from the Middle Ages to the cusp of the Renaissance: Hildegard of Bingen, John Duns Scotus, Julian of Norwich, and Nicholas of Cusa. At the outset, it is important to acknowledge that, while these thinkers contribute important resources to a theology of flourishing, over eight centuries separate the birth of Gregory of Nyssa from the death of Hildegard. Historically, these centuries included the expansive growth of Christianity

113

A Theology of Flourishing

in imperial Rome, the fall of the Roman Empire, the birth of monasticism, and the rise of the Holy Roman Empire—a development that inaugurated the long association of the Catholic Church with European monarchy. In this period, too, the seeds of a paradigm that places personal salvation from sin at the heart of soteriology sprouted. This new approach increasingly framed humanity and creation as fallen, with the debt of sin paid and heavenly salvation assured through the crucifixion of Christ.[1] Important social and ecological developments accompanied these shifts. Urbanization and new agricultural practices (for example, the scratch plow) centralized human communities and expanded demand for agricultural resources.[2] As the nascent intellectualism of early accounts of deification prospered, hierarchical dualism wove itself ever more securely into the fabric of theology and philosophy. Patriarchal linkages of intellect and rationality with masculinity prospered, further silencing and subjugating women and gender minorities in church and society. The same associations enabled the Baconian plunder of "Mother" Earth in the name of human "progress."[3]

---

[1] In *Creation and the Cross*, Johnson offers a detailed analysis, evaluation, and critique of Anselm's satisfaction atonement paradigm. This analysis illustrates how Anselm's theology reflects the developments I have named. Elizabeth A. Johnson, *Creation and the Cross: The Mercy of God for a Planet in Peril* (Maryknoll, NY: Orbis Books, 2018).

[2] Lynn White uses the example of the scratch plow to illustrate the correspondence between agricultural practices and anthropocentric perspectives on creation. Lynn White, "The Historical Roots of Our Ecologic Crisis," *Science* 155, no. 3767 (1967): 1203–7. Wirzba offers an insightful introduction to factors such as urbanization and agriculture in view of humanity's relationship to creation. Norman Wirzba, *The Paradise of God: Renewing Religion in an Ecological Age* (Oxford: Oxford University Press, 2007), 1–18.

[3] Johnson and numerous others have observed the intrinsic relationship between the subjugation of women and the treatment of the earth. For a brief treatment, see Elizabeth A. Johnson, "Turn to the Heavens and the Earth: Retrieval of the Cosmos in Theology," in *Proceedings of the Catholic Theological Society of America* 51 (1996): 11–12.

Creation, Life, and Love in and beyond the Medieval Period   *115*

Admittedly, a cursory snapshot cannot capture the nuanced historical development that took place from the fourth to eleventh centuries. Still, this brief glance at history provides an important contextual frame for reading Hildegard, Scotus, Julian, and Nicholas, because their contributions to a theology of flourishing are conditioned and constrained by the times and places in which they lived. At the same time, these thinkers' contributions to a theology of flourishing most clearly appear against this historical backdrop—and often in contrast to its predominant values.

Hildegard of Bingen

Ecological imagery and an abiding sense of God's action as the power of life working in all things pervade the writings of Hildegard of Bingen—especially the *Scivias* and *The Book of Divine Works*.[4] Unsurprisingly, these two facets of her writings are closely interrelated. An expert in herbal medicine, Hildegard knew firsthand the work of cultivation and the life-giving power of plants.[5] For Hildegard, the life-giving order and function of ecosystems and the diverse flora they produce attest to a "universal proportion," or "an underlying order, harmony, or proportion in the nature of all things."[6] In keeping with the interpretations

---

[4] I am working from Hildegard of Bingen, *Scivias*, trans. Mother Columba Hart and Jane Bishop (New York: Paulist Press, 1990), and Hildegard of Bingen, *The Book of Divine Works*, trans. Nathaniel Campbell (Washington, DC: Catholic University of America Press, 2018). For a brief study of the relationship between Hildegard's life and mystical visions, see Barbara Newman, "Hildegard of Bingen: Visions and Validation," *Church History* 54, no. 2 (June 1985): 163–75. For Newman's longer treatment of Hildegard's theology, see *Sister of Wisdom: St. Hildegard's Theology of the Feminine* (Berkeley: University of California Press, 1987).

[5] Hildegard's *Physica* and *Causae et Curae* contain written accounts of her encyclopedic knowledge of nature.

[6] Pozzi Escot, "Hildegard von Bingen: Universal Proportion," *Mystics Quarterly* 19, no. 1 (March 1993): 36.

116   *A Theology of Flourishing*

of the Hebrew Bible (chap. 1), Hildegard does not interpret this God-given order as order for its own sake. Rather, she comes to behold universal proportion by observing the *fruitfulness* of creation—its ability to produce life in keeping with God's own being as life.

To wit, the identification of God as "wholly Life" in association with the fruitfulness of creation is a hallmark of Hildegard's writings. For example, in the prologue to the second book of the *Scivias*, Hildegard envisions God as "a blazing fire, incomprehensible, inextinguishable, wholly living and wholly Life, with a flame in it the color of the sky, which burned ardently with a gentle breath."[7] Here, the flame represents the force of creation, which—in ways that evoke God's ordering of the *tohu wabohu* in Genesis 1—strikes a "dark sphere" until "Heaven and earth stood fully formed and resplendent." God then gives life to mud to create the human person, and dawn comes to creation. "And thus in the radiance of that dawn," she concludes, "the Supreme Will was enkindled."[8]

Hildegard's vision of creation attests that God is the God of life and that creation possesses a God-given capacity to bring forth life. The flame striking the dark sphere represents creation's own coming to be through God's action, and the first dawn radiates God's own will for creation to be. This theme continues throughout the *Scivias*, with God as the fire that enlivens all things, or as Hildegard puts it once again, "wholly Life, for everything that lives takes its life from Him."[9] In all this, Hildegard parses divine power in cosmic-ecological terms, seeing the "universal proportion" of the created order as revelatory of God.

In the passages that follow, Hildegard elaborates on her vision in dialogue with Job 12:10, "In His hand is the soul of

---

[7] Hildegard, *Scivias*, prologue to Book II.
[8] Hildegard, prologue to Book II.
[9] Hildegard, II.1.

Creation, Life, and Love in and beyond the Medieval Period 117

every living thing and the spirit of all human flesh."[10] Vitally, the Hebrew uses *nefesh* and *ruah*, respectively, where translators have supplied soul and spirit. Although she was likely not reading in Hebrew, this translational decision deserves mention because, by Hildegard's time, "soul" and "spirit" were encoded in a dualistic paradigm that is inconsistent with the Hebrew Bible imaginary. Nevertheless, her take on this passage attests to the life-giving power of *ruah* as both the source of life and as that which brings creatures—both living and nonliving—to achieve the fullness of their potential in keeping with their unique creaturely constitutions. She writes:

> No creature is so dull of nature as not to know what changes in the things that make it fruitful cause it to attain its full growth [viz., *to flourish*]. The sky holds light, light air, and air the birds; the earth nourishes plants, plants fruit, and fruit animals; which all testify that they were put there by a strong hand, the supreme power of the Ruler of All, Who in His strength has provided so for them all that nothing is lacking for them for their use. And in the omnipotence of the same Maker is the motion of all living things that seek the earth for earthly things like the animals and are not inspired by God with reason, as well as the awakening of those who dwell in human flesh and have reason, discernment and wisdom.[11]

Three observations bear mention here. First, the whole of creation is included in Hildegard's vision of "full growth." As in Genesis 1, the fulfillment of a particular creature, or aspect of creation, corresponds with the fulfillment of God's life-giving intentions. The skies are included insofar as they hold light and

---

[10] Hildegard, II.2.
[11] Hildegard, II.1.2.

118   *A Theology of Flourishing*

air and thus provide space for birds to fly; the earth puts forth vegetation, bearing fruit that feeds animals; and all this reflects the Creator's providential purposes, manifested in the flourishing of each creature in keeping with its unique form.

Second, despite this vision, the preceding reflection explicitly separates humans from other creatures on the basis of "reason, discernment and wisdom." Consistent with the elevation of the intellect in the theology of her time, this separation pervades her writings, finding further development in *The Book of Divine Works*. There, while still identifying God with life, she sees God saying, "I am also rationality, possessing the breath of the resounding Word through which every created thing was made."[12] In what follows, Hildegard again elevates humans on the basis of rationality and speaks of nonhuman creatures as being made to serve human ends. In all this, Edwards observes, "Hildegard has an exalted view of the human as at the center of God's plan of the creation and the incarnation."[13] On the one hand, such a perspective is to be expected from a thinker of her time; it is not altogether uncommon, even today. On the other hand, per Jantzen's concerns about the exaltation of the intellect in mystical discourse, this perspective appears a bit at odds with Hildegard's broader vision of creation.

This may well be the case, yet a third observation arises here. Despite the anthropocentric and sometimes instrumentalist tenor of her theology, Hildegard consistently imagines the human person in terms of creation and, in the spirit of Job, carefully admonishes humans to know their place in the created order. Immediately following the reflection quoted above, she observes parallels between the makeup of the human person and the created order: "Man . . . has a circle, which contains his

---

[12] Hildegard, *The Book of Divine Works,* I.1.2.

[13] Denis Edwards, *Christian Understandings of Creation: The Historical Trajectory* (Minneapolis: Fortress Press, 2017), 101.

Creation, Life, and Love in and beyond the Medieval Period 119

clarity, breath, and reason, as the sky has its lights, air and birds; and he has a receptacle containing humidity, germination and birth, as the earth contains fertility, fruition and animals." After making this comparison, she adds: "What is this? O human, you are wholly in every creature, and you forget your Creator; you are subject to Him as was ordained, and you go against His commands?"[14] While the elevation of the human intellect might have led to a tyrannical anthropocentrism or hard instrumentalism that authorizes the exploitation and degradation of creation, in Hildegard we find a reassertion of the similarity between humans and other creatures and an admonition to humans not to forget their Creator or place in creation—a forgetting that, by implication, other creatures do not do.

This observation finds fulfillment shortly thereafter, where Hildegard, reflecting on why Jesus is called the Word of God, writes, "Just as a word of command uttered by an instructor among local and transitory human dust is understood by people who know and foresee the reason he gave it, so also the power of the Father *is known among the creatures of the world, who perceive and understand in Him the source of their creation*."[15] In keeping with her vision of God as the fire that breathes all things into life, Hildegard envisions all creatures as able to "perceive and understand" God as Creator. This may not be the rational understanding humans possess, but still she attests to a kind of innate creaturely knowledge of God's life-giving presence and action in all things.

As Constant Mews observes, this creational perspective sets Hildegard apart from her contemporaries, philosophically and theologically. Mews writes, "Whereas Anselm takes for granted the capacity of reason to come to terms with static philosophical concepts like 'being,' 'substance,' and 'accident,' Hildegard develops her thought from organic concepts like 'life' and 'greenness'

---

[14] Hildegard, *Scivias*, II.1.2.
[15] Hildegard, II.1.4. Emphasis mine.

120   *A Theology of Flourishing*

or 'viridity' (*viriditas*)."[16] Rather than prioritizing concepts, her reflections on God and the world center livingness—the actuality of life. Moreover, while "universal proportion" is a key concept for Hildegard, it is important to reiterate that this idea does not stem from abstract reflection on the created order. Rather, it is rooted in a lived awareness of the fruitfulness of creation, life as it is experienced: in the fragrance of flowers, the vision of soaring eagles, the rush of cool air on a hot day, and in love shared among friends, human or otherwise.

This analysis brings us to Hildegard's best-known idea: *viriditas*, typically translated as "greenness" or "viridity." Hildegard's writings abound with talk of *viriditas*. Although at face value the term may seem predisposed to ecological matters—and that has been its most common application in recent theology—*viriditas* has a wide semantic range. As Edwards observes, "Greenness captures the life, the energy, the dynamic newness of things, in an abundance of multivalent resonances."[17] Various snapshots from Hildegard's writings illustrate this range. In a passage with ecological overtones, Hildegard envisions God saying:

> I am also the fiery life of the essence of divinity; I flame above the beauty of the fields, and I shine in the waters,

---

[16] Constant Mews, "Religious Thinker: 'A Frail Human Being' on Fiery Life," in *Voice of the Living Light: Hildegard of Bingen and Her World*, ed. Barbara Newman, 52–69 (Berkeley: University of California Press, 2008), 56.

[17] Edwards, *Christian Understandings of Creation*, 96. Cf. Mews, "Religious Thinker," 57. "Translators sometimes supply a range of terms to capture its meaning, which relates much more than the color green: freshness, vitality, fertility, fecundity, fruitfulness, verdure, growth. She uses the word as a metaphor of health, both physical and spiritual. Thus she understands the Word of God as a flame within the divine fire which became incarnate through the viridity of the Holy Spirit. The Word gives life to humanity by pouring into it 'warmth in viridity,' 'just as a mother gives milk to her children' (II.1.7). Through the incarnate Word, divine viridity is seen (II.i.11). Indeed Creation itself would not have been possible without this viridity (II.2.1)."

Creation, Life, and Love in and beyond the Medieval Period 121

and I burn in the sun, the moon, and the stars. With the airy wind I quicken all things with some invisible life that sustains them all. For the air lives in viridity and in the flowers, the waters flow as if alive, and the sun lives within its own light.[18]

Here, *viriditas* shines in blossoming flowers, rushing waters, air, and light, all of which reflect God's being, the fire of life. Later in the same chapter Hildegard builds upon these images in relational terms, writing: "I saw also that from the thin air, moisture bubbling forth upon the earth roused the earth's viridity and made all the fruits to sprout and grow. It also bore certain clouds above, which sustained all the things above and were strengthened by all those things above."[19] Here, *viriditas* appears in the interaction of air, water, and clouds, which "rouse," "sustain," and "strengthen" earth's generative capacity.

While the notion of *viriditas* is surely rooted in the ecosystems Hildegard inhabited and the plants she tended, Edwards observes that she likewise applies the term to "the God-given livingness of the spiritual journey."[20] An illustrative passage states:

These signify that thought proceeds from the faithful person's right desire to the useful fruitfulness that brings forth good works, touching his viridity to produce the many fruits of holiness and lift up human minds to heavenly things, so that they yearn for them and are strengthened by them. For so long as a person tends with right desire to the fruit of good works, he despises earthly things and so affixes himself to what is above in heaven that he reveals

---

[18] Hildegard, *The Book of Divine Works,* I.1.2.
[19] Hildegard, I.4.1.1.
[20] Edwards, *Christian Understandings of Creation,* 97.

122   *A Theology of Flourishing*

himself to be no longer the same person, but one wholly transformed.[21]

In ways that closely parallel Gregory's account of *epektasis*, Hildegard sees the spiritual journey of the human person as a journey into *viriditas*, whereby the Spirit's greening power transforms the human person, raising the mind to "heavenly things." Despite the somewhat intellectualist tone of this passage, it is crucial to observe how the flourishing of nonhuman creatures functions for Hildegard as a grounding metaphor for Christian life—a life that culminates in bearing the fruit of love. Hildegard herself states, "The elements that sustain humankind do not urge them to sin, but rather judge them in sin by God's judgment; and in good works, they reveal sweetness and pleasantness upon them."[22] In all these cases *viriditas* evokes abundant life.

Thus, despite occasional anthropocentric tendencies, Hildegard's visions situate the human person within the broader creation and see God's intention that each creature may "attain its full growth," may flourish, as extending to all things. Moreover, although Hildegard's occasional soteriological statements characterize humanity as "fallen" and in need of salvation from sin, this characterization must be situated beside, if not within, her statements about God's desire that all creatures may flourish.[23] By no means is Hildegard's world a place of ruin; it is a place of abundance, in which human creatures strive to realize their own *viriditas* in communion with plants, animals, one another, and God. As such, Hildegard contributes important resources for constructing a theology that links social and ecological concerns

---

[21] Hildegard, *The Book of Divine Works,* I.4.8.

[22] Hildegard, I.4.32.

[23] Hildegard, *Scivias*, II.8. Hildegard's soteriology emerges episodically throughout her writings. She speaks explicitly of heavenly salvation in *Scivias* II.1.15.

Creation, Life, and Love in and beyond the Medieval Period 123

into a holistic socio-ecological paradigm, wherein God—who is "wholly Life"—intends all creatures to flourish.

—A Biographical Coda: Thinking about Hildegard with Grace Jantzen—

To conclude this section, I offer a brief reflection that relates Hildegard's life as a woman mystic and theologian living in a profoundly patriarchal context to illustrate one manifestation of flourishing—in Hildegard's own *viriditas*. As Jantzen notes, Hildegard's writings are replete with reflections on gender. Time and again Hildegard questions how she—a woman—could possibly speak with authority of God and God's intentions. In Jantzen's view this is not just rhetorical play. Hildegard seems to believe that no woman could speak as she spoke. Reflecting on this point, Jantzen writes, "It would be going much too far to see Hildegard here as striking a blow for feminism. . . . Although she herself found her voice and claimed her authority, she never treated this as anything other than extraordinary."[24]

Yet, even so, she spoke. Under the yoke of medieval European patriarchy, surrounded by the "learned men" of the schools, Hildegard's visions and theological commentaries communicate truths of faith that remain relevant today. In this way she achieved a degree of self-actualization that was impossible for most women of her time. Jantzen makes the point well, illustrating how Hildegard both flourished through her writings and found in her own theological insights reason to critique the men of her day. She writes: "In hearing God's voice, Hildegard is finding her own; and furthermore finding herself rebuking her male counterparts. They should be the real mystics . . . but they are 'lukewarm and sluggish in serving God's justice.'"[25] Moreover,

---

[24] Grace M. Jantzen, *Power, Gender, and Christian Mysticism* (Cambridge: Cambridge University Press, 1995), 171. For Jantzen's analysis of gender in Hildegard's writings, see 161–63.

[25] Jantzen, 171.

as Jantzen also observes, beyond wondering why the men of her day are not practicing what they preach—why despite their words and ideas they are not bringing about a world that reflects God's intentions—and by making her critique in terms of "God's justice," Hildegard imparts a practical orientation to her thought.

In addition to providing a check on the often-intellectualist flavor of her writings, this reading of Hildegard provides an important glimpse into what flourishing might look like in the concrete conditions of human life. In finding her voice and speaking amid and against forces that subjugated and silenced voices like hers, Hildegard blooms as an icon of self-actualization. Her life attests to the possibility of an alternative socio-ecological order where all voices are welcomed, heard, and heeded as vital contributors to a symphony of reflection on the Spirit's work in the world. To heed these voices, those with power must, of course, have ears to hear.

John Duns Scotus

Driven by the emergence of the medieval university, the century after Hildegard's death marked a period of great growth in Scholastic theology. Founded in 1150, the University of Paris provided a special locus for this flourishing—a place where teacher-scholars including Albertus Magnus, Thomas Aquinas, and John Duns Scotus debated perennial questions in theology and philosophy and produced masterworks that continue to shape theological discourse.

To my mind, amid the countless questions asked and answers proposed, Duns Scotus's answers to the question *Cur deus homo?*—Why did God become human?—and his distinctive view on *haecceitas*, the particularity of creatures, make important contributions to a theology of flourishing. Scotus's answers stand out for two reasons. First, in keeping with the warp and

Creation, Life, and Love in and beyond the Medieval Period 125

weft of his Franciscan heritage, his account of the reason for the incarnation demonstrates greater consistency with the biblical vision of divine love than the Thomistic synthesis. Second, as Horan observes, Scotus's account of "thisness," or *haecceitas*, offers an invaluable basis for recognizing creaturely uniqueness as beloved by God and, thus, for valuing creatures as they are in themselves, according to their God-given, embodied particularity. Both recognizing and valuing creatures in these ways are foundations of the proposed theology of flourishing.[26]

The Reason for the Incarnation

In the *Summa Theologica* Thomas Aquinas asks, "Whether it was fitting that God should become incarnate in the beginning of the human race?"[27] Taking up what contemporary scholars term the "absolute predestination of Christ," Thomas queries whether the incarnation would have happened if humanity had not sinned.[28] Although it would be reductionistic and incorrect to claim that Thomas altogether rejects the view that God desires for all things to be united to their Creator irrespective of sin or that the incarnation is a contingent response to human sin, his

---

[26] Horan makes this argument with respect to humans and other-than-human creatures. See Daniel P. Horan, "Beyond Essentialism and Complementarity: Toward a Theological Anthropology Rooted in *Haecceitas*," *Theological Studies* 75, no. 1 (2014): 94–117, and "*Haecceitas*, Theological Aesthetics, and the Kinship of Creation: John Duns Scotus as a Resource for Environmental Ethics," *Heythrop Journal* 59, no. 6 (November 2018): 1060–76.

[27] Thomas Aquinas, *Summa Theologica,* trans. Fathers of the English Dominican Province (Cincinnati, OH: Benziger Brothers, 1947), III.1.a5. Hereafter *ST.* For a historical study of medieval perspectives on the incarnation, see Justus H. Hunter, *If Adam Had Not Sinned: The Reason for the Incarnation from Anselm to Scotus* (Washington, DC: Catholic University of America Press, 2020).

[28] For a historical perspective on the genesis of "absolute predestination," see Daniel P. Horan, OFM, "How Original Was Scotus on the Incarnation? Reconsidering the History of the Absolute Predestination of Christ in Light of Robert Gosseteste," *Heythrop Journal* 52 (2011): 374–91.

126   *A Theology of Flourishing*

answer to this question explicitly links the incarnation to human
sinfulness. He writes:

> Since everywhere in the Sacred Scripture the sin of the
> first man is assigned as the reason of the Incarnation, it is
> more in accordance with this to say that the work of the
> Incarnation was ordained by God as a remedy for sin; so
> that, *had sin not existed, the Incarnation would not have been.*
> And yet the power of God is not limited to this; even had
> sin not existed, God could have become incarnate.[29]

Shortly after this, Thomas ponders a related question: whether
it was fitting that God should become incarnate before humanity's first sinful act.[30] The first objection offered in this question
argues that "the work of the Incarnation sprang from the immensity of Divine charity,"[31] such that it would be appropriate
for the incarnation to coincide with the emergence of the first
humans, before "the fall." The immensity of divine love notwithstanding, Thomas rejects this view, arguing that "since the work
of the Incarnation is principally ordained to *the restoration of the
human race by blotting out sin*, it is manifest that it was not fitting
for God to become incarnate at the beginning of the human
race before sin. For medicine is given only to the sick."[32] Here
as before, Thomas presents the incarnation as merely a remedy, a
corrective to a problem. While he does not state that this remedy is wholly contingent on the problem—a divine reaction of
sorts—he presents human sin as logically prior to the incarnation, concluding that the incarnation would not have happened
without sin.

---

[29] *ST* III.1.a3. Emphasis mine.
[30] *ST* III.1.a5.
[31] *ST* III.1.a5.
[32] *ST* III.1.a5. Emphasis mine.

Creation, Life, and Love in and beyond the Medieval Period 127

This summary of the Thomistic position provides important context for understanding Scotus's contrasting view. The importance of this context is twofold. First, reading Scotus against a Thomistic backdrop highlights his distinctive emphasis on divine love and freedom in the logic of the incarnation. Second, the contrast between Thomas and Scotus on the reason for the incarnation reflects the same issues that are at play in the contrast between heavenly salvation and flourishing. To wit, does the incarnation function primarily as a remedy that enters creation from the outside to save the world from sin, or does it arise from within creation as an expression of the same love that created all things? This question seems especially crucial given the continued dominance of the Thomistic synthesis in Roman Catholic theology.

And so, following the hints offered above, we arrive at Scotus's view. In contrast to the logical priority that Thomas affords human sin vis-à-vis the incarnation, Scotus absolutely rejects the idea that sin—or anything else—could impose necessity on the divine will. For Scotus, God is utterly free, and this freedom comes to expression in divine love. As Étienne Gilson explains, for Scotus, in God, the necessity of love involves no diminution of freedom because God is love—and eternally so. On this basis Gilson concludes, "Duns Scotus's whole theology is marked by this key thesis, that the first free act found in all being is an act of love."[33]

Scotus's understanding of the incarnation follows this same logic. If God's first free act is to love, then the incarnation of the one whom the New Testament describes as "before all things" (Col 1:17) must express that same love. Scotus explains this point in terms of a hierarchy of divine priorities, or goods. He writes,

---

[33] Étienne Gilson, *John Duns Scotus: Introduction to His Fundamental Positions,* trans. James Colbert (London: Bloomsbury, 2018), 452.

128 A Theology of Flourishing

> Neither is it likely that the highest good in creation is something that was merely occasioned only because of some lesser good; nor is it likely that He predestined Adam to such good before He predestined Christ; and yet this would follow [were the Incarnation occasioned by Adam's sin].[34]

In other words, if Christ is creation's highest good, the fullest expression of divine love, then it cannot be the case that so great a good could be occasioned, even logically, by a lesser good. As Mary Beth Ingham observes, "This means that God's choice to become incarnate is logically prior and intentionally superior to the traditional response that God became human as a result of the sin of our first parents."[35] In short, for Scotus, the incarnation is not solely a response to sinfulness within created reality but is a preparation for and enactment of God's communion with creation through Jesus Christ.

Scotus's account of the incarnation has much to offer a theology of flourishing. First, in centering divine love and God's desire for communion with creation in Christ, he appears better aligned with the biblical presentation of a God who collaborates with creation to bring forth life and foster a living communion of creatures. In this way, too, Scotus demonstrates how much the logic of the incarnation matters for how Christians see the world and themselves. For if the incarnation follows the logic of divine love and expresses a divine will that seeks the flourishing and communion of all things, then Christ's life manifests and reinforces a sense of creation's goodness before God. If the incarnation is seen only as a remedy for sin, then Christ's redemptive work suggests that the world is corrupt, fallen, no longer

---

[34] John Duns Scotus, *Ordinatio*, III, d.7, q.3, 4–6.

[35] Mary Beth Ingham, CSJ, *Understanding John Duns Scotus: "Of Reality the Rarest-Veined Unraveller"* (St. Bonaventure, NY: Franciscan Institute Publications, 2017), 127.

Creation, Life, and Love in and beyond the Medieval Period   129

good—and the incarnation appears as a response to a "lesser" good. This need not be an either-or, for linking the incarnation to love does not negate or downplay the reality of sin. Rather, despite the obvious need for atonement for and forgiveness from sin, in contrast with a paradigm that sees salvation primarily as cleansing from sin in a fallen world, Scotus's approach puts sin in its proper place. Sin is not an ontologized force in competition with divine goodness. For Scotus, sin is a disruption of God's intention that all creation may flourish in the fullness of life. In this approach the incarnation is more than just a remedy. The incarnation is a revelation and manifestation of divine love that reorients the cosmos toward the fullness of life in communion with God.

Second, as Béraud de Saint-Maurice observes in an early commentary on Scotus, the Scotistic position raises important qualitative questions about God's character and will. Seeing the incarnation as primarily a remedy for sin centers humanity rather than Christ in the narrative of God's relationship to the world, subordinating God's will to human acts. In Saint-Maurice's assessment, such a view leads naturally to the paradigms of satisfaction and substitutionary atonement, as the crucifixion of Christ provides a bloody means to an end within a "drama of avenging justice."[36] Pushing this point further, and anticipating feminist critiques of the idea that God the Father "sent" Jesus to his death, Saint-Maurice writes,

In the anthropocentric picture, it is an Eternal Father, a kind of executioner athirst for blood . . . whom we see lifting an avenging hand against His Son, an innocent

---

[36] Béraud de Saint-Maurice, *John Duns Scotus: A Teacher for Our Times*, trans. Columban Duffy, OFM (St. Bonventure, NY: Franciscan Institute, 1955), 268. For the feminist critique of this point, see Joanne Carlson Brown and Carole R. Bohn, eds., "For God So Loved the World?" in *Christianity, Patriarchy and Abuse* (New York: Pilgrim Press, 1989).

130 *A Theology of Flourishing*

> Victim dying upon the Cross . . . dedicated to be this
> kind of victim *by a fate*, as it were, from which He cannot
> extricate himself.[37]

Beyond anticipating the feminist critique of violence in traditional accounts of Jesus's mission, here Saint-Maurice also anticipates Jantzen's critique of necrophilia. Interpretations of Jesus's mission that see sin as necessitating the bloody death of an innocent victim quietly subjugate the proclamation of abundant life to the necessity of death, glorifying violence. But this is not the way of a God who is love. Scotus's logic thus has the potential to ripple out beyond Christology to theologies of God, soteriologies, and so on, resituating Christian views on sin and salvation within Christ's promise of abundant life—one primary aim of a theology of flourishing.

Haecceitas, or "Thisness"

Scotus's account of *haecceitas*, or "thisness," constitutes a second aspect of his thought that sets him apart from the predominant theologies of his time—and most theologies since his time. The perennial question of the relationship between universals and particulars received significant attention from the theologians of the schools. Yet, where most understood particulars in terms of universals—understanding a specific "this" in terms of its "thisness"—Scotus centers his reflections on the concrete particularity of a "this." He refers to this "thisness" as *haecceitas*, from the Latin *haec*, for "this."

Explaining this principle, Scotus defines a

> designated unity as a *this*, so that just as . . . an individual
> is incompossible with being divided into subject parts . . .

---

[37] Saint-Maurice, *John Duns Scotus*, 269.

Creation, Life, and Love in and beyond the Medieval Period 131

> so too I say here that an individual is incompossible with not being designated a *this* by this singularity and the cause [of its thisness] is asked not of singularity in general but of *this designated singularity in particular*—that is, as it is determinately *this*.[38]

As Mary Beth Ingham explains, Scotus locates the cause of individuation, or particularity, in "an intrinsic positive principle," such that the singularity of an individual entity is real and true in itself, not derivable from its belonging to a particular genus.[39] As Scotus develops this point, he argues that even two instantiations of a single species (for example, two parakeets) are not derivatively distinct in view of their belonging to a higher form. Rather, each parakeet is a "this" in and of itself, by virtue of its concrete existence.[40]

Before considering the potential implications of *haecceitas* for a theology of flourishing, it is important to note that, in Scotus's own writings, this concept provides a philosophical answer to a philosophical question: the principle of individuation, the answer to the question, What makes this *this* rather than *that*? Although Scotus himself does not draw specific theological conclusions from *haecceitas*, as the coming engagement with Nicholas of Cusa will show—and as numerous commentators suggest—*haecceitas* takes on great significance when seen through an incarnational lens.

In Ingham's view, *haecceitas* grounds a perspective in which "each being exists to grow into an authentic expression of itself, of himself, of herself." On this basis, she concludes, "The beauty of each being is particular and intended. It is precisely insofar as

---

[38] Duns Scotus, *Ordinatio* II, d.3, p.1, q.4, n.76.

[39] Mary Beth Ingham, *The Philosophical Vision of John Duns Scotus: An Introduction* (Washington, DC: The Catholic University of America Press, 2004), 113. Ingham offers an in-depth analysis of *haecceity* in this volume, 101–16.

[40] Duns Scotus, *Ordinatio* II, d.3, q.5–6, n.188.

132   *A Theology of Flourishing*

each individual is itself that it is able to express (indeed, proclaim) its inner beauty."[41] Indeed, given Scotus's view of the incarnation, one might conclude that, just as the embodied Word gives concrete expression to the love that created all things and that holds them in existence, so, too, all things—as expressions of God's love—are destined in their particularity toward fulfillment by virtue of God's life-giving will independent of their "usefulness" to humans or any other such factor. Here, *haecceitas* takes on a qualitative dimension that synthesizes Scotus's theology and philosophy into a holistic vision of all things "as beings of enormous value, creatures of a loving God."[42]

Following a similar logic, Horan argues that *haecceitas* enables us to interpret "the value of human personhood . . . within the context of the principle of individuation, which is really identical with, yet formally distinct from, a person's actual existence or being."[43] Here, Horan adds a vital point: while Scotus is concerned with the idea of individuation, the actuality of individuation subsists within a "matrix of relationships beginning with that between creation (in each aspect and writ large) and the Creator, that emphasizes the fundamentality of our alterity and inherent relationality."[44] In other words, it would be a mistake to understand *haecceitas* as a foundation for any sort of individu*alism*; while as a philosophical concept it explains the unique, God-given "thisness" of every creature, creatures do not exist in isolation. Quite the contrary, in the concrete, *haecceitas* possesses a radically interdependent character, as countless creatures co-inhabit and are mutually co-conditioned by their socioecosystems. For a theology of flourishing that links the social and ecological under the rubric of God's life-giving will, *haecceitas* provides a key resource for valuing the flourishing of everything that is "because

---

[41] Ingham, *Understanding John Duns Scotus*, 23.

[42] Ingham, 24.

[43] Horan, "Beyond Essentialism and Complementarity," 114.

[44] Horan, 115.

Creation, Life, and Love in and beyond the Medieval Period **133**

everything that exists has been intentionally loved into existence by a Creator that desires each particular being exist when it could otherwise not."[45] Such a vision of creaturely life offers a firm foundation for thinking about flourishing, as God both loves every creature into existence and wills its fulfillment, as it is held and sustained in being by the love that created all things.

Julian of Norwich and Nicholas of Cusa

The final two figures in this exploration of medieval thought lived on the cusp of a new era. The English anchoress and visionary theologian Julian of Norwich lived in the late fourteenth century, at the end of what we now call the Middle Ages. Born just over fifty years after Julian, the life of German philosopher and spiritual writer Nicholas of Cusa stretched from the end of this period into the period we now call the Renaissance. Despite their different contexts, Julian and Nicholas both put heavy emphasis on the possibility of creaturely fulfillment through the love of God in the concrete, embodied conditions of material reality. In doing so, their writings place a capstone on the contributions to a theology of flourishing made by Hildegard and Duns Scotus.

Julian of Norwich

Like Hildegard and Scotus, Julian sees all things as expressions of God's love. Yet Julian takes this commitment further, setting love at the core of her entire theological perspective. Love grounds her theology, anthropology, and understanding of creaturely reality to such a degree that, Philip Sheldrake observes that, for Julian, "the meaning of everything is 'love.'"[46] In an illustrative

---

[45] Horan, "*Haecceitas*, Theological Aesthetics, and the Kinship of Creation," 1063.

[46] Philip Sheldrake, *Julian of Norwich: In God's Sight* (Hoboken, NJ: John Wiley and Sons, 2018), viii.

134   A Theology of Flourishing

passage from her *Showings*, or *Revelations of Divine Love*, Julian reflects that in all her visions God's love "was never abated and never will be." Linking this love to creation and human life, she adds, "And in this love he has done all his works, and in this love he has made all things profitable to us, and in this love our life is everlasting."[47] The link between love and creation pervades Julian's thought. In one representative passage God shows Julian "something small, no bigger than a hazelnut," which represents the whole of creation. Julian is baffled at the sight and wonders how something so small could avoid "[falling] into nothing." Her questioning is met by a realization: "It lasts and always will, because God loves it; and thus everything has being through the love of God." The love of God gives life to all things, sustains them in being, and seeks to draw them to fulfillment through what she terms "substantial union" with God.[48] This emphasis on love comes to fuller expression in the conclusion of *Showings*, wherein Julian—writing at least fifteen years after her vision of Christ's Passion—reflects anew on the meaning of what she had seen. She writes: "And it was said: What, do you wish to know your Lord's meaning in this thing? Know it well, love was his meaning. Who reveals it to you? Love. What did he reveal to you? Love. Why does he reveal it to you? For love. Remain in this, and you will know more of the same."[49] Love was the meaning of all Julian had seen.

Julian's vision of God as love also grounds her anthropology. Her visions depict God as waiting patiently for humanity,

---

[47] Julian of Norwich, *Showings*, trans. Edmund Colledge and James Wash (New York: Paulist Press, 1978), LT 86, p. 342. In scholarship on Julian of Norwich, it is conventional to use "ST" to represent the "Short Text" and "LT" to represent the "Long Text" of her *Showings*, or *Revelations of Divine Love*. I use this convention, followed by the chapter number and the page on which the chapter is located in the volume cited above.

[48] Julian, LT 5, p. 183.

[49] Julian, LT 86, p. 342.

Creation, Life, and Love in and beyond the Medieval Period 135

unchanging in love, "[wanting] for us to be converted and united to him in love, as he is to us."[50] Yet, she observes, it can be difficult for humans to recognize and accept the radical character of God's love. She writes: "Yes, and he wants us in all things to have our contemplation and our delight in love. And it is about this knowledge that we are most blind, for some of us believe that God is almighty and may do everything, and that he is all wisdom and can do everything, but that he is love and wishes to do everything, there we fail."[51] Here, Julian expresses a recognition of God's intentions for humanity, stating that God wants us to see and delight in divine love in all things. At the same time, she observes that we humans often fail in our ability to see and accept God's love for us and for creation. She writes: "But our passing life which we have here does not know in our senses what our self is. . . . And when we know and see, truly and clearly, what our self is, then we shall truly and clearly see and know our Lord God in the fullness of joy."[52] And what will we perceive when we see "truly and clearly"? For Julian, the answer is that God loves us and that there is "no difference between God and our substance, but, as it were, all God."[53] Despite our inability to perceive it amid the conditions of finitude and sin, the truth of creaturely existence is that all things are substantially united to God as God, and—as in Irenaeus and Gregory—the fulfillment

---

[50] Julian, LT 78, p. 332.

[51] Julian, LT 73, p. 323.

[52] Julian, LT 46, p. 258. Emphasis mine. These divergent ways of seeing, which Sheldrake defines as seeing "'in my sight' and 'in God's sight,'" correspond with a second pair of contrasting terms that lie at the heart of Julian's anthropology: *substance* and *sensuality*. To see "in God's sight" is to see oneself and others as united in their very essence to the love of God. Again, for Julian, substantial union with God's love is the basic fact of existence. In contrast, to see "in my sight" is to see oneself and others through the lens of sensuality, or sense perception, with a kind of vision that often cannot perceive divine love at the heart of all things. See Sheldrake, *Julian of Norwich*, 75. Julian's fullest treatment of substance and sensuality takes place in LT 54–59.

[53] Julian, *Showings*, LT 54, p. 285.

136   *A Theology of Flourishing*

of human life comes in seeing ourselves and all things as God sees them. As Jantzen puts it in her commentary on Julian's life and work, "Julian argues that this ignorance of the love of God is paralleled by an ignorance of our own souls as created and restored in that love. . . . Thus, according to Julian, to come to know ourselves, we must come to know God."[54]

This account of divine love seeking the fulfillment of all things amid the fragmentation of creaturely vision also grounds Julian's soteriology—a category with significant importance for a theology of flourishing. Foundational here is Julian's claim that "sin is nothing," because, in her vision of creation in God's sight, she "did not see sin."[55] Here, Julian does not intend to deny the reality of sin. Rather, from the standpoint of God's vision, there is no sin because God sees only the substance of things, and the substance of things is God's love. On this basis Julian can conclude that, when she saw things as God sees them, she did not see sin.[56] As Sheldrake notes, this observation explicitly contrasts with the idea that humanity is "fallen" and leads toward a "revised and positive theology of the meaning of sin and the process of salvation."[57]

Within this process of redemption, which Jantzen insightfully characterizes as "human whole-making," the fundamental truth is that humanity "is a reflection of divine wholeness"—what I would simply term *love*.[58] Seen in this way, the human journey toward fulfillment is at its most basic a journey into oneself

---

[54] Grace M. Jantzen, *Julian of Norwich: Mystic and Theologian* (New York: Paulist Press, 1988), 93.

[55] Julian, *Showings*, ST 8; LT 34.

[56] Neither is there anger or blame in God. In LT 46, Julian writes that anger only exists in sensuality. Since, as love, God is absolute substance, there is no anger in God. This also means that God does not blame humanity for sin, because it results from distorted vision. On this point, see Sheldrake, *Julian of Norwich*, 73–76.

[57] Sheldrake, *Julian of Norwich*, 121.

[58] Jantzen, *Julian of Norwich*, 92–93.

Creation, Life, and Love in and beyond the Medieval Period   *137*

and into the world, where God waits, calling all things to fulfillment. In our fragmentation and brokenness, humans are, Jantzen writes, "at odds with ourselves until this orientation is the focus of our whole life, integrating our sensuality with our substance, which is always united with God."[59] Even amid fragmentation, then, the basic fact does not change: all things are created in and for the love that constitutes the innermost essence of *everything*.

Julian's claim that "sin is nothing" denies sin anything approximating an ontological status. This move resituates sin within human experience, as a privation that distorts our vision, inhibiting our ability to see God's love at the heart of creation. In and of itself, sin is "nothing." For Julian, then, Christ's redemption is first about opening eyes to God's love and bringing creatures into the fullness for which they were created. Salvation from sin will happen along the way, because sin obstructs our ability to attain self-actualization according to our God-given "substance." Here again, flourishing is a constituent expression of salvation, as the human journey toward wholeness culminates in experiencing the fullness of what one is by seeing as God sees and acting in accordance with this vision.

Julian herself makes a turn toward action in the final chapter of *Showings*. There she writes, "This book is begun by God's gift and his grace, but it is *not yet performed*, as I see it."[60] For both Jantzen and Sheldrake, this practical orientation is part and parcel of Julian's vision. In discovering our substantial unity with God and seeing as God sees, Christians discover a call to act as God acts, in a radical praxis of love for all things. As Jantzen notes: "There is no indication that she expected further understanding to come upon her in blinding flashes or in additional visions. . . . It was only *in living by what she already understood* that she could

---

[59] Jantzen, 148.

[60] Julian, *Showings*, LT 86, p. 342.

138   *A Theology of Flourishing*

hope to come to understand more deeply."[61] Similarly, Sheldrake writes that Julian's integration of vision and praxis leads to an anthropology in which "we humans are called upon to be agents of love in our own world," a point he describes as "frequently a deeply uncomfortable message."[62] Taking this point a step further, Frederick Bauerschmidt sees in Julian's writings an implicit foundation for a radically transformative, political "performance" of God's love. In Bauerschmidt's view, such a performance "would seem to undercut any neat division of the world into spiritual and temporal realms" and paves the way toward "a new kind of polis, a pilgrim city defined not by borders or geography but by the practice of ongoing discernment of the mystery of God in Christ."[63] Whether applied individually or collectively, Julian's theology proffers a powerful vision of divine love working at the heart of things—a love that seeks to draw all things into the fullness of what they are in an unchanging, unending communion of love.

Nicholas of Cusa

Where Julian's writings offer a more implicit account of human deification in relationship to divine love, Nicholas of Cusa's writings—especially *On the Vision of God*—cast the journey toward fulfillment in God in terms of intellectual awakening. This fact is important to name up front because it both captures the basic orientation of Nicholas's writings and recognizes that his writings manifest the intellectualist bias of most theologies of deification observed and critiqued by Jantzen. Even so, the

---

[61] Jantzen, *Julian of Norwich*, 92. Emphasis mine.

[62] Sheldrake, *Julian of Norwich*, 92.

[63] Frederick Christian Bauerschmidt, *Julian of Norwich and the Mystical Body Politic of Christ* (Notre Dame, IN: University of Notre Dame Press, 1999), 195; 197. For Bauerschmidt's full treatment of the "performance" of love, see 191–202.

Creation, Life, and Love in and beyond the Medieval Period 139

specific character of Nicholas's account of deification resonates closely with those of Julian, Gregory, and other authors, and so offers further resources for building a theology of flourishing on the threefold foundation of scripture, theology, and spirituality.

Like Scotus, Nicholas affords primacy to particulars—what he calls "quiddities"—rather than universals. In his philosophical treatise *On Learned Ignorance* he makes the uniqueness of things the basic fact of existence. He writes:

> Since no one person is like another in anything, not in sense, or imagination, or intellect, or in an activity, whether writing, painting, or a craft, even if for a thousand years someone zealously attempted to imitate another in anything, one would never arrive at precision, although at times a perceptible difference may go unnoticed.[64]

No amount of imitation can ever attain to the deepest core of what a person is. This uniqueness is not, however, a humans-only affair. As in Scotus, all things are both radically unique in their own right and radically interrelated by virtue of their participation in God's being, on the one hand, and the universe, on the other. Put another way, while in an absolute sense all things take their being from God, Nicholas holds that, in a finite, or "contracted" sense, all things take their being from creation. Within this framework, Nancy Hudson observes, "creation is not a fabricated object apart and against God, but is intimately related to the divine."[65]

This model of quiddity and divine-creaturely relationship also grounds Nicholas's account of creaturely fulfillment, or salvation.

---

[64] Nicholas of Cusa, "On Learned Ignorance," in *Nicholas of Cusa: Selected Spiritual Writings* (New York: Paulist Press, 1997), II.1, 94, p. 129.

[65] Nancy Hudson, "Divine Immanence: Nicholas of Cusa's Understanding of Theophany and the Retrieval of a 'New' Model of God," *Journal of Theological Studies* 56, no. 2 (October 2005): 455.

140   *A Theology of Flourishing*

Where Julian envisions creaturely fulfillment "in God's sight," Nicholas—in a riff on Genesis—interprets creaturely fulfillment through the lens of the divine declaration, "Let it be made." Amid a lengthy discourse on the relationship between the finite and the infinite, he writes that "every creature is, as it were, a *finite infinity* or a *created god.*" On this basis, he concludes that the Creator molds each thing

> that it exists in the way in which this *could best be* . . . as much like God as possible. The inference, therefore, is that every created thing as such is perfect, even if by comparison to others it seems less perfect. For the most merciful God communicates being to all *in the manner in which it can be received.*[66]

This passage has important implications for a theology of flourishing, as it attests—in ways that make explicit what was implicit in Scotus—that the particularity of creatures is beloved by God and is intended by God as *perfect* in its own right. From this perspective none can judge the perfection of this or that, because all things manifest a particular perfection simply by being what they are. As Hudson summarizes, "Each individual thing is as much like God as possible; nothing can be said to be more perfect than another."[67] This point alone is significant, but Nicholas presses on, concluding that "every created being *finds its rest in its own perfection*, which it freely holds from divine being."[68] Therefore, for Nicholas, the essence of a creature's fulfillment lies not in external validation but in actualizing its particular perfection in union with God, flourishing precisely as it is, as God made it to be.

---

[66] Nicholas of Cusa, "On Learned Ignorance," II.2, 104, p. 134. Emphasis mine.

[67] Hudson, "Divine Immanence," 456.

[68] Nicholas of Cusa, "On Learned Ignorance," II.2, 104, p. 134.

Creation, Life, and Love in and beyond the Medieval Period   *141*

If *On Learned Ignorance* articulates Nicholas's philosophical and theological framework, *On the Vision of God* deploys this framework in a model of deification wherein self-realization and self-actualization function as markers of creaturely fulfillment. In a key passage, the speaker addresses God:

> And, even more, how will you give me yourself if you do not also give me myself? And when I thus rest in the silence of contemplation, you, Lord, answer me within my heart, saying: "Be yours and I too will be yours!" . . . Hence, unless I am my own, you are not mine, for you would constrain my freedom since you cannot be mine unless I am also mine. And since you have placed this in my freedom, you do not constrain me, but you wait for me to choose to be my own.[69]

Here Nicholas equates "being one's own" with "belonging to God." But what does it take to "be one's own," to attain self-actualization within the contours of creaturely life? Read in the context of a spiritual journey toward God, to "be one's own" is to discover one's true self, one's God-given quiddity, and, through discernment in relationship with God and the world, to come to know what it means to be a beloved creature of God. As Andrea Hollingsworth writes in a commentary on this text, for Nicholas,

> the God who is infinite possibility-in-actualization, the form of forms (*forma formarum*) which constitutes the deep structure of creaturely becoming, is imaged as humans actualize their ownmost possibilities. Said another way, my coming-to-be that which I most deeply am coincides with my coming-to-reflect (and be ever more united with) the

---

[69] Nicholas of Cusa, "On the Vision of God," in *Selected Spiritual Writings*, trans. H. Lawrence Bond (New York: Paulist Press, 1997), VII.25–26, p. 247.

142   *A Theology of Flourishing*

God in whom all possibilities for being, including my being, are enfolded.[70]

Notably, Nicholas places this journey in the context of human freedom. God does not constrain freedom, he writes, because constraint would obstruct the authenticity of the journey
toward the fullness of life that accompanies finding one's true
self. Within this journey, he—like Julian—characterizes God as
"waiting" and "seeing," patiently longing for the full realization
of those who seek. Indeed, for Nicholas, as for Irenaeus and
Julian, all this is about experiencing the fullness of life in the vision of God, whose "seeing is nothing other than your bringing
to life, nothing other than your continuously imparting your
sweetest love."[71]

Finally, it is important to note that Christ, whom Nicholas
dubs the "maximum contracted individual" of the human species, stands at the center of this framework as the perfected
union of the infinite and finite. Because all things are linked by
co-participation in the universe, Christ—the perfect union of
the divine and creaturely—is the one being who can "enfold
in its fullness the perfections of all the things in the species."[72]
In other words, as Hudson explains, because human nature is
a microcosm, or micro-cosmos, "divine union with humanity
would infuse the entire created order with absolute value."[73]
The redemptive work of the incarnation thus ripples out from
Christ's blessed body, enfolding all creation in God's redeeming
work. Though Nicholas casts his account of the spiritual journey

---

[70] Andrea Hollingsworth, "The Faces of Possibility in Nicholas of Cusa's *De
Visione Dei*," *Modern Theology* 32, no. 3 (July 2016): 350. Hollingsworth's essay
offers an insightful analysis of the way the Latin "posse" functions in Nicholas's
text.

[71] Nicholas of Cusa, "Vision of God," IV.12, p. 240.

[72] Nicholas of Cusa, "On Learned Ignorance," III.2, 191, p. 173.

[73] Hudson, "Divine Immanence," 469.

Creation, Life, and Love in and beyond the Medieval Period 143

in intellectual, anthropocentric terms, when linked to his broader philosophical framework, his vision clearly extends the incarnation to all things, forging a vital link between the human journey toward God and the redemption of all creation through Christ.

Key Insights for the Path Ahead

Following the thread of flourishing through the tapestry of the medieval period elicits key concepts and insights that inform my theology of flourishing. Hildegard's account of God as "wholly Life" and her notion of *viriditas* orient the Christian imagination to God's life-giving presence in all things precisely as that which draws things to fulfillment through the work of the Holy Spirit. When coupled with Nicholas's reflections on creaturely self-actualization, Scotus's account of the incarnation and notion of *haecceitas* resituate sin and salvation within God's life-giving will for each creature in its beloved "thisness," reinforcing the biblical vision that the created order is and always has been meant for the fullness of life. Julian's account of seeing things "in God's sight" and her discussion of love as God's meaning lend further support to this view, providing invaluable resources for constructing a nuanced understanding of flourishing as the principal intention of a God who speaks, "*Amo, volo ut sis*—'I love you, I will that you be.'"[74] Together, these contributions ground a Christian praxis of justice, peace, and *amor mundi* that generates conditions in which all creatures may flourish in their particular perfection.

Building on the scriptural and historical foundations established thus far, the next chapter leaps forward to the twentieth century, examining how Karl Rahner's theology of the incarnation and account of self-transcendence further ground a theology of flourishing. After considering Rahner's writings, the chapter

---

[74] Hannah Arendt, *The Life of the Mind: Thinking and Willing*, vol. 2 (New York: Harcourt Brace Jovanovitch, 1978), 136.

presents two key developments of Rahner's thought from two of his most important students: Johann Baptist Metz and Ignacio Ellacuría. Together, these thinkers help to deepen understanding of how the *haecceitas* of human experience shapes the contexts in which flourishing and degradation, life and injustice, occur. This analysis paves a way toward the construction of a theology of flourishing in its own right.

7

Rahner and Beyond

*Twentieth-Century Foundations
for a Theology of Flourishing*

The preceding explorations of scripture and history have presented life and love, wisdom and justice, *haecceitas* and deification, creation and incarnation as foundations for a theology of flourishing. As a last step in this journey through history, this chapter takes a quantum leap into the twentieth century, utilizing a close reading of the German Jesuit theologian Karl Rahner and two of his most significant students—Johann Baptist Metz and Ignacio Ellacuría—to weave together the theological and practical insights that have emerged thus far. In doing so, this chapter paves the way for the next chapter's development of a theology of flourishing in its own right.

This chapter begins by engaging Rahner's cosmic-evolutionary Christology as a further basis for situating the incarnation within the sweep of cosmic history, providing christological foundations for a holistic vision of socio-ecological flourishing. Analysis of Rahner's theological anthropology follows. This analysis highlights how his account of transcendence in history fosters a lived awareness of God's intentions for creation and a

145

146   *A Theology of Flourishing*

praxis of life-giving love amid the conditions of creaturely life.
This analysis gives special attention to how Rahner's framework
fosters a perceptual awareness of injustice vis-à-vis God's desire
that all creatures flourish, toward a praxis of socio-ecological
justice for all. The chapter then returns to Christ, linking the
cosmic-evolutionary foundations of the incarnation to his redemptive function as the exemplar of divinized humans, who, in
their own self-actualization, serve as conduits of God's love and
so act as co-participants in the divine work of flourishing. The
chapter concludes by reflecting on critiques and developments
of Rahner's theology offered by Metz and Ellacuría. Together,
these thinkers build on the foundations established by Rahner
to ponder more directly the realities of injustice, suffering, and
oppression as concrete obstructions to God's life-giving will.

Toward a Cosmic Christianity: Rahner's Evolutionary Christology

Although his reputation for using abstruse language may seem
to belie the claim, Rahner consistently frames Christology, and
indeed all theology and doctrine, in terms of Christian life.
Making this point clear, he consistently expresses concern that
doctrinal claims too often devolve into over-definition and over-
simplification, reducing complex theological truths to statements
with little relevance for Christian praxis.[1] Swimming against
these currents, Rahner describes the incarnation as "the very
center of the reality from which we Christians live" and insists
that—far from being ends in themselves—doctrinal statements
emerge from prayer and are tools for encountering the living
God in everyday experience.[2] Elucidating this point, he writes:

---

[1] See Karl Rahner, "Current Problems in Christology," *Theological Investigations I*, trans. Cornelius Ernst, 149–200 (New York: Crossroad, 1982), 149–50.

[2] Karl Rahner, "On the Theology of the Incarnation," *Theological Investigations IV*, trans. Kevin Smyth, 105–20 (New York: Crossroad, 1982), 105.

Rahner and Beyond

> The degree of theoretical precision and existential vitality with which man understands what he hears depends on the degree to which he comprehends it within the total content of his spiritual being. . . . Man's unique standpoint in history . . . helps to determine the perspective within which we have to consider God's eternal truths too, if we are really going to let them become a reality of mind, heart and life in our personal existence.[3]

Here, Rahner indicates that the theoretical precision of theological claims depends on the extent to which Christians can grasp and apply their content to life. Here again, doctrine is not developed for theoretical reasons alone. Doctrine is practical. Advancing this claim, Rahner explicitly connects the meaning of doctrine to history, such that if doctrines are matters of everyday life, then the circumstances of everyday life condition their meaning. In addition to being practical, then, doctrines are contextual. Applied to a theology of flourishing, Rahner's framework suggests that the meaning of Christ's proclamation of abundant life necessarily emerges within the conditions of concrete, embodied reality—in relationship to all creatures' *haecceitas*. How might we conceptualize the link between Christ, whom Rahner names "the mysterious goal of God's plans and activity for his creation from all eternity," and creation with a view toward flourishing?[4]

In "Christology within an Evolutionary View of the World," Rahner retrieves the cosmic Christology articulated in the prologue to John and Colossians 1 in an evolutionary age, situating Christ within cosmic-evolutionary history. His essay opens with a reflection on the relationship between spirit and matter—a

---

[3] Rahner, "Current Problems in Christology," 152. The translation of the German "Mann" as "man" (meaning "the human person") is pervasive.

[4] Rahner, "Current Problems in Christology," 164.

148 *A Theology of Flourishing*

relationship that Rahner, explicitly aligning himself with Duns Scotus, sees as achieving its fullness in the hypostatic union, such that the incarnation serves as an icon of the eschatological union of God and creation.[5] As he puts it, "The Incarnation appears as the necessary and permanent beginning of the divinization of the world as a whole."[6] Building on this point, Rahner speaks of Christ as the "climax" of creation:

> Truly a part of the earth, truly a moment in the biological evolution of this world, a moment of human natural history . . . a receiver of that self-communication of God by grace which we affirm of all men—and hence of the cosmos—as the climax of development in which the world comes absolutely into its own presence and into the direct presence of God.[7]

As the perfect union of spirit and matter, the incarnation signals the beginning of a cosmic deification—the movement of all creation toward union with God.[8] In addition to its consistency with the biblical and historical perspectives considered in the preceding chapters, Rahner's account of Christ and creation elicits three conclusions with implications for a theology of flourishing.

---

[5] For a treatment of Rahner's correspondence with Bonaventure, another Franciscan, on creation and incarnation, see Michael Rubbelke, "Reading Rahner's Evolutionary Christology with Bonaventure," *Philosophy and Theology* 30, no. 2 (2018): 507–29. As Rubbelke observes, for Rahner as well as Bonventure (and Scotus), "The Incarnation is embedded in the design of creation and human beings, even apart from the infralapsarian need for redemption."

[6] Karl Rahner, "Christology within an Evolutionary View of the World," *Theological Investigations V*, trans. Karl-H. Kruger, 157–92 (New York: Crossroad, 1983), 160–61.

[7] Rahner, "Christology within an Evolutionary View," 176.

[8] Although his focus differs from mine, Denis Edwards comments on Rahner's account of the deification of the cosmos in various texts. See, for example, Denis Edwards, *How God Acts: Creation, Redemption, and Special Divine Action* (Minneapolis: Fortress Press, 2010), 152–59.

Rahner and Beyond 149

First, Rahner's understanding of the hypostatic union as the union of spirit and matter throughout cosmic history provides a christological foundation for reflecting on the intersecting realities of social and ecological injustice and a basis for a holistic model of socio-ecological flourishing. As Rahner writes, thinking redemption through the lens of a cosmic Christology means that the "materiality of man and of the cosmos . . . must not be simply eliminated from this consummation as if it were a merely temporary element."[9] Whether we are speaking of the human body or the cosmos, redemption arises in and through materiality, producing concrete effects that foster flourishing in the present. Indeed, as Rahner writes,

> It follows from this that it would be quite wrong and unchristian to conceive matter and spirit as realities simply existing side by side in the actual order of things while being really quite unrelated to each other, the spirit in its human form having—unfortunately—to utilize the material world as a kind of exterior stage.[10]

Far beyond being an add-on to the drama of heavenly salvation, material reality mediates redemption. The union of Christ's flesh with material reality offers hope that all materiality will be in some sense redeemed, orienting Christian thought and praxis toward the flourishing of all things.

Second, the unity of matter and spirit indicates that matter is, and always has been, the medium of spirit—not in an extrinsic way, but intrinsically. In Rahner's view this observation calls us to see matter as the medium of "intercommunication" between subjects in history.[11] If cosmic-evolutionary history is

---

[9] Rahner, "Christology within an Evolutionary View," 162.

[10] Rahner, 161.

[11] Rahner, 163.

150 *A Theology of Flourishing*

the history of matter and spirit, then such "intercommunication" involves creatures of all types and stripes, alongside whom we have evolved and with whom we share this earth. Moreover, in this intercommunication we humans are not observers but agents who are called by God to carry out God's life-giving will here and now. Truly, we are making history. Furthermore, this history-making takes place in and through a cosmic communion with countless other creatures. There is no room for human exceptionalism here. We are, and always have been, embedded in material reality along with all God's creatures.

Third, Rahner's evolutionary Christology orients theology toward the particularity of socio-ecological contexts. The meaning of the incarnation may be universal in that it brings about redemption, but precisely what redemption *means* depends on the particular configurations of matter and spirit into which the mystery of Christ enters. This particularity matters because it provides a basis on which we can talk about how the conditions of material history shape the experience of salvation vis-à-vis cosmic deification. For Rahner, this means that salvation "must not be confused with the escape of a spiritual soul—an alien in this cosmos—from the totality of that world which is always also material (and is so precisely in the service of the spirit) and has always had and still has also a material history."[12] Immortality is, then, shaped by the way grace works through freedom in materiality and history. The history of the material world is both the history of grace-working-in-freedom and the history of the free rejection of grace. In all this, salvation consists not in escape but in deeper entry into the world, in its beauty and complexity. Here, Rahner likewise concludes that the incarnation includes the fact that

> man can realize his transcendental future, his attainment of God in himself, only by means of the material of this

---

[12] Rahner, 171.

Rahner and Beyond

world and its history. . . . The promise of a supra-historical consummation in the absoluteness of God himself—a promise given together with Christology—does not diminish man's task in this world but provides it with its ultimate dignity, urgency and danger. Because man cannot effect his salvation apart from his worldly task but only *through it.*[13]

The consummation of creation made manifest in the self-realization of creatures in relationship with God and others happens in the world, in history, in creaturely life—and never apart from it. As such, this consummation proceeds according to the logic of flourishing. We do not experience salvation from the world but within it, such that the fruit of redemption is the self-actualization of creatures in this world on the way toward the final fulfillment of all things in union with God.

Rahner's Transcendental Anthropology— A Closer Look at Humanity

As the preceding quotation shows, Rahner's cosmic Christology provides foundations for his account of human life in relationship to God and creation—an account that, in keeping with the Gospel of Matthew, finds fulfillment in the love of neighbor, an action Rahner describes as "the all-embracing basic act of man which gives meaning, direction, and measure to everything else."[14] For Rahner, to reflect on what it means to be human is

---

[13] Rahner, 191.

[14] Karl Rahner, "Reflections on the Unity of the Love of Neighbor and the Love of God," *Theological Investigations VI*, trans. Karl-H. Kruger and Boniface Kruger (Baltimore: Helicon Press, 1969), 241. For an appreciative analysis of Rahner's account of the unity of love, see Gerald J. Beyer, "Karl Rahner on the Radical Unity of the Love of God and Neighbour," *Irish Theological Quarterly* 68, no. 3 (2003): 251–80.

152   *A Theology of Flourishing*

to reflect on what it means to love as Christ loved. In this way, love provides the answer to the question that the human person *is* and so constitutes humanity's fulfillment.

Humanity's journey toward this fulfillment in love takes place through transcendental experience, what Rahner defines as "the subject's openness to the unlimited expanse of all possible reality" within the conditions of materiality.[15] Here again, as in Gregory's *Life of Moses*, it is crucial to recognize that Rahner's account of transcendence does not mean transcendence away from the world, as if the encounter with "unlimited expanse" effects an escape into a world of ideas. Rather, for Rahner, transcendental experience always precipitates deeper immersion into oneself and creation, leading humans into a thoroughgoing attentiveness and deep discernment amid the needs of the world. This attentiveness subsequently fosters deeper entry into reality through the experience of transcendence. Like love of God and love of neighbor, transcendence and attentiveness to the world are inextricably intertwined.

Rahner's explanation of the process and fruits of transcendence elucidates this point. He describes personhood as the "self-possession" of a human subject "in a conscious and free relationship to the totality of itself."[16] Here, in harmony with Scotus and Nicholas, Rahner locates the journey toward self-actualization not in a universal idea of "humanity" but in the particularity of each and every experiencing subject. As Rahner explains:

> Man's subjectivity and his free, personal self-interpretation take place precisely in and through his being in the world, in time, and in history, or better, in and through world, time and history. The question of salvation cannot be answered

---

[15] Karl Rahner, *Foundations of Christian Faith: An Introduction to the Idea of Christianity*, trans. William V. Dych (New York: Crossroad, 2010), 20.

[16] Rahner, 30.

Rahner and Beyond 153

by bypassing man's historicity and his social nature. Transcendentality and freedom are realized *in history*.[17]

Seeking the infinite totality of fulfillment thus orients persons toward the world, such that they experience in what Rahner terms the "categorical"—the concrete circumstances of materiality and history—an awareness of something utterly transcendent, holy, and mysterious: that which Christians name God.

Yet despite his emphasis on God's otherness—as Holy Mystery, God is unlike anything we can imagine—Rahner is emphatic that humans know God as Mystery only because God has revealed Godself through the "categorical" in the mode of infinite, unspeakable love. Thus, just as the human experience of transcendence happens in the categorical, the categorical self-communication of the God who is utterly transcendent takes place in and through the world. This is what Rahner describes as "mediated immediacy." He writes:

> And when according to the understanding of the Christian faith the most radical and absolutely immediate self-communication of God in his very own being is given to us, namely, in the immediate vision of God as the fulfillment of the finite spirit in grace, this most radical immediacy is still mediated in a certain sense by the finite subject experiencing it, and thereby also experiencing itself. The finite subject does not disappear in this most immediate manifestation of God and is not suppressed, but rather it reaches its fulfillment and hence its fullest autonomy as subject.[18]

On Rahner's account, then, the encounter with the living God in the world—an expression of the Ignatian mantra "finding God

---

[17] Rahner, 40. Emphasis mine.
[18] Rahner, 83.

154   *A Theology of Flourishing*

in all things"—constitutes the basis for the fulfillment of human persons in graced self-actualization, orienting us toward the totality of what we are. In other words, in being grasped by Mystery and seeking it, the human person experiences "the movement toward liberating freedom, and the responsibility which imposes upon him real burdens and also blesses them."[19]

This "burdened liberation" lies at the heart of Rahner's contribution to a theology of flourishing, as transcendence toward God in the categorical frees persons for authentic self-actualization. Such freedom liberates them to become who they truly are, alongside other humans and other-than-human creatures in the socio-ecological contexts they inhabit, and places upon them the responsibility to live freely and fully as the people God created them to be. In this way, Rahner writes, transcendental freedom constitutes "a person's ultimate responsibility for himself, not only in knowledge . . . but also as self-actualization."[20] Self-actualization is, then, a concrete, embodied, and contextual expression of personhood wherein a subject, acting in freedom, does not simply act but "does *himself*."[21] This is what it means for the human person to be the "event" of God's self-communication. In relationship with God, we humans do not only exist and act. Through the journey of discernment inaugurated within this relationship, we discover, seek, and become what we truly are. And we do so alongside countless other creatures, from air and water to animals and plants, who are co-partners in the categorical and who—perhaps imperceptibly to us—are likewise seeking fulfillment.

In keeping with his stance that transcendence happens in the concrete circumstances of materiality and history—the

---

[19] Rahner, 33.

[20] Rahner, 36. Here, it bears repeating that this self-actualization is not the individual making oneself but becoming the creature God wants them to be in deep, intentional relationship with God and the world—that is, flourishing.

[21] Rahner, 94.

Rahner and Beyond 155

categorical—Rahner does not view human subjects as blank slates. Rather, he recognizes that talk of freedom and responsibility necessarily entails reflection on sociocultural conditioning and structural dynamics. In dialogue with the social sciences, he observes that every human person is born "in a situation which he finds *prior to himself,* which is imposed on him . . . in a situation which itself is always determined by history and other persons."[22] We humans are conditioned creatures, living under the influence of social, biological, psychological, and ecological forces. Even so, Rahner is careful to assert that we cannot see ourselves as wholly determined by these forces, "as able to be analyzed and reduced into antecedents and consequences."[23] Still, these forces bear down on our freedom and shape the meaning of responsibility. Consider, for example, the influence of patriarchy and homophobia, internalized and structural racism, differing abilities, and mental health on a person's experience in and of the categorical. In shaping the conditions of human life, these factors and myriad others shape our experiences of transcendence and the exercise of freedom.

At the same time, Rahner notes, no one is reducible *to* these factors. He writes: "So even when a person would abandon himself into the hands of the empirical anthropologies, he still remains in his own hands. He does not escape from his freedom, and the only question can be how he interprets himself, and freely interprets himself."[24] While they condition human life, awareness of such factors gives rise to new possibilities for self-understanding and self-actualization. Rahner uses the example of buying a banana to illustrate the point in terms of the condition of being born into the "collective guilt" of humanity:

---

[22] Rahner, 107.
[23] Rahner, 39.
[24] Rahner, 39.

When someone buys a banana, he does not reflect upon the fact that its price is tied to many presuppositions. To them belongs, under certain circumstances, the pitiful lot of banana pickers, which in turn is co-determined by social injustice, exploitation, or a centuries-old commercial policy. The person himself now participates in this situation of guilt to his own advantage. Where does this person's personal responsibility in taking advantage of such a situation co-determined by guilt end, and where does it begin?[25]

The dynamics of transcendence, freedom, responsibility, and social conditioning thus also inform Rahner's account of *guilt*—the existential condition into which humans are born on account of the collective history of human wrongdoing—and *sin*, which he defines as "the free self-destruction of the subject and an intrinsic contradiction of oneself."[26] This two-fold analysis emerges naturally from his account of God's self-communication to the world. In remarkable correspondence with Julian, he writes that, in communicating Godself to the world, "God in his own most proper reality makes himself the *innermost constitutive element of man*."[27] As such, sin involves an intrinsic self-contradiction that occludes the truth of what one is by virtue of God's life-giving presence and action in all things. Sin is, as a result, contrary to authentic human being. As the example of buying a banana shows, sin does not lie in the violation of objective moral codes imposed from without but in the destruction of possibilities for self-actualization—for

---

[25] Rahner, 110–11.

[26] Rahner, 102. For an in-depth examination of Rahner's notion of sin as a "no" to God and his account of the sacrament of penance vis-à-vis the concrete consequences of human sinfulness, see Peter J. Fritz, "Placing Sin in Karl Rahner's Theology," *Irish Theological Quarterly* 80, no. 4 (November 2015): 294–312.

[27] Rahner, *Foundations of Christian Faith*, 116. Emphasis mine.

Rahner and Beyond   157

example, in the plight of workers whose freedom is constrained by an unjust system of trade or in a Christian's responsibility to those workers. Here, then, lies a basis for denouncing racism, gender-based violence, oppressive economic and labor practices, and ecological degradation as sinful, as all these factors obstruct the possibility of flourishing by contradicting God's primary intentions for the created order.

In a passage that is anything but idealistic, the challenges of social conditioning and sin lead Rahner to argue for a certain "historical pessimism" within Christianity, which he sees as "the best service towards improving the world here and now."[28] Here, as before, Rahner offers an important recognition: just as hope is empty if it does not attend to the multifaceted realities of injustice and suffering in this world, ideas of salvation that do not promote action in faith on behalf of a better world are similarly bereft. Invoking Marx, he writes, "Such a pessimism, of course can become the excuse for not doing anything, for offering the consolation of eternal life, and really for offering a religious attitude not only as the opiate of the people, but also as an opiate for the people."[29] Salvation is a matter of this world—a matter of flourishing.

Although not always explicit, this call to contemplation in action pervades Rahner's writings, grounding his answer to the question of how God could allow evil to occur and his understanding of Christian social responsibility. Taking up the former, he argues that people today are "more likely to have the impression that God has to justify the unhappy condition of the world before man, that man is the sacrifice and not the cause of the condition of the world and of human history."[30] Amid suffering and hardship, humanity cries out to God, "How could

---

[28] Rahner, 110.

[29] Rahner, 110.

[30] Rahner, 92.

158   *A Theology of Flourishing*

you let this happen?" This perspective is understandable in view
of a religion that speaks of God in terms of life, love, justice,
and liberation. Yet here, in concert with his justified concern
about Christian faith functioning as an opiate for the people,
Rahner takes a different view. He argues that Christians, and
indeed all people, should in fact be asking how *we* permit suffering and hardship to continue while professing faith in a God
of life, love, justice, and liberation. Elaborating on this point, he
writes, "This is still true even when the wrong seems indeed
to be caused by man as a free subject, but this agent is once
again the product of his nature and of his social situation."[31]
Practically, this again suggests that even structural factors that
silently produce sin through the operation of the status quo do
not excuse humanity from responsibility. Attempts to write off
human responsibility for evil by asking God "why?" amount
to a refusal to look our own darkness in the face. In this situation, too, heavenly salvation functions as an opiate that numbs
our senses to the perdurance of injustice and suffering. Applied
socially, this same logic allows the transformative potential of
Christ's revolutionary love to be subordinated to moral codes
and institutional concerns. Written after World War II, Rahner's
observation that "under National Socialism . . . [German office-
holders and clerics] thought considerably more about ourselves
and about upholding what belonged to the Church and its
institutions, than about the fate of the Jews," makes the point
all too well.[32] A theology of flourishing must chart a different
course, taking responsibility for understanding the genesis of
virulent cultural and structural conditions and promoting material conditions that make abundant life possible.

---

[31] Rahner, 92.
[32] Karl Rahner, "A Church Concerned with Serving," in *The Shape of the
Church to Come*, trans. Edward Quinn (New York: Crossroad, 1974), 61.

Rahner and Beyond 159

Love of Christ, Heart of Creation

This analysis brings us back to Christ. The cosmic-evolutionary dimensions of Rahner's Christology follow a trajectory that runs from the New Testament through Irenaeus and Athanasius and up to the present. The anthropological dimensions of his thought interpret the idea of deification that links Gregory, Julian, and Nicholas through the lens of transcendental analysis.[33] As Rahner explains, "Transcendental Christology appeals to a person who . . . has at least unthematically a finality and a dynamism imparted by God himself towards God's self-communication, and it asks him whether he could not appropriate this orientation as his own in freedom and from out of his own inner experience."[34] As human persons receive God's self-communication in faith, beginning the journey toward self-actualization in union with God through the categorical, so the witness of Christ asks—following Athanasius's maxim—whether we humans really can become God in the actualization of our truest selves. The basis for this idea lies in Christ's own life: in becoming "what we ourselves are, what

---

[33] Brandon Peterson offers an in-depth study of patristic influences on Rahner's soteriology in *Being Salvation: Atonement and Soteriology in the Theology of Karl Rahner* (Minneapolis: Fortress Press, 2017). For a treatment of the importance of deification in Rahner, see Francis J. Caponi, "Karl Rahner: Divinization in Roman Catholicism," in *Partakers of the Divine Nature: The History and Development of Deification in the Christian Tradition*, ed. Michael Christensen and Jeffery A, Wittung, 259–80 (Madison, NJ: Fairleigh Dickinson University Press, 2007).

[34] Rahner, *Foundations of Christian Faith*, 208. Rahner's use of "unthematically" here is important. A person may not consciously be aware of the dynamism that leads toward God—it may be only implicit. Rather than being a basis for judgmentalism or arrogance—a way of evaluating who is and who isn't "saved"—Rahner deploys this "unthematic" quality as a basis for deep humility, a recognition that because God's ways are not our ways, we can never plumb the depths of God's mercy and love expressed toward a transcendental human subject. We can only love.

160   *A Theology of Flourishing*

we experience in daily life, what has been experimented with and lived out a million times in the history to which we belong, what we are familiar with from the inside, each one in himself, and from the outside, in the world of persons around us," Christ reveals to us the fullness of what we can be.[35] Here, the connection to Athanasius becomes clearer. Rahner sees Christ as a person like us in all things but sin, who lived a life "orientated towards the God who is incomprehensible" and in freedom accepted "the mystery which we are . . . the mystery of fullness."[36] Here again, a vision of fullness, flourishing, takes center stage within Rahner's anthropology, now with Christ revealing to us the fulfillment of human life—and thereby also revealing what it means to be God.

In his historically-conditioned flesh and blood, Jesus of Nazareth accepted his humanity in its fullness, and—in seeking the full realization of his personhood in faithful discernment and radical love—came to "the unique and highest instance of the actualization of the essence of human reality, which consists in this: that man is insofar as he abandons himself to the absolute mystery whom we call God."[37] According to Rahner, Christ's life offers an unsurpassable model of what it means to be human. He is the *event* of the fulfillment of humanity. For Christians, then, he exemplifies what it means to "bring to radical actualization in the living out of man's whole existence throughout the whole length and breadth and depth of man's life."[38] Furthermore, per the connection of his body to the sweep of cosmic-evolutionary history, Christ also inaugurates what Rahner describes as "the irreversible and embryonically final beginning of glorification and divinization of the *whole* reality."[39] Through his enfleshed

---

[35] Rahner, 215.

[36] Rahner, 217.

[37] Rahner, 218.

[38] Rahner, 306–7.

[39] Karl Rahner, "Dogmatic Questions on Easter," in *Theological Investigations IV*, 129.

Rahner and Beyond

161

connection to the whole cosmos, the flourishing of creation also finds fulfillment in Christ's redeeming work, challenging Christians to work on behalf of creation's fulfillment amid the challenges and complexities of categorical existence—in view of Christ, creation and salvation are inseparable.

In Rahner's analysis, this returns us once more to the unity of love of God and neighbor as "an ultimately single and all-encompassing actualization of existence."[40] For if Christ reveals unsurpassably the love of God, then the unity of love of God and neighbor—a unity that includes love of self—lies at the heart of self-actualization and represents a core dimension of flourishing. Indeed, flourishing happens when life and love meet, and the mature fruit of their union emerges in a world-changing praxis of the fullness of life. When, through our orientation toward the Holy Mystery of love, we humans actualize ourselves in practices of compassionate care for all things in their *haecceitas*, we make known the love of Christ at the heart of creation. This is, for Rahner, the essence of redemption, "empowered and fulfilled by the divinizing self-communication of God."[41] And what this actualization brings about is nothing other than the fulfillment of God's will for every person, every creature, and the whole of creation, testifying through Christian life and community that "the absolute and living God is victorious in his self-giving love throughout the whole length and breadth of his creation."[42]

Beyond Rahner: Critique, Development, and the Birth of Political and Liberation Theologies

Rahner's theology provides fertile soil for cultivating an account of God, Christ, creation, and humanity that is oriented toward

---

[40] Rahner, *Foundations of Christian Faith*, 309.
[41] Rahner, 138.
[42] Rahner, 401.

162   *A Theology of Flourishing*

flourishing. His account of transcendence in and through the categorical provides a basis for thinking about how human life is conditioned by forces that are often predisposed toward sin and guilt. His writings also operate with an eye toward suffering and injustice, explicitly calling Christians to account for these realities. The writings of two of Rahner's most significant students, Johann Baptist Metz and Ignacio Ellacuría, provide critical developments of his approach, appropriately critiquing Rahner and making explicit what is often implicit in his writings with a view toward realities that obstruct self-actualization, liberation, and the fullness of life in and beyond the human community.

Johann Baptist Metz: Idealism, the "Hedgehog Trick," and Political Theology

In *Faith in History and Society*, Metz offers what may still be the most significant extant critique and development of Rahner's thought. Metz uses a German folktale about a hare and a hedgehog to demonstrate dangers implicit in the German Idealist account of history that informs Rahner's theology.[43] In the folktale, an identical-looking hedgehog couple rigs a footrace against a hare. One hedgehog starts the race, while his wife hides in the bushes near the finish line. Once the race begins, the wife leaps out from the bushes and crosses the finish line, "winning" the race. But in Metz's interpretation, the race was never really run. On Metz's account, the folktale offers a fitting illustration of problems associated with the forgetfulness of history—the race— in German Idealist thought. Applying this critique to Rahner's transcendental method, he writes:

---

[43] Johann Baptist Metz, *Faith in History and Society: Toward a Practical Fundamental Theology*, trans. J. Matthew Ashley (New York: Crossroad, 2007), 150–52. The Hegelian understanding of history conceives of history teleologically, as a process by which universal "Spirit" progressively evolves toward self-realization.

Rahner and Beyond 163

The "running"—in which one can also get left behind—is an integral part of securing one's identity, together with the dangers it brings; it cannot be compensated for transcendentally by anything else. . . . History itself—with its ever threatened, vulnerable, and at any rate endangered forms of identity—barely intervenes at all. The transcendental spell is complete, and it is (like the two hedgehogs) unbeatable. It thus becomes hard to avoid the suspicion that the transcendentalization of the Christian subject could be guided by a tendency to disburden and immunize that subject.[44]

Although Metz and Rahner both speak at length about history, and although Rahner gestures toward the realities of injustice, suffering, and oppression, Metz proffers an important practical critique. Despite Rahner's acknowledgment of unjust realities, the idea of transcendence, even amid the categorical, may well "immunize" Christians to the real suffering borne by the victims of history, rendering Christianity nothing more than a religion of "bourgeois subjects" removed from the cares of the world.[45]

Although Rahner acknowledged and accepted Metz's critique, he also insisted that his emphasis on the categorical mediation of transcendence implies Metz's concern. He states:

If one not only sees and takes seriously these necessary mediations of transcendental experience but also fills it out in a concrete way, then one already practices in an authentic way

---

[44] Metz, 152.

[45] Bourgeois subjectivity functions as Metz's presenting concern. For a treatment of Metz's critique and Rahner's clarification of the political implications of his thought in view of the critique, see Declan Marmion, "Rahner and His Critics: Revisiting the Dialogue," *Irish Theological Quarterly* 68 (2003): 195–212. Marmion observes, "Rahner's later awareness of the political dimension of Christianity, then, can be traced to his early writings on the unity of the love of neighbour and the love of God, an awareness that subsequently became more explicit."

164   *A Theology of Flourishing*

political theology, or in other words, a practical fundamental theology. . . . Therefore, I believe that my theology and that of Metz are not necessarily contradictory. However, I gladly recognize that a concrete mystagogy must, to use Metz's language, be at the same time "mystical and political."[46]

Rahner's response notwithstanding, Metz's critique led to a crucial development of Rahner's thought with important implications for a theology of flourishing. The concrete contexts in which transcendence takes place—in a word, history—shape both the experience of transcendence and how the subject experiences transcendence in a reciprocal manner. Attending to dynamics of power and subjugation—the relegation of some to the underside of history—sharpens the critical importance of attentiveness to suffering and exploitation in a theology of flourishing. Without such attention, talk of flourishing is little more than bourgeois fluff. Yet when seen through the lens of the political, and especially the lens of oppression, Christ's promise of the fullness of life takes on sharper significance as a "no" to oppression that demands action in the form of ecclesial and socio-ecological transformation in step with God's redeeming work for *ta pánta*, all things.

Concretely, then, a theology of flourishing—like political theology—aims to "negotiate a process of translation between the Kingdom of God and society," with an explicit focus on what it means for all creatures to flourish given the networks of relations they inhabit, as they are held in being and called to fulfillment by God.[47] By seeing creation as a fundamental expression of God's love and the foundational gift in which all other gifts find fulfillment, a theology of flourishing thus seeks to "translate" the whole creation as a locus of God's reign, in keeping with God's

---

[46] Karl Rahner, "Introduction," in James J. Bacik, *Apologetics and the Eclipse of Mystery: Mystagogy according to Karl Rahner* (Notre Dame, IN: University of Notre Dame Press, 1980), x.

[47] Metz, *Faith in History and Society*, 99.

Rahner and Beyond   165

intentions that all things may "be fruitful and multiply." Such a vision naturally entails what Metz—in terms that radicalize Rahner's discussion of freedom and responsibility—terms the "radical *democratization* of the base of society, constructing and animating freedom and efficacious responsibility from below," but with an expanded, holistic vision of society that unites the social and ecological under God's reign.[48] In short, Metz calls for the rebuilding of our networks of relations on the order of God's reign—an order of justice, peace, and flourishing.

As a basis for praxis, this democratization necessarily entails a critique of violence and exploitation that begins from attentiveness to the concrete links between Christ and the most vulnerable of creation—what Metz terms a "practical hermeneutics." In the context of a theology of flourishing, such a hermeneutic interprets religious truth claims, and claims on experience in general, on the basis of their ability or inability to promote creaturely flourishing. Interpretation thereby translates into action. Metz writes, "This perduring ethical dimension of social praxis . . . becomes concrete as a *critique of violence*, or a critique of extrapolating from violence and logic of violence and hate, according to which the only way violence can be overcome is by violence."[49] For, if the thief comes only to kill and steal and destroy, then—as Jantzen likewise recognizes—violence appears as inherently opposed to the promise of life and realization of God's reign enacted through the dangerous memory of the Word made flesh.

Ignacio Ellacuría:
Deepening the Meaning of the Historicity of Salvation

Likely a natural consequence of the time he spent under the theological mentorship of Rahner, Ellacuría's writings employ a

---

[48] Metz, 100.
[49] Metz, 66.

166 *A Theology of Flourishing*

Rahnerian framework that centers history and experience.[50] At the same time, as Martin Maier observes, differences in context and philosophical background lead Ellacuría to center *praxis*, which Maier defines as "the active commitment to the realization of the kingdom of God in history," in ways that go well beyond Rahner.[51]

While Rahner points toward the interlocking realities of social, political, and economic oppression, Ellacuría places these realities, in their concrete forms, squarely at the center of his theology. In terms of the Ignatian tradition to which he and Rahner both belonged, we might say that while Rahner contemplates injustice phenomenologically and sketches implications of this contemplation for Christian life, Ellacuría reflects explicitly on how such contemplation should shape action in service of God's reign.

Making this point clear, in an essay titled "The Historicity of Christian Salvation," Ellacuría suggests that human participation in divine life—what we might also name deification—is a primary means by which God participates in the life of the world. He writes, "God's participation does not occur without some form of human participation, and human participation does not occur without God's presence in some form."[52] Here,

---

[50] Martin Maier, SJ, "Karl Rahner: The Teacher of Ignacio Ellacuría," in *Love That Produces Hope: The Thought of Ignacio Ellacuría*, ed. Kevin F. Burke and Robert Lassalle-Klein, 128–43 (Collegeville, MN: Liturgical Press, 2006). Maier describes Rahner as "the theologian who had the most impact on the thought of Ignacio Ellacuría."

[51] Maier, 134–35. Differences notwithstanding, Maier notes that Rahner defended early liberation theologians, including Gutiérrez and Ellacuría, in the face of Ratzinger's critiques. For Rahner's perspective, see "We Must Protest," *Cross Currents* 28, no. 1 (1978): 66–70. For an appreciative analysis of Rahner's impact on liberation theology, see Jon Sobrino, "Karl Rahner and Liberation Theology," *The Way* 43, no. 4 (2003): 53–66.

[52] Ignacio Ellacuría, "The Historicity of Christian Salvation," in *Ignacio Ellacuría: Essays on History, Liberation, and Salvation*, ed. Michael E. Lee, 137–68 (Maryknoll, NY: Orbis Books, 2013), 142.

Rahner and Beyond

as in Rahner, God works through the free human acceptance of grace, collaborating with humanity to harmonize reality with God's reign. Salvation happens *in history*. Yet, like Metz, Ellacuría centers praxis in ways not found in Rahner, with a particular emphasis on how liberation from injustice serves as an *a priori* condition for the realization of God's reign. In liberationist perspective, deification without justice is "pie in the sky." No one is truly "like God" unless all experience the material conditions that enable them to become like God. In a representative passage Ellacuría calls special attention to the reality of poverty, uniting contemplation and action in a commentary on the "crucified people." He writes:

> What I would ask—because the word "demand" sounds too strong—involves two things. First, that you look with your eyes and heart at these peoples who are suffering so much—some from poverty and hunger, others from oppression and repression. Then, because I am a Jesuit, I would bid you pray the colloquy of St. Ignatius . . . before this crucified people, asking yourself: What have I done to crucify them? What am I doing to end their crucifixion? What should I do so that this people might rise from the dead?[53]

Amid such crucifixion, he writes elsewhere, "The needs [of humanity] can be seen as the outcry of God made flesh in human suffering, as the unmistakable voice of God, who moans in pain in God's own creatures, or more exactly, in God's own children."[54] The qualitative character of God's intentions that all

---

[53] Ignacio Ellacuría, *Escritos Teológicos,* trans. Kevin F. Burke, vol. 2 (San Salvador: UCA Editores, 2000–2002), 602.

[54] Ignacio Ellacuría, "Church of the Poor, Sacrament of Liberation," in *Mysterium Liberationis: Fundamental Concepts of Liberation Theology*, ed. Ignacio Ellacuría and Jon Sobrino (Maryknoll, NY: Orbis Books, 1993), 544.

168 *A Theology of Flourishing*

creatures may flourish is, for Ellacuría, revealed in cries of pain from creatures who suffer under the yoke of oppression—and they cry out with God's own voice.

Building further on themes sketched but not developed in Rahner, Ellacuría situates his understanding of the historicity of salvation in the context of creation. After appealing directly to Rahner's analysis of the unity of "profane" and salvation history—the foundation for his cosmic-evolutionary Christology—Ellacuría states that "profane history is the condition of possibility for the history of Christ, which is also the history of God, just as natural history in its materiality and vitality is the condition of possibility for the emergence of finite spirit."[55] Applying this point to praxis, Ellacuría takes up questions of justice under the rubric of sin, grace, and freedom, using the idea of life to interrogate how sociopolitical systems operate in view of God's aims. In what may be an implicit evocation of John 10:10, he writes: "Some actions kill (divine) life, and some actions give (divine) life. Some social and historical structures objectify the power of sin and serve as vehicles for that power against humanity, against human life; some social and historical structures objectify grace and serve as vehicles for that power in favor of human life."[56] In ways that correspond with Irenaeus's and Scotus's accounts of creation as the basis for incarnation and redemption, he writes, "Everything depends on how we understand creation."[57]

Here, Ellacuría follows the logic of Rahner's account of the inner unity of spirit and matter. In so doing, he upholds the fullness of participation in divine life—what I term flourishing—as the surest sign of the realization or suppression of God's reign. Ellacuría's view of creation as the locus of life's meaning and the condition of possibility for Christ's relationship to reality

---

[55] Ellacuría, "Historicity of Christian Salvation," 145.

[56] Ellacuría, 150.

[57] Ellacuría, 151.

Rahner and Beyond 169

challenges us to consider how theological claims, and especially soteriological claims, shape Christian praxis in relationship to socio-ecological realities. If Christians profess faith in a savior whose body bears the whole history of the cosmos in its wonder and ugliness, then our ideas of Christ and salvation must actualize that faith by interrogating how claims to truth intersect with the play of natality and necrophilia. Put differently, Ellacuría's praxiological development of Rahner's account of the hypostatic union challenges us to ponder the conditions of material reality—of creation—in terms of the dynamics of injustice and justice, oppression and liberation, death and flourishing, just as Ellacuría did while living among the poor of El Salvador. Seen in this light, creation and humanity are not fallen except insofar as we humans make them fallen or allow them to fall through participation in and indifference toward systems that churn out death. Perhaps in reflecting on the brokenness of the Body of Christ, we might see anew the brokenness of the "crucified people" and the "crucified earth." Perhaps in proclaiming the resurrection of Christ, his glorified body, we might find inspiration to work for the flourishing of all bodies—*ta pánta*—amid logics that kill, steal, and destroy. Such a vision stands at the very heart of a theology of flourishing.

Toward a Theology of Flourishing

The preceding chapters have pursued the precious thread of flourishing through scripture and tradition, illustrating how—despite its sometimes latency or suppression—flourishing has functioned and continues to function as a grounding principle of Christian theology and praxis. This chapter's engagement with Rahner, Metz, and Ellacuría draws together and builds upon these foundations, demonstrating how the thread of flourishing weaves its way through the twentieth century, providing a grounding basis for articulating the principles and practices of a theology of flourishing in its own right. The following chapters take up this task directly, first by articulating a framework for thinking about flourishing theologically within the *haecceitas* of creaturely life. With this theological basis in place, the following chapter proposes a framework of discernment in relationship to God and the world as a means toward actualizing flourishing in Christian life—recognizing that, as the work of the Spirit, self-actualization in relationship to God and the world is inviolable. On this basis, the final chapter considers the potential of a theology of flourishing for addressing several pressing questions in contemporary life.

Granting that the meaning of "abundant life" must emerge from the particularity of creaturely experience and cannot be predetermined and imposed from the outside, these chapters engage a wide swath of contextual theological methods to suggest ways that theology might understand flourishing. Just as Metz and Ellacuría offered constructive developments of Rahner's thought, numerous theologians have advanced the insights of political and liberation theologies, reflecting from diverse perspectives on the meaning of the Christian witness to God's self-communication in Christ and the Spirit. Though their perspectives vary, these theologies all ponder the mystery of Christ from the concrete particularity of experience, offering variations on a theme of the categorical. Applied theologically, this particularity functions as a principle for interpreting the core claims of Christian faith in view of distinct ways of living as creatures made and loved by their Creator.

Part III

INTEGRATIONS

*A Theology of Flourishing
in Vision and Praxis*

8

A Theology of Flourishing

Envisioning Christianity for the Fullness of Life

On April 3, 2021, as the world cautiously emerged from the virulent circumstances of the COVID-19 pandemic, I found myself at the piano for the Easter Vigil at Santa Clara University. It was a familiar place. I came to the study of theology after years of working as a liturgist and liturgical musician. Yet, after more than a year of online liturgies, this celebration—which came just a few weeks after our community returned to in-person worship—felt unusual, even strange. This sense of strangeness was heightened by one factor in particular: like all our liturgies at the time, our celebration of the vigil took place entirely outside, on a plaza in front of Mission Santa Clara de Asís.

After the blessing of the new fire, one of the SCU Jesuits proclaimed the Exsultet: Christ risen, creation renewed, all things rejoicing in the promise of life's fullness. This proclamation was unlike any I had witnessed before. A warm California evening offered conditions that made it possible for the proclamation's rich image of the paschal candle as "the work of bees and of your servants' hands"—the fruit of socio-ecological collaboration— to be accompanied by actual bees buzzing about in flowering

173

174 *A Theology of Flourishing*

bushes outside the church, united with cawing crows, a red-pink sunset, and God's people in celebrating the resurrection, the fulfillment of God's life-giving will.

Then came the First Reading, the creation narrative from Genesis 1. As the sky settled into evening and stars twinkled overhead, we heard the story of God's collaboration with the earth in the work of flourishing. This setting immediately brought to mind Wendell Berry's description of the Bible as "an outdoor book . . . a book open to the sky."[1] Indeed, hearing this reading and celebrating the mystery of dying and rising outdoors in a world reeling from the consequences of a global pandemic shed brilliant light on the idea that God is a God who intends that all things may flourish in their beloved *haecceitas*—their absolute uniqueness—and in communion with one another. In Berry's terms, this celebration in word and sacrament prompted me to see anew that "we are holy creatures living among other holy creatures in a world that is holy."[2]

And yet, Berry's next sentence also deserves contemplation: "Some people know this, and some do not."[3] Despite the great evocative potential of an Easter Vigil celebrated outside, the ability to find God in buzzing bees and blooming flowers, in cawing crows, bread and wine, wax and water, depends on humanity's ability to see things "in God's sight," to use Julian's phrase. Given the perdurance of social and ecological injustice, such a celebration might rightly call to mind the question that punctuates Berry's discussion of creation's holiness: "How can modern Christianity have so solemnly folded its hands while so much of the work of God was and is being destroyed?"[4]

---

[1] Wendell Berry, "Christianity and the Survival of Creation," in *The Art of the Commonplace: The Agrarian Essays of Wendell Berry*, ed. Norman Wirzba (Berkeley, CA: Counterpoint, 2002), 311.

[2] Berry, 308.

[3] Berry, 308.

[4] Berry, 309.

A Theology of Flourishing 175

Weaving together the previous chapters' retrieval of the precious thread of flourishing with an appreciative reading of several contemporary theologies, this chapter proposes a vision for Christian thought and praxis that takes flourishing as its starting point and center of gravity.[5] This vision centers the Christian imagination on God's life-giving will for all things, a will that is worked out among and through all creatures, including deified humans, by the outpouring of the Holy Spirit. By retelling what Berry names "the story in which we are taking part," this theology offers a renewed context for thinking about creation and humanity and resituates sin under the rubric of God's life-giving will.[6] In practice, this theology aims to attune the Christian imagination to the Spirit's stirrings, sharpening Christians' capacity to perceive and redress social injustice and ecological degradation as interlocking violations of the Creator's will, in service of a holistic vision of the fullness of life. After laying out the contours of this theology, the chapter analyzes key aspects in greater detail to illustrate how flourishing might orient Christian theology and praxis toward action on behalf of the fullness of life. The chapter concludes by considering the implications of this approach for broader theological discourse and rethinking sin and salvation. All of this points a way toward the final chapters' discussions of discernment and praxis.

Contours of a Theology of Flourishing

A theology of flourishing is rooted in a renewed understanding of the symbol of creation. God is "wholly Life," and the

---

[5] This "appreciative reading" intends to illustrate key aspects of the proposed theology of flourishing and show how this theology intersects with various aspects of the contemporary conversation. This reading prescinds from debates and may sometimes err on the side of generosity.

[6] Berry, "Christianity and the Survival of Creation," 315.

176   *A Theology of Flourishing*

fullness of life is God's primary intention for creation. A theology of flourishing takes Christ's proclamation of abundant life in John 10:10 as a starting point and center of gravity for Christian thought and praxis.

In Christ, whose flesh unites materiality to divinity and so witnesses to the fulfillment of human deification through a praxis of liberating and life-giving love, this theology orients Christianity toward the cultivation of a socio-ecological order in which all things may flourish. Guided by the Spirit, this journey toward the fullness of life is an open-ended adventure, wherein the self-actualization of creatures in relationship to God and each other, according to their beloved *haecceitas*, serves as a primary marker of the realization of God's intentions. Because *haecceitas* is absolutely unique—it describes *this* creature's relationship to the Creator and the creation—no one can define, much less prescribe, what flourishing means in the concrete conditions of categorical existence. Ways of understanding flourishing as self-actualization can be shared and developed in dialogue and relationship, but they cannot be imposed from the outside.

As the next chapter will discuss, this paradigm makes discernment in relationship to God and other creatures (and God in other creatures) the foundation of Christian life. What it means to live in Christ—or to have Christ live in us—emerges in and through each creature's absolutely unique relationship to the Spirit, the power of *viriditas* that draws all things to fulfillment. As in Irenaeus's axiom and Rahner's account of self-transcendence, this framework necessarily entails a positive appraisal of materiality and embodiment, an understanding of creation as a mediator of God's grace. For humans, the fruit of such self-actualization is the interior freedom to discern their unique paths toward deification, becoming the persons God intends them to be. Although we humans do not and cannot know the interiority of other-than-human creatures, such a theology calls Christians to work in faith on behalf of a socio-ecological order of *viriditas*—a

A Theology of Flourishing   177

"new creation"—characterized by justice and peace, conditions that make flourishing possible.

Applied theologically, this focus on flourishing reframes questions of God, Christ, Spirit, anthropology, ecology, ethics, and other loci in terms of God's life-giving intentions. Further, by making the fullness of life the primary norm for theological claims, such a theology sees sin—in its individual and collective manifestations—as a disruption of God's life-giving will that blocks creaturely self-actualization. In this way a theology of flourishing intrinsically interrogates the whole socio-ecological reality vis-à-vis the fullness of life, asking what enables deifying self-actualization and what obstructs it. Correlatively, a theology of flourishing avoids over-spiritualizing tendencies that enable Christians to remain indifferent to the necrophilic march of theft, death, and destruction. In practice, this orientation attunes Christian consciousness to suffering and the needs of others from the very first moment, fostering the work of justice and liberation in the here and now through a revolutionary praxis of hospitality, compassion, humility, justice, and love on behalf of the fullness of life for all creation.

Rooted in a Renewed Understanding of the Symbol of Creation

A theology of flourishing begins with the conviction that creation is fundamentally good and made to flourish. Seen in this light, the fullness of life for every creature and for creation as a whole manifests the realization of God's intentions. The life-giving interplay of creatures and habitats, plants and animals, wind, land, sunlight, and rain proclaims a divine order that is oriented toward abundant life—in direct correspondence with John 10:10. And, in keeping with Elizabeth A. Johnson's maxim, this way of symbolizing creation attunes Christian understandings of the God-world relationship to God's self-communication to and through all things, strengthening the view that creation is

178   *A Theology of Flourishing*

good, blessed, "itself a dwelling place of God."[7] Such attunement likewise imparts to the Christian imagination a lived awareness that all creatures and socio-ecological contexts are expressions of the love that God is. They bear out divine love in their fruitfulness and flourishing, recognizing—as Nicholas Lash writes—that "the life God gives is nothing other, nothing less, than God's own self. Life is God, given."[8]

This vision stands in contrast to any claim that the created order is fundamentally fallen, or sinful. Quite the contrary, the Hebrew Bible proclaims that creation is a place of life wherein God "lets be," collaborating with creation to draw out every creature's potential to "be fruitful and multiply and fill" in keeping with its beloved particularity. Attuning human hearts and minds to God's love thus means attuning ourselves to creation, and vice-versa. In observing the work of bees, pollinating crops and preparing wax for candles, and in accepting our place in the created order—not as "lords and masters, entitled to plunder [earth] at will" (*Laudato Si'*, no. 2), but as partners in the work of life—we humans come to see God's presence and action abounding all around us, drawing all things toward the fullness for which they are created, individually and collectively. In practice, such attunement calls humans to behold all things "in God's sight" and orients us toward what Pope Francis terms "a new and universal solidarity" (*Laudato Si'*, no. 14) that fosters care for all creatures, human and otherwise, in their embodied materiality—as Matthew 25 would have it. Such solidarity entails a fundamental reorientation of the Christian imagination toward the wonderful world we share with other creatures, providing a new lens on the journey of faith. Our journey is not a quest for otherworldly salvation apart from the world but is a wholehearted commitment to entering "more

---

[7] Elizabeth Johnson, *Ask the Beasts: Darwin and the God of Love* (London: Bloomsbury, 2015), 124.

[8] Nicholas Lash, *Believing Three Ways in One God: A Reading of the Apostles' Creed* (Notre Dame, IN: University of Notre Dame Press, 1994), 104.

A Theology of Flourishing   179

deeply into the movements of love that nurture and heal and celebrate the gifts of God."[9]

Yet there is also brokenness and corruption in creation, the result of humanity's disregard for the life-giving order God established, symbolized in the eating of the forbidden fruit. Even so, as Julian attests, in God's sight there is "no sin," only love. As the first fruits of God's love for all creatures, flourishing thus provides an indispensable backdrop for understanding what sin is and how it functions. Sin is an affront to the goodness of creation that obstructs the realization of God's life-giving aims. In other words, attunement to creation's fundamental orientation toward life—declared by cawing crows, blooming flora, and all creatures' hymns of praise—challenges us to see sin not as the human condition or an inescapable existential state. Rather, as Colin Gunton writes, echoing Julian and Rahner, "Sin is not part of what it is to be human, but a distortion of our humanity," an existential *contradiction* to what we are created to be.[10]

Corresponding to the Psalmist's vision, reimagining the symbol of creation also links us to the rest of creation in our common praise of the Creator. Our glorification of God, as Irenaeus proclaims, arises through the full "aliveness" of every creature when it beholds God in its own way. This imparts to Christian consciousness a recognition that praise is universal and ongoing; it does not occur in liturgy or hymnody alone. Rather, these media sacramentally enact the praise in which all creatures are already engaged simply by being what they are within the socioecosystems they inhabit. As Margaret Adam notes, such praise of God is the basic purpose of creaturely life, the basic action that unites all things in a dynamic of "mutual formation" that

---

[9] Norman Wirzba, *From Nature to Creation: A Christian Vision for Understanding and Loving Our World* (Grand Rapids, MI: Baker Academic, 2015), 1.

[10] Colin E. Gunton, *Christ and Creation* (Eugene, OR: Wipf and Stock, 1990), 26.

enables creatures to flourish ever more fully according to their *haecceitas*. She writes:

> Praise does not require a particular age, capacity, strength, productivity, intelligence, self-sufficiency: all life, as life, is created by God, for the glory of God. Life that fulfills its purpose of praise is flourishing life, and the context of Christian praise is participation in Christ. . . . Christians mutually form themselves into their participatory purpose, and then hold each other accountable for constancy in flourishing praise. That mutual formation includes learning to praise with the rest of creation.[11]

In light of this vision the brokenness of creation must not be accepted as a status quo description of the way things are, and it certainly must not be seen as the way things are *meant to be*. Quite the contrary, as Pope Francis states, "to commit a crime against the natural world is a sin against ourselves and a sin against God" (*Laudato Si'*, no. 8). Framing humanity's relationship to the rest of creation in this way naturally implies attention to the suffering of other creatures, especially suffering that is caused by the operation of human social systems. The unchecked extraction of natural resources through practices such as clear-cutting

---

[11] Margaret B. Adam, "The Purpose of Creatures: A Christian Account of Farmed Animal Flourishing," *Sewanee Theological Review* 62, no. 4 (2021): 738. Although his account of individuation charts a different path from Scotus and Nicholas of Cusa, Thomas Aquinas shares this view. As Johnson explains, "An influential principle used by Thomas Aquinas clarifies this insight further: 'whatever is received, is received according to the mode of the recipient,' or more colloquially, each creature receives and responds to the love of God according to its own nature. By virtue of their being created and continually empowered by the Creator Spirit, animals give praising glory to God simply by living according to their natures, which are oriented to God. In their very existence, their concrete quiddity, the way they interact in an evolving universe, they extol the excellence of their Maker." Elizabeth Johnson, "Animals' Praise," *Interpretation: A Journal of Bible and Theology* 73, no. 3 (2019): 270.

A Theology of Flourishing

that cause immense biodiversity loss, the industrial farming system's heartless commodification of land and animals, as well as the general ease with which humans kill and eat other creatures without a thought toward their suffering—all these illustrate the ethical gap that a theology of flourishing aims to address.

In keeping with the interpretation of the symbol of creation that grounds this theology of flourishing, thinkers reflecting on animal suffering contribute important resources for addressing this gap. For example, Andrew Linzey observes a close connection between the suffering of helpless animals, including those humans consume, and Christ's suffering. The Christlikeness of animal suffering does not lie in its redemptive significance, as sacrificial soteriologies might have it. Rather, the link between Christ and suffering animals emerges through recognition of the cruelty we show other creatures, such that their suffering

> ought to compel a moral response, as ought the sufferings of Christ himself. We are right to be, in [John Henry] Newman's words, "moved" and "sickened" because that kind of suffering—whether of humans or of animals—of the innocent, unprotected, and vulnerable is morally unconscionable.[12]

In view of Genesis's vision of the cooperation of God and creation—a vision that includes God's prohibition of violence and prescription of a bloodless diet—I wager that taking flourishing as the starting point for retelling the Christian story will reframe questions of violence and suffering, orienting Christians away from seeing the circumstances of Christ's death according to a necrophilic logic of sacrifice and toward seeing it as an event that illustrates a deep contradiction to God's life-giving intentions. Following this logic the brokenness and suffering

---

[12] Andrew Linzey, *Why Animal Suffering Matters: Philosophy, Theology, and Practical Ethics* (Oxford: Oxford University Press, 2009), 39–40.

182 A Theology of Flourishing

that result from humanity's rejection of the life-giving order of creation—whether in strained relationships with other creatures, gender-based discrimination, or a contentious relationship with land—should enact a call to protest against all forms of brokenness, all obstructions to the enfleshed glorification of God, and orient Christians toward action on behalf of God's reign—to which the life, death, and resurrection of Christ attest in an unsurpassable way.

In Christ, Whose Flesh Unites Divinity and Materiality

Inspired by the Prologue to John's Gospel and the creation hymn of Colossians 1, a theology of flourishing understands the incarnation as coextensive with creation. From the depths of the Mariana Trench to the summit of Everest, from the sparrow's nest to the farthest reaches of the universe, the incarnation extends God's work on behalf of "new creation" to all things. This is indeed a cosmic, "deep" interpretation of the incarnation, which finds in the Word made flesh not a means to paying a debt or satisfying an angry Lord but "the presence of divine love in the flesh enacting a historical solidarity with all who suffer and die." as Johnson writes in a commentary on Scotus's Christology.[13] In this way, too, the incarnation lends support to a holistic, socio-ecological account of flourishing. Just as the incarnation permeates all things, drawing them into communion with God, so it sees the human and other-than-human, the social and ecological, drawn together within the sweep of God's reign.

Correlatively, just as the author of 1 John aimed to overcome the spiritualization of the incarnation by emphasizing the fleshly reality of Jesus as the Word made flesh, so the incarnation reinforces a positive assessment of materiality and embodiment. Christ is in all things through his *sarx*. As Wirzba notes,

---

[13] Johnson, *Ask the Beasts*, 226.

A Theology of Flourishing

reflecting Julian's vision, "That means that when Christians look carefully at the world, when they peer beyond the surface of things, what they should see is Jesus and his love moving through everything."[14] This view offers further grounds for cultivating a nondualistic view of creation, wherein spirit and matter, humans and other creatures, are united in their flesh. This, too, entails a call to action, wherein fostering the enfleshed flourishing of others, all of whom are "in Christ," functions as a principal expression of Christian faith. To feed the hungry and give drink to the thirsty, to liberate captives, clothe the naked, and provide homes for those in need—from unhoused persons to species facing extinction due to habitat loss—all of these actions demonstrate faith working through love in service of new creation.

Guided by the Spirit

While creation and incarnation provide the foundation for a theology of flourishing, the practice of such a theology is fundamentally pneumatological. As the one whom Christians name "Lord and giver of life," the Holy Spirit advocates unceasingly for flourishing, actualizing God's life-giving intentions throughout the cosmos and in human life. As Wolfhart Pannenberg explains:

> The Spirit is at work already in creation as God's mighty breath, the origin of all movement and all life, and only against this background of his activity as the Creator of all life can we rightly understand on the one hand his work in the ecstatics of human conscious life, and on the other hand his role in bringing forth the new life of the resurrection of the dead.[15]

---

[14] Wirzba, *From Nature to Creation*, 20.

[15] Wolfhart Pannenberg, *Systematic Theology,* vol. 3, trans. Geoffrey W. Bromiley (Grand Rapids, MI: Eerdmans, 1997), 1.

184   *A Theology of Flourishing*

The Spirit's work is the work of life, functioning as the medium of God's self-communication in every nook and cranny of the cosmos and in the depths of the human heart. In all creation, "the Spirit is the breath of God thrumming through the lifeblood of every living thing," as Jane Linahan writes.[16]

In the life of faith, the Spirit thus actualizes the attunement of Christian consciousness to God's presence and action in all things with a specific orientation toward the fullness of life in the conditions of embodied existence. As Grace Ji-Sun Kim puts it:

> The Spirit of God helps human beings to perceive *God in the midst of creation*, to experience God under the conditions of earthly life relations, and to live in a secure, strengthened, and dignified manner in God's community. The Spirit of God makes it possible to live lovingly, responsibly, and honorably precisely under the conditions of fleshly-perishable existence.[17]

This is not only a matter of intellectual interest or spiritual awareness. In keeping with the hermeneutics of the fullness of life, perceiving the Spirit's work necessarily entails critical evaluation of material conditions vis-à-vis flourishing. As Lash notes, this perspective has deep roots in scripture. Recognizing the unceasing, life-giving movements of *ruah*—later rendered as "Spirit"—compels us toward prophetic analysis of the conditions of creaturely life. Lash writes, "Throughout both Testaments, at the heart of talk of God as Spirit (and of the world as effect of, and as affected by, the Spirit that is God) the contrast drawn is that between not-life, or lesser life, or life gone wrong, and life:

---

[16] Jane E. Linahan, "Breath, Blood, and the Spirit of God: The Kenotic Cost of Giving Life," in *God, Grace, and Creation*, ed. Philip J. Rossi, 107–23 (Maryknoll, NY: Orbis Books, 2010), 113.

[17] Grace Ji-Sun Kim, *Reimagining Spirit: Wind, Breath, and Vibration* (Eugene, OR: Cascade Books, 2019), 334.

A Theology of Flourishing 185

true life, real life, God's life and all creation's life in God."[18] Attunement to the Spirit in creation—or to creation's silent witness to the Spirit—guides those who profess faith in Christ Jesus toward action on behalf of the flourishing of all things.

The movement of attunement, discernment, and action—the subject of the next chapter—imparts a dynamism to theology and praxis that is consistent with the Spirit's life-giving work in and through creation. As the Sequence for Pentecost proclaims, the Spirit is ever the Spirit of the new, the one who seeks new ways to actualize the gift of life, enlivening *viriditas* amid the ever-changing circumstances of creaturely existence. The Spirit is indeed the one who pours dew upon dry places in creation and upon the heart, who washes away guilt, bends the stubborn will, melts what is frozen and warms what is chill, who guides human steps toward the fullness of life, drawing us away from what is deadening or demeaning and toward that which brings all things to fulfillment in the vision of God that is, always has been, and ever will be available to us—if we have eyes to see.[19] Jantzen reflects on the Spirit's work in similar terms:

> The Spirit of God immanent in the created world dismantles the cosmic dualism that sets God apart from the universe. The Spirit of God in the incarnation liberates us from fear of the body and sexuality. The Spirit poured out upon all flesh, women and men, slaves and free, deconstructs myths of superiority and fearsomeness, and enables mutuality and inclusiveness.[20]

The great equalizer, *ruah elohim* does not play by the rules of the systems and structures we humans establish. The breath of

---

[18] Lash, *Believing Three Ways in One God*, 85.

[19] Roman Missal, *Sequence for Pentecost*.

[20] Grace M. Jantzen, "Healing Our Brokenness: The Spirit and Creation," *The Ecumenical Review* 2, no. 2 (April 1990): 140.

186   *A Theology of Flourishing*

life blows as it wills, calling all to radical humility and openness before the world's wonders. Indeed, as Pope Francis concludes in *Laudato Si'*, "The Spirit of God has filled the universe with possibilities and therefore, from the very heart of things, something new can always emerge" (no. 80).

Despite the great contributions that a Spirit-centered theology might make to Christian thought, spirituality, and praxis, Yves Congar rightly notes that "the Holy Spirit has sometimes been forgotten."[21] Here, it is noteworthy that this forgetting of the Spirit, its marginalization in theological discourse and liturgical practice, corresponds closely with the suppression of the paradigm of flourishing in theological history. Indeed, a Christianity that understands salvation primarily as the work of a human for humans will implicitly marginalize views that link Christ's redeeming work to the Spirit's work of life, rendering the Spirit something of a suppressed other in theology, in direct parallel with the suppression of flourishing.

This may be an understandable outcome of the fact that we humans are the ones telling the story of Christ, who was human. When we consider the dominance of hierarchical dualism in history and theology, however, other questions emerge. Why has the hypostasis who is traditionally represented in images drawn from nature—bird, fire, wind, water—and thus associated with femininity, not been given its due?[22] A similar question arises when we consider Christianity's links to colonial and imperial history. Many traditional accounts of the Spirit's work correspond with Indigenous worldviews that were forcibly suppressed by European colonizers. Has the Spirit been similarly suppressed—even unwittingly—in part due to its incoherence

---

[21] Yves M. J. Congar, *I Believe in the Holy Spirit,* vol. 1: *The Holy Spirit in the "Economy,"* trans. David Smith (New York: Seabury Press, 1983), 159.

[22] See Johnson, *Ask the Beasts,* chapter 5, for a study of these biblical images. Nature and materiality are associated with the feminine in Greco-Roman hierarchical dualism.

A Theology of Flourishing   187

with a colonial-imperial paradigm? Unlike Christ, who can be incorrectly imaged as other than a first-century Palestinian—for example, as white to support colonial claims to power—an incorporeal, invisible force that divinizes all things cannot easily be seen in this way. Neither can the rushing *ruah* be used as a warrant for seizing lands or eradicating peoples. Nor can one easily crown the head of an incorporeal force of life and associate it with empire.[23]

Quite the contrary, the Spirit attests to the fullness of life in ways that inherently interrupt systems of oppression. Discussing the implications of this view, Mary Grey states that the Spirit of life is "the very ground of our hope of cracking open the death-dealing symbols causing the suffering of millions."[24] Elsewhere she states, "The Holy Spirit, in the root meaning of *pneuma* as life and breath, creates awareness of the woundedness of bodies and spirits inflicted all through history by culturally-sanctioned violence, poverty, caste discrimination, and many forms of sickness and disability."[25] In step with Metz's analysis of the suffering of historical victims, attentiveness to the Spirit's life-giving work in creation—in the concrete relationships between thriving ecosystems and just, peaceful societies—also attunes us to the realities of injustice, degradation, and oppression and calls us to protest.

Therefore, insofar as the fullness of life is the basic point of God's creative work, carried out in Christ and the Spirit, a theology centered on flourishing necessitates critical interrogation of systems that oppress or deal death, stealing and destroying the possibility of fulfillment. A new awareness of the places theology

---

[23] Much more could be said about this point. I offer it here as an illustration of the Spirit's suppression and hope to pursue it in future research.

[24] Mary Grey, "Survive or Thrive? A Theology of Flourishing for the Next Millennium," *Studies: An Irish Quarterly Review* 88, no. 352 (Winter 1999): 405.

[25] Mary Grey, "*Natality* and *Flourishing* in Contexts of Disability and Impairment," in *Grace Jantzen: Redeeming the Present,* ed. Elaine Graham (Routledge, 2010), 203.

188 *A Theology of Flourishing*

must go—the peripheries to which it must attend—so that all may be liberated from conditions that obstruct their ability to flourish as God intends emerges through such interrogation. This may be an uncomfortable, even destabilizing process, especially for those who hold power, but it is the Spirit's work and must be respected as such.

Ponder the story of Eldad and Medad, on whom the spirit of God rests despite their absence from a gathering of the elders of Israel. To the alarm of a young member of the community, they prophesy among the people, leading Joshua to implore Moses to stop them (Nm 11:27–28). But Moses offers an instructive reply, relinquishing his authority to make room for the Spirit: "Are you jealous for my sake? Would that all the Lord's people were prophets and that the Lord would put his spirit on them!" (11:29). Again, we humans do not determine the scope of the Spirit's work, and—as the story of picking grain on the Sabbath attests—even the norms established by religious authorities do not norm the Spirit of Life. Rather, that which gives life to creatures and communities, providing the conditions that make flourishing possible, is the surest sign of the Spirit's presence. Ever the advocate for abundant life, the Giver of Life stands opposed to sinful forces that kill, steal, and destroy—that oppress or suppress. The Giver of Life calls Christians to attend ever more fully and to work to realize God's intentions for creation, even, or especially, when they are proclaimed by the Eldads and Medads of creation.

But how does the Spirit draw things to fulfillment? The one who dwells innermostly in all things, advocating on behalf of their flourishing, proclaims God's glory, the fullness of life, in all things. We humans may perceive this proclamation as the Psalmist did, attuning ourselves to the Spirit's presence and action in the categorical. As the next chapter explains, the movements of the Spirit can be found in a unique way in discernment, as the innermost stirrings of hearts attuned to God's mediated immediacy reveal what it means for people to become what God intends

A Theology of Flourishing

us to be: deified creatures who "pledge ourselves in service to the labour of what might be called the politics and ecology of the world's peacemaking."[26] Although ineffable, the Spirit's work in otherkind can be discerned in their holistic flourishing, as well—in the *viriditas* of healthy ecosystems, the fulfillment of plants and animals in keeping with their *haecceitas*, and the harmony of creation as a whole. The work of the Spirit is, to put it simply, that which generates life for ones's self and others, just as that which does not generate life must be rejected as contrary to the Spirit's aims.

Toward the Self-Actualization of Creatures, according to Their Beloved Haecceitas

Though the Spirit's work is universal, it is mediated through each creature's embodied, embedded particularity. Such mediation has two dimensions: the *haecceitas* of the creature as it is created and loved by God, and the socio-ecological contexts the creature inhabits. If *haecceitas* is the basic principle of creaturely existence and if a creature's uniqueness is oriented toward its fulfillment, as Nicholas of Cusa states, then the work of the Spirit in each creature is inviolable because it is perfectly conformed to its uniqueness.

Emphasizing the importance of first-person narratives as a source for theology, *mujerista* theology gives force to this point. As Ada María Isasi-Díaz explains, *mujerista* theology begins with the conviction that first-person narratives of "Latina grassroots women" are an invaluable source for theology, calling on theology as a whole to "[take] seriously the religious understandings and practices of Latinas." In practice, bringing the particularity of Latina women's experiences to bear on all theology will "challenge theological understandings, church teachings, and religious

---

[26] Lash, *Believing Three Ways in One God*, 119.

190   *A Theology of Flourishing*

practices that oppress Latina women, that are not life-giving, and, therefore, cannot be theologically correct."[27] This requires deep respect for the voices of Latina women, who say *permítanme hablar*, permit me to speak, "asking for a respectful silence from all those who have the power to set up definitions of what it means to be human, a respectful silence so others can indeed hear our cries denouncing oppression and injustice, so others can understand our vision of a just society."[28] To speak theologically in the first person from one's *haecceitas* is to speak the Spirit's word of life from one's beloved particularity.

Isasi-Díaz's theological vision corresponds closely with the hermeneutics that guides a theology of flourishing. Following this correspondence, a theology of flourishing suggests that, if fullness of life operates as the orienting center for theological discourse and the primary criterion for interpreting theological claims, then theology must attend authentically to the experiences of all people, especially those who suffer oppression, because oppression blocks creaturely flourishing. But we must not be idealistic. Theology can only attend to the experiences of all people if those who hold power are, like Moses, willing to make room for the Spirit by empowering all to speak with prophetic authority, as Hildegard did in her own time and place. To begin with flourishing is, then, to hear the Spirit speaking through the voices of all who cry out for the fullness of life as they narrate their first-person experience from the standpoint of their God-given, inviolable, and beloved particularity.

Moreover, within a framework that bridges the social and ecological, including all voices extends to all creatures. Humans can listen to the first-person testimony of other creatures as they speak from their *haecceitas*, recognizing that each creature's way

---

[27] Ada María Isasi-Díaz, *Mujerista Theology: A Theology for the Twenty-First Century* (Maryknoll, NY: Orbis Books, 1996), 1.

[28] Isasi-Díaz, 136.

A Theology of Flourishing

191

of being communicates its unique, inviolable dignity and right to flourish. As Linahan puts it, "The Spirit not only gives life, but also empowers all things to live the life that is distinctively and authentically their very own. . . . The Spirit provides what is necessary to make possible this 'other' life of creatures, to make it possible for them to be, to live, and to actualize their own potential."[29] Deepening this observation, Pope Francis reflects that the Spirit works within all creatures, irrespective of who they are or how long they exist. "Even the fleeting life of the least of beings is the object of his love, and in its few seconds of existence, God enfolds it with his affection" (*Laudato Si'*, no. 78). What it means for a creature to flourish is absolutely unique. It flows from *haecceitas* and cannot be defined on the basis of principles imposed from the outside. While it may be possible to discern common characteristics of flourishing, these characteristics can only be discovered in dialogue, community, and relationship. No one but the Spirit "knows" what it means for a specific creature to experience the fullness of life.

That said, as Horan's analysis of Scotus shows, *haecceitas* must not be seen as a basis for individualism. Although it functions philosophically to explain individuation, as a basis for self-actualization, *haecceitas* does not support the Enlightenment ideal of an individual person apart from others, making its own radical claim to existence. Rather, particularity emerges in relationship, as creatures move together toward their particular perfections. Gunton argues, "A satisfactory conception of particularity depends upon an acceptance of the fact that persons also are constituted in their particularity both by their being created such by God and by the network of human and cosmic relatedness in which they find their being."[30] Particularity subsists and develops

---

[29] Linahan, "Breath, Blood, and the Spirit of God," 112.

[30] Colin Gunton, *The One, the Three, and the Many: God, Creation, and the Culture of Modernity* (Cambridge: Cambridge University Press, 1993), 203.

192 *A Theology of Flourishing*

within a framework of relationality. A creature comes to know itself, what it is called to be, what it means to live fully, how it can contribute to the categorical contexts it inhabits only in relationship. *Haecceitas* and relationality walk together.

Here, caution is again in order. Humans cannot determine what it means for other creatures to flourish except through this same relational orientation. As any animal lover knows what it looks like for a beloved dog to romp joyfully about with a friend, human or otherwise; as any gardener knows what it looks like for a healthy plant to sprout, flower, and bear fruit; so attunement to the emergence of joy, life, and holistic well-being points toward the realization of the Spirit's work through a creature's embodied particularity. Rather than leading to assertions of human power over other creatures, such attunement should "develop the sympathetic capacity that encourages us to see things in their particularity, their wholeness, and their (often hidden) potential."[31] Here again, humans do not and cannot set limits around how the Spirit works. With humility and openness, we can only work to perceive and be surprised by God's life-giving action in creation. In all this, *haecceitas* comes to clarity and finds fulfillment relationally, as creatures come to know their unique calling, their potential, their own flourishing by testing the spirits in the conditions of categorical existence to discover the full meaning of what it means to be *this*.

In the Concrete Conditions of Categorical Existence

While *haecceitas* is absolutely unique, its relational constitution suggests that it is, as Rahner observes, conditioned by the circumstances of creaturely life. In pneumatological terms this means that "God's vivifying Spirit relates to human beings in

---

[31] Wirzba, *From Nature to Creation*, 4.

A Theology of Flourishing

their existential present. In its many manifestations, the vivifying Spirit reflects God's commitment to the flourishing of creatures in their finite, embodied lives *now*," as Colleen Griffith observes.[32] Just as divine self-communication is mediated by the categorical, so particularity is mediated in and conditioned by the circumstances in which a creature lives, such that every creature exists, as Gunton puts it, in "a network of mutually constituting *particularities.*" He goes on,

> To take a simple illustration, we can say that a relatively small and short-lived creature like an insect is constituted for a brief span of time out of the reservoir of being by certain causes—procreative, sustaining, and the rest—and returns to that reservoir once its brief cycle of life is complete, possibly after sharing in the constitution of others of its own species.[33]

Seen in this light, factors such as race, gender, ability, economic status; social, biological, and psychological conditioning; water and air quality; access to healthy food; and countless other forces condition *haecceitas* and may enable or foreclose possibilities for flourishing. Indeed, as Grey reflects,

> "Flourishing" situates us in time and place, with all the specificity of cultural and historical memories constituting community identity: these memories are enshrined in bone and blood, in frayed garments, in the silent stories of a landscape, stumps of lost trees in the desert, in texts of stone and wood, in fragments of ruined houses, in the drawings

---

[32] Colleen Griffith, "The Spirit and Nearness of God," in *The Holy Spirit: Setting the World on Fire*, ed. Richard Lennan and Nancy Pineda-Madrid, 3–12 (New York: Paulist Press, 2017), 10. Emphasis mine.

[33] Gunton, *Christ and Creation*, 37.

194   *A Theology of Flourishing*

of children as they crouched in cellars hearing the bombs drop on their city.[34]

Such considerations heighten the importance of understanding *haecceitas* as a uniqueness that cannot be comprehended fully by another. In large part because it subsists within the categorical, *haecceitas* remains ineffable, partial, untranslatable, for only the God who can count the number of hairs on a person's head (Lk 12:7) can know fully what it means for someone to experience reality as the unique creature they are in a specific context.

Theologians writing about disability and mental health illustrate and offer qualifications to this point, elucidating how the categorical can mediate non-belonging and unhomelikeness—often due to the imposition of "normative" social expectations and theological categories. These experiences may nuance or altogether alter the meaning of self-actualization as it arises from the interplay of *haecceitas* and the categorical, giving force to the recognition that flourishing must not be thought of in a univocal manner and providing a further warrant for a praxis of flourishing that is rooted in deep awareness of and care for others. Nancy Eiesland writes that "normative" understandings of human persons and human experience have led many Christian communities to fail to recognize and promote the full humanity of all people. Where churches might function as spaces of radical hospitality and care for people with disabilities, she writes that they more often treat "people with disabilities as objects of pity and paternalism. For many disabled persons the church has been a 'city on a hill'—physically inaccessible and socially inhospitable."[35] At issue here is failure to respect how the *haecceitas* of a person with disabilities interfaces with "normative"

---

[34] Grey, "Survive or Thrive," 404.

[35] Nancy L. Eiesland, *The Disabled God: Toward a Liberatory Theology of Disability* (Nashville, TN: Abingdon Press, 1994), 20.

A Theology of Flourishing

expressions of ecclesial life—one aspect of the categorical—that are rooted in specific, and often unrecognized, ideas of what it means to be human. Rather than being places that nurture fullness of life for people with disabilities, churches and communities become places of marginalization that force people with disabilities "to conform to crippling theological categories" that are incompatible with their distinctive ways of being human.[36] In so doing, churches become spaces that foreclose possibilities for flourishing, not only by denying the full dignity of people with disabilities, but also by refusing to hear their voices, their accounts of what it means for them to flourish in their unique, beloved *haecceitas*—to be cared for and to care for others, expressing the love of the "disabled God" in their embodied particularity.

Relatedly, Jessica Coblentz's groundbreaking study of theology and life with depression characterizes depression as "unhomelikeness," as a state in which the categorical functions as a "wilderness" like the wilderness into which Hagar fled (Gn 16) and was later sent (Gn 21)—and in which, amid her plight as the rejected mother of Ishmael, she also met God.[37] Seeing the categorical as wilderness radically changes possible meanings of self-actualization, demanding sensitivity to objective, material conditions as well as the subjective experience of the categorical, as it is shaped by the interplay of sociocultural, ecclesial, political, cultural, and scientific assumptions about the meaning of human life. As with Eiesland, a central issue here is the alignment, or lack of alignment, between "normative" views of human experience and the experience of unhomelikeness. A key element of this misalignment emerges around the meaningfulness of depression, the possibility of understanding it as "fruitful," a basis for flourishing. As Coblentz explains, "One

---

[36] Eiesland, *The Disabled God*, 20.

[37] On depression as a wilderness experience, see Jessica Coblentz, *Dust in the Blood: A Theology of Life with Depression* (Collegeville, MN: Liturgical Press, 2022), 124–27.

196   *A Theology of Flourishing*

cannot presume depression to be inherently fruitful and meaningful, for those suffering with it often long to make meaning of their experience but cannot find or generate this meaning in their present state; some will never."[38] This point has important implications for a theology of flourishing and theology as a whole, as it calls theology to account for the stigmatization of people suffering mental illness, as well as the lack of models of the human person that are capacious enough to include "sufferers who are often doing the best they can to interpret their suffering in a life-affirmation fashion."[39] On this basis Coblentz poses a critical challenge to theology: to reject theologies that stigmatize and, in a vital self-critical practice, ask whether and to what extent existing theological models can accommodate the actual reality of depression sufferers. Such a perspective sees that "sufferers are not only accepting the limitations of depression but also affirming that possibilities of dignity, meaningfulness, and goodness might be compatible with it—possibilities previously unforeseen when they were singularly invested in liberation from their condition."[40]

Indeed, while liberation from depression may not be possible, liberation from views that stigmatize depression sufferers—demanding that they conform to standards that are incongruous with their experience of the categorical—is. That is, of course, if theologians—and indeed all Christians—are willing to practice radical hospitality that hears others as they give voice to their experience in the midst of the distinctive configurations of the categorical that they inhabit—even those that do not quite feel like home. This hospitality moves once more from radical attention to radical care in a praxis of flourishing that "enables Christians to 'stay with' unresolved suffering" and provide support and

---

[38] Coblentz, *Dust in the Blood*, 9.
[39] Coblentz, 110.
[40] Coblentz, 187.

A Theology of Flourishing

love that meets the needs of others precisely as they are.[41] Staying with suffering enables us to give full attention to how others narrate their experience of the categorical in which—like Hagar in the wilderness—they see God, are seen by God, and come to discern how they might live fully in view of their circumstances, not in spite of them.

We must become attuned to the reality of others as they describe it, and we must actively confront forces that deaden, demean, and stigmatize with a vibrant proclamation that flourishing is for all creatures as they are. The conditions of categorical reality—from time and place to social and ecclesial conditions to spoken and unspoken assumptions about what it means to be human—shape what it means to flourish according to one's *haecceitas*. In view of the gospel call to care for the embodied needs of all, recognizing the impact of the categorical on the possibility of flourishing calls Christians to foster the conditions that make possible the fullness of life for all creatures, so that the church can truly be a house for all people—a living witness to divine love made manifest in diverse "heres" and "nows."

Liberating Them to Become Fully What God Intends Them to Be

Giving attention to dynamics of power and agency vis-à-vis flourishing also necessitates that we attend to the ways that the categorical shapes *haecceitas*. For, while it is true that "the Spirit makes possible the conditions and provides the potential that enable creatures to develop according to their own nature and to work out their own history and destiny," realizing this possibility depends also on the existence of social and ecological conditions that enable the Spirit's work to come to fulfillment.[42]

---

[41] Coblentz, 205.

[42] Linahan, "Breath, Blood, and the Spirit of God," 114.

198   *A Theology of Flourishing*

A creature that exists under unjust conditions, conditions of degradation, will find its opportunities to flourish diminished by the same forces that numb privileged others to its suffering, allowing death to triumph where life should abound. As Black and womanist theologians observe, this remains the reality for many Black persons and communities in the United States, who experience constrained opportunities for flourishing due to the perdurance of anti-Black racism and white indifference.[43] The legacy of slavery, lynching, and Jim Crow, which continue today under the guise of police brutality, environmental racism, educational inequality, and so on, constitute a death-dealing "background theory" for much of Black experience in the United States. As a result, the socio-ecological status quo functions as a constraint on flourishing, fostering what M. Shawn Copeland describes as a "racial alienation" with deep roots in the construction of blackness by white Enlightenment philosophers.[44]

Amid such a history, James Cone writes, the "lynching tree" functions preeminently as a symbol of death—what he names "America's cross." Cone explains:

> Lynched black bodies are symbols of Christ's body. If we want to understand what the crucifixion means for Americans today, we must view it through the lens of mutilated black bodies whose lives are destroyed in the criminal justice system. Jesus continues to be lynched before our eyes. He is crucified wherever people are tormented. That is why I say Christ is black.[45]

---

[43] For one such study, see Kelly Brown Douglas, *Stand Your Ground: Black Bodies and the Justice of God* (Maryknoll, NY: Orbis Books, 2015).

[44] M. Shawn Copeland, *Enfleshing Freedom: Body, Race, and Being* (Minneapolis: Fortress Press, 2010), 15.

[45] James H. Cone, *Said I Wasn't Gonna Tell Nobody: The Making of a Black Theologian* (Maryknoll, NY: Orbis Books, 2018), 140.

A Theology of Flourishing 199

This reality is stark enough to illustrate how possibilities for self-actualization are diminished by injustice that is mediated in the material and social conditions that constitute categorical reality. Liberation from oppression is a fundamental condition of the possibility of flourishing. Correlatively, any denial of this reality by white Christians amounts to an authorization of crucifixion, a willing complicity in the necrophilic logic of defilement and destruction that took Christ's life and continues to destroy Black personhood—in direct contradiction to God's life-giving will.

Simply, suffering caused by injustice must be ended so that all may experience the fullness for which they are created. This entails a twofold liberation: liberation from forces that oppress, suppressing the realization of *haecceitas* by constraining discernment and imposing limits on the Spirit's life-giving work; and liberation to discern what flourishing means in view of one's *haecceitas*, one's relationship to God and other creatures amid the socio-ecological reality one inhabits. We must attend and respond to reality in all its beauty and brokenness, for only through such attentiveness can creatures and communities discern how they may contribute to the flourishing of all, confronting powers that oppress with God's own promise of abundant life. Thus, liberation from oppression and interior freedom to discern what it means to flourish and foster the flourishing of others walk hand in hand.

On this journey, what we might simply call the journey of deification, human persons enter ever more fully into the vision of God, becoming more and more fully what God created us to be—to be Christ in our own particularity. Such liberation enables creatures to live fully in the ways they are intended to live. Ultimately, together we cultivate a world in which Christ, living in and through Christians, builds a "new creation" that "enables individuals to arrive at their destiny, and in the end enables the whole world and its history to be rightly ordered in justice and peace."[46]

---

[46] Elizabeth Johnson, *She Who Is: The Mystery of God in Feminist Theological Discourse* (New York: Crossroad, 1991), 90.

200

A Theology of Flourishing

And Fostering a Praxis of Justice and Peace, on Behalf of "New Creation," a World in which the Fullness of Life Abounds

A radical call to action on behalf of the fullness of life emerges from attunement to reality: reject forces of death, theft, and destruction and act as agents of flourishing. To become agents of flourishing we must retell the Christian story, reorient Christian consciousness, and see things as God sees them, not as fallen or inherently sinful but as good and created to flourish. As a context for discernment, such attunement orients Christian thought and praxis toward the needs of the world, fostering a "relational embrace of diversity" that sees "human beings and the earth with all its creatures intrinsically related as companions in a community of life."[47] Fostering this relational embrace, in turn, produces a praxis of radical hospitality that, in keeping with the Spirit's aims, welcomes others as the Spirit welcomes them, "precisely in their radical otherness."[48] Here, we must practice deep humility and openness as we recognize that God is present within every creature and that God wills the flourishing of all things in ways that defy comprehension.

From this hospitality, humility, and openness flows a praxis of justice, peace, and love that denounces forces that impede or obstruct the realization of God's aims and takes action to enable all creatures, individually and collectively, to dwell in the fullness of life. Moreover, as Linahan observes, recognizing justice as a precondition for flourishing requires attention to the needs and the suffering of others, especially the "least of these." She writes, "If God is love and if the Spirit is the power of God's love giving life to all things, it means that the Spirit is self-invested in the life of all things, not only in the lives that succeed and flourish but also in those countless ones that, unseen and unheard, are

---

[47] Elizabeth A. Johnson, *Women, Earth, and Creator Spirit* (New York: Paulist Press, 1993), 30.

[48] Linahan, "Breath, Blood, and the Spirit of God," 113.

A Theology of Flourishing

agonizing and blighted."[49] Inspired by this vision and led toward fulfillment by the Spirit who "gives life to all things and makes them holy," deified Christians become practitioners of *amor mundi*, conduits of "new creation," in and with creatures of myriad stripes.[50] Far from being a way to an otherworldly heaven alone, this praxis makes possible the full actualization of each creature in this world, in its beloved uniqueness, on the way to the final consummation of all things in perfect union with God.

Implications for Theological Discourse

A theology that sees the flourishing of all creatures as the original divine intention, an intention borne out by Christians in faith through practices of hospitality, love, justice, and peace, orients Christian theology to search the tradition for "signs of life" in two key ways. First, theologians can probe scripture and tradition anew, undertaking a *ressourcement* of sources that lie at the fringes of theology—possibly because of their emphasis on flourishing. Such sources might include theologians like Hildegard and Julian, as well as thinkers like John Duns Scotus and Nicholas of Cusa, whose contributions never entered the mainstream. Such a *ressourcement* has potential to deepen awareness of the presence of the theme of flourishing throughout Christian theology, spirituality, and praxis. Similarly, theologians can reread sources that constitute the theological mainstream, assessing their potential to contribute to a holistic, socio-ecological paradigm of flourishing. Here, as in all the theological methods this chapter has engaged, sources and interpretations that see the fullness of life as the realization of God's aims—especially as descriptions of this fullness arise from first-person narratives—take precedence over those that envision creation and humanity in a state of lack or aim to

---

[49] Linahan, 119.
[50] Roman Missal, *Eucharistic Prayer III.*

202   *A Theology of Flourishing*

preserve the status quo. For God's intentions to be realized, all must be liberated and empowered to speak prophetically from their experience. Conversely, sources and interpretations that suppress flourishing must be reconsidered in light of Christ's proclamation of abundant life. In this way, too, while ecclesial teachings should be read as normative, they cannot be taken as determinative of the full meaning of creaturely life. Moreover, ecclesial teachings that foreclose possibilities for the Spirit to realize God's will to life, flourishing, and communion must be subjected to critical evaluation. All in all, a theology of flourishing resituates sources of the tradition—theology, ecclesial teaching, scripture, and so forth—within the *sensus fidelium*, using collective discernment about what fosters liberation to the fullness of life as a primary norm for theological claims, a method of testing the spirits to discern what Christ's promise of abundant life means in diverse times and places.

Pope Francis's emphasis on synodal listening and collective discernment fits well with this paradigm. While some may experience synodality as a threat to the centralized authority of the church's teaching magisterium, within a framework of flourishing, concerns about ecclesial authority are only valid insofar as exercises of authority foster the fullness of life for all creation. Preserving authority or institutional structures for their own sake, even for the sake of tradition, will not suffice. For, as the church has always taught, the central authority of the tradition is the Holy Spirit, who guides the church and all creatures toward fullness in union with Christ, the Creator God, and one another. In a theology that centers the Spirit's work of *viriditas*, of making all things new, trusting in the Spirit—even amid disagreement, dissent, and protest—reflects the central Christian belief that "the Lord has done [and continues to do] great things for us" (Ps 126:3). As a principal expression of this belief, theology has the potential to further trace the precious thread of flourishing on behalf of fullness for all creatures. But first, we must listen and trust.

A Theology of Flourishing

Resituating Sin and Salvation

Coming full circle, the theological approach proposed here resituates sin in relationship to flourishing, defining it as a contradiction to the life-giving order God established. If flourishing constitutes the default orientation of all things, then sin is an obstruction to the realization of this orientation. Sin is a direct contradiction to the salvific intentions at work around, within, and among us.

A theology of flourishing thus recognizes that, through the Spirit, creation is and always has been capable of realizing God's purposes because it is empowered in existence and action by a Creator who labors infinitely to bring all things to the fullness of life. Therefore, whereas many traditional soteriologies overstressed "the divine action *towards* the creation at the expense of that action *within* the structure of time and space," a theology of flourishing situates salvation within the broader logic of creation, not apart from it, such that the Spirit can be seen "as the one enabling the creation truly to *be itself*."[51] As I have already noted, this vision calls us to action on behalf of abundant life. Yet to act on behalf of abundant life is always and already to reject sin in all its forms. Confronting forces that obstruct flourishing in this world likewise means cooperating with grace in fostering the fullness of life for all things. Lash puts it pithily: "In the end, God heals absolutely, but we work in the meantime."[52]

As a test case for applying this framework to the relationship between flourishing, sin, and salvation, consider Romans 3:23, arguably one of Paul's most influential statements on sin: "All have sinned and fall short of the glory of God." In many theologies, sermons, and homilies, this statement has been and continues to be used to characterize humanity as fallen, in a

---

[51] Gunton, *Christ and Creation*, 51. Emphasis mine.

[52] Lash, *Believing Three Ways in One God*, 120.

204

A Theology of Flourishing

state of lack, on the basis of the existential operation of sin. However, when interpreted through the lens of flourishing, using a hermeneutics of the fullness of life, this text appears differently. Taking seriously the idea that creation is a locus of divine presence and action, that God's glory enfolds all things, and expanding Irenaeus's axiom about the glory of God to all creatures, the "glory" of which Paul speaks takes on new meaning. No longer is this glory a goal that lies beyond the life of creatures, something rendered unattainable by sin. This glory is the glory for which humans and all creatures are created—the very presence of God in all things.

To fall short of *this* glory is, then, is to fall short of the divine glory that creation mediates to us at all times—the foundation of the fullness of life for which all things are made. When we see God as wholly life, the one in whom there is no sin and whose only meaning is love, sin indeed appears as a privation of the good. But this good is the goodness of creation itself, of each and every creature, of the grace that comes to us humans and to all things as it has from the very beginning. A disruption of this graced order, sin consists in humanity's unwillingness to accept and execute our life-giving calling to be caretakers of one another and all things, to be people who work in love for justice and peace on behalf of flourishing, both individual and collective. Our calling entails a call to protest against forces that degrade and demean, against thieves of life who obstruct creation's capacity to flourish out of self-interest or indifference. The final chapters of this book suggest ways of putting this vision into practice.

Onward, toward a Praxis of Flourishing

In the final analysis a theology of flourishing does not see Christianity primarily as a tradition that seeks to pay a moral

A Theology of Flourishing   205

debt on behalf of heavenly salvation but as a radical, deifying living-unto-God that confronts sin by proclaiming and acting on behalf of God's reign. In step with Johnson's discussion of God as SHE WHO IS, this theology affirms that

> in a surpassing and originating sense God is not undialectically the ground of everything that is but is the ground of *what should be and we hope will be*, the power of being over the ravages of nonbeing . . . as pure aliveness in relation, the unoriginate welling up of fullness of life in which the whole universe participates.[53]

This vision of God elicits a deep call to action for justice and peace as conditions of possibility for the "welling up of fullness of life" in, with, and for all creation, so that bees and crows, water and trees, all creatures may praise God in their beloved *haecceitas*, empowered by the Spirit and liberated from socio-ecological constraints to offer hearts and voices—their deified selves—in praise of the living God. Retelling the Christian story with this vision in mind is the primary aim of the theology of flourishing that this chapter has proposed.

How does this deifying self-actualization in the Spirit take place in human life, and how does it relate to the flourishing of other creatures? This chapter has already gestured toward the tradition of discernment—of forming persons with deep awareness of God's intentions for themselves in relation to God's intentions for all creation—as a means toward this end. Building on the foundations established here, the next chapter offers a tripartite framework of dialogue, discernment, and decision as a foundation for a human practice of flourishing. After presenting this framework, which must be adapted to various contexts

---

[53] Johnson, *She Who Is*, 240.

206 *A Theology of Flourishing*

and purposes on the basis of the particularity of every person's *haecceitas* and categorical context, the conclusion ponders praxis: what it looks like for Christians attuned to the Spirit to foster the fullness of life for all things.

9

Dialogue, Discernment, Decision

A Framework for Flourishing

Building upon the earlier study of the theme of flourishing in scripture and history, the preceding chapter articulated the shape and scope of a theology that takes flourishing—the self-actualization of all creatures in relationship with God and others—as a starting point and center of gravity for Christian theology and praxis. How does flourishing come to fulfillment in the circumstances of human life? How does the Spirit's invitation to the fullness of life come to us as we walk with others through the joy and brokenness, the beauty and struggle, of the everyday?

Linking the proposed theology of flourishing to the Ignatian tradition of discernment, this chapter presents a three-part framework for actualizing flourishing in theology, spirituality, and Christian life. Moving from dialogue to discernment to decision, this approach aims to cultivate attunement to the Spirit's life-giving intentions, guiding individuals and communities to discover through sustained dialogue with reality what it means for them to flourish and, in flourishing, to foster the flourishing of others. Given the priority that the proposed theology affords to narratives of suffering and oppression, this approach understands humble,

207

208   *A Theology of Flourishing*

compassionate listening to the cry of the earth and the cry of the poor as a precondition for authentic discernment. After all, one cannot discern what it means to flourish in isolation, apart from or indifferent to the cares of the world. On the path toward fullness of life, the love of self, love of God, and love of neighbor—human and other-than-human—remain inextricably intertwined.

How, concretely, does the self-actualizing encounter with God take place, and how does one's own self-actualization reach out to foster the flourishing of other creatures? Rooted in Rahner's account of God's self-communication in the full sweep of cosmic history, a theology of flourishing operates on the conviction that God really is at work *in all things*, such that by entering into dialogue with the world, we enter into dialogue with God. Mediating the Spirit's invitation to deifying self-actualization, engagement with material reality thus functions as a path toward individual and collective discernment of God's life-giving intentions for all things. Seen in this way, every moment of every day offers an opportunity to actualize the Spirit's life-giving aims—or to reject those aims in favor of something else: the comfort of the status quo, empty pity or piety, wealth or prestige, or countless other powers that kill, steal, and destroy. In all this there are no predetermined outcomes. On the path toward flourishing, the Spirit blows as it wills. Yet we trust that the Spirit is there, speaking through our beloved *haecceitas* and guiding us, and all things, toward deification—the fullness of life. Reflecting on the path toward flourishing begins, then, with consideration of how dialogue with the world mediates dialogue with the Spirit's aims in every corner of creation.

Dialogue as Method of Attunement and Context for Discernment

As a foundation for actualizing the vision of a theology of flourishing, dialogue begins with deep attunement to reality. Dialogue

Dialogue, Discernment, Decision

Dialogue, Discernment, Decision 209

requires an active, informed, compassionate consciousness of reality that bridges self-awareness with awareness of the entities, processes, and relationships at work in the concrete socioeco-systems a person inhabits, from the operation of sociopolitical and cultural systems to ecological relationships and everything in between. Such attunement can be grounded in many sources of knowledge: firsthand experience and reflection on experience, conversations with friends and family, relationships with animal kin, the natural and social sciences, adventures around the world, witnessing or experiencing suffering and oppression, and so on.[1] Theologically, attunement includes awareness of God's presence and action in categorical reality and recognition of forces that obstruct the realization of the Spirit's work of life. As an expression of what Pope Francis dubs a "theology of welcoming," this vision of dialogue is grounded in radical openness and hospitality to others and to reality as a whole. It manifests a willingness to let every creature speak from its *haecceitas*—*permítanme hablar*—and be heard authentically, with priority given to suffering and oppression.[2] Such dialogue calls theology, and indeed all Christians, beyond biases and preconceived notions about others, especially those who narrate experiences of marginalization and exclusion, to genuine mutuality, love, and trust in the Spirit's deifying work in all things.

Through such dialogue, persons and communities expand, clarify, and enrich their sense and understanding of reality. Dialogue may elicit deeper awareness of socioeconomic realities, the impacts of oppressive social and ecclesial structures, the degradation of the environment, the loss of biodiversity, and

---

[1] My definition of attunement builds on Stoeger's phenomenology, as articulated in William R. Stoeger, "Our Experience of Knowing in Science and in Spirituality," in *The Laws of Nature, the Range of Human Knowledge, and Divine Action* (Tarnow, Poland: Biblos, 1996).

[2] Pope Francis, "Meeting on the Theme 'Theology after *Veritatis Gaudium* in the Context of the Mediterranean,'" June 21, 2019.

210   *A Theology of Flourishing*

so on. It may also deepen awareness of what people hope for, what elicits joy and compassion, what they dream the world *can* be—what fosters the fullness of life. At the same time, dialogue is self-reflexive. Authentic dialogue with reality invites persons and communities to understand ever more deeply who they are and what they are called to be.

A vision of the world as the medium of the Spirit's invitation to the fullness of life, itself the mature fruit of discernment, grounds such an understanding of dialogue. Dialogue with the world thus facilitates dialogue with the Spirit. As Rahner would have it, human transcendence is actualized and fulfilled—humans *flourish*—in and through categorical reality. It is, then, through dialogue with reality that we come to know ourselves and God, that we attune ourselves to the Spirit's stirrings within and around us and discover what it means to flourish in keeping with God's intentions—intentions that extend to creation as a whole. In other words, when dialogue with reality attunes us to God's work within us and within the world—when it leads us to understand who we are called to be and how we are called to collaborate in realizing the Spirit's work—we set out on a journey of deification that leads toward fullness of life.

As Pope Francis writes, such dialogue requires both a "bottom-up" approach that listens deeply to the needs of individuals and communities, and a "top-down" approach that—rather than asserting "what the church teaches"—interprets reality through the lens of the reign of God, fostering a prophetic sensibility. He writes:

> Both movements are necessary and complementary: a *bottom-up* movement that can dialogue, with an attitude of listening and discernment, with every human and historical instance, taking into account the breadth of what it means to be human; and a *top-down* movement where "the top" is that of Jesus lifted up on the cross that allows, at the

Dialogue, Discernment, Decision 211

same time, to discern the signs of the Kingdom of God in history and to understand prophetically the signs of the anti-Kingdom that disfigure the soul and human history. It is a method that allows us in a dynamic that is ongoing to confront ourselves with every human condition and to grasp what Christian light can illuminate the folds of reality and what efforts the Spirit of the Risen Crucified One is arousing, from time to time, here and now.[3]

Here we must also recognize the possibility that a Christian, or a theology, may prescind from dialogue and thereby proceed with a lack of awareness—whether willful or unwitting—that implicitly rejects the idea that reality mediates the Spirit's work of new creation. Such a rejection forecloses possibilities for discernment and, therefore, flourishing. Dean Brackley makes the point well:

> Many decent people are unaware of the scope of structural poverty in the world; the dimensions of our environmental crisis; the scale of violence against women, child abuse, and abortion in our societies; inhumane sweatshop conditions at home and abroad; the danger of proliferation of weapons of mass destruction; and the pervasiveness of racism and patriarchy.[4]

Thus, just as dialogue fosters awareness of the Spirit's intentions for persons and communities in view of suffering, injustice, and oppression, so lack of dialogue enables these evils to continue, in direct contradiction to God's life-giving aims. A theology of flourishing calls for dialogue with reality—from *lo cotidiano*, everyday life, to *la realidad*, the total sociopolitical and

---

[3] Pope Francis, "Meeting on the Theme 'Theology after *Veritatis Gaudium* in the Context of the Mediterranean.'"

[4] Dean Brackley, *The Call to Discernment in Troubled Times: New Perspectives on the Transformative Wisdom of Ignatius of Loyola* (New York: Crossroad, 2004), 157.

socio-ecological reality—with this negative possibility in view. Just as genuine hope is rooted in awareness of the evils that plague our world, so the meaning of flourishing emerges through dialogue with the realities of socio-ecological degradation and injustice as a concrete expression of faith in a God who desires that all creatures may flourish in the fullness of life.

In practice, such dialogue must remain anchored in a commitment to flourishing. As we listen and respond, we do so always with flourishing in heart and mind, partnering with others in discerning the Spirit's intentions. Therefore, while dialogue may appeal to an array of sources—scripture, tradition, science, the news, the beliefs and practices of other religious traditions, and so forth—any such appeal must be rooted in a commitment to discerning what fosters fullness of life for every creature and creation as a whole. A hermeneutics of the fullness of life thus imparts a critical sensibility to dialogue, orienting human engagement with reality to discern what actualizes Christ's proclamation of abundant life and what obstructs or suppresses it.

Insofar as the whole scope of human experience can be understood as mediating dialogue with God, any experience may confront us with the question of who we are called to be and what we are called to do in view of the promise of flourishing. What might hiking to a misty mountain peak or swimming toward the horizon on a hot day at the beach teach us about who we are? What can films that break open the imagination and touch the heart, and artistic interpretations of the world's joy and sorrow, teach us about who we are called to become? How do we recognize and live into the promise of flourishing when praying with others at Eucharist or at the bedside of a dying friend, traveling to distant lands, being moved to solidarity by stories of suffering and survival? Through dialogue with reality, we attune ourselves to the Spirit's work of new creation in us and in all things.

Dialogue, Discernment, Decision

213

The shadow side of human experience, especially the operation of life-destroying powers under the guise of the status quo—"just the way things are"—is equally revelatory. For example, in a society where white supremacy is or ever has been constitutive of structures and institutions, dialogue centered on flourishing demands critical reflection on how the "regular operation" of social systems perpetuates racial alienation and the oppression of people and communities of color, even to the point of authorizing violence against them.

Societies whose grounding narratives mythologize weapons of war as necessary for the protection of fundamental human rights will be predisposed toward the same necrophilic logic that resulted in Christ's death. This logic leads naturally to the conclusion that the crucifixion of innocent persons and communities, as well as anthropogenic extinction and the destruction of the biosphere, is somehow permissible—even compatible with the gospel.

Patriarchal, heterosexist, and ableist systems follow suit. The perdurance of violence against women and children, including sexual violence; the exclusion of women from spaces of authority in church and society; the ecclesial characterization of homosexuality as "a more or less strong tendency ordered toward an intrinsic moral evil" and dismissal of gender dysphoria and transgender experience as "ideology"; the marginalization of people with disabilities and the stigmatization of mental illness all provide opportunities to retell the Christian story with flourishing as the foundation for theological discourse and Christian life.[5]

Dialogue must also attend to the intersection of these realities. To offer one illustration of this point, Chung Hyun Kyung

---

[5] Congregation for the Doctrine of the Faith, "Letter to the Bishops of the Catholic Church on the Pastoral Care of Homosexual Persons" (October 1, 1986). On the denial of transgender experience, see Congregation for Catholic Education, "Male and Female He Created Them: Towards a Path of Dialogue on the Question of Gender Theory in Education" (February 2, 2019).

214   *A Theology of Flourishing*

attests to the virulent intersection of colonization and patriarchy in the experience of Asian women. In addition to suppressing and remaking Asian cultures in the image of White European Christianity, colonial-imperial systems empowered further patriarchal subjugation of and violence against women. Asian women's theology arises from the death-dealing cooperation of these forces. Chung explains:

> Asian women's theology was born out of Asian women's tears and sighs and from their burning desire for liberation and wholeness . . . from Asian women's cries and screams, from the extreme suffering in their everyday lives. They have shouted from pain when their own and their children's bodies collapsed from starvation, rape, and battering. Theological reflection has emerged as a response to women's suffering.[6]

Whether as a seedbed for theological reflection or a call to protest and action, dialogue rooted in a vision of flourishing elicits discernment of how the self-actualization of Christian persons and communities meets the concrete realities of others vis-à-vis the promise of abundant life. Given the priority that a theology of flourishing affords to experiences of suffering and marginalization, the mutuality of dialogue necessitates a willingness to really listen as others speak from positions of diminished power or pain. Those who hold power cannot cling to certainty or privilege; in love, they must be willing to relinquish power and privilege if it enables another to flourish. After all, a person cannot be fully human, or fully Christian, and sit comfortably with the dehumanization of others. Centering dialogue with reality on God's life-giving intentions thus fosters "good discomfort"

---

[6] Chung Hyun Kyung, *Struggle to Be the Sun Again: Introducing Asian Women's Theology* (Maryknoll, NY: Orbis Books, 1991), 22.

Dialogue, Discernment, Decision 215

that leads to conversion. When generalized, Chung's observation that "only when Asian men in the liberation movement incorporate the liberation of women as an intrinsic ingredient for Asia's struggle for full humanity can their claim for people's liberation have integrity," illuminates this conclusion and becomes a paradigm for Christian life.[7]

With flourishing in view, reflecting individually and communally on reality may entail protest against or even action for the abolition of systems and structures and mediate death. Such abolition is not so much an act of tearing down as it is an opening of space for the Spirit's work of new creation, for building up the reign of God in ways that were unimaginable given the hold of existing systems and long-held assumptions on humanity's collective vision of what can be. Just as Christ heard and responded to the cries of those who called out to him even when it meant transgressing the socioreligious status quo, so Christians must enter into dialogue with reality and discern who we are called to be and what we are called to do as co-partners in the Spirit's deifying work.

Discernment: Discovering the Spirit's Will in Relationship with God and Creation

Dialogue opens persons and communities to the Holy Spirit's work of life in experience, history, and creation as a whole, deepening understanding of what is and opening new horizons for imagining what can be when flourishing is the starting point and center of gravity for theology and Christian life. Rooted in Ignatian spirituality, discernment—the second facet of the proposed approach—contemplates and evaluates understandings and possibilities that emerge from dialogue in the concrete circumstances of creaturely life. Authentic discernment draws out from these

---

[7] Chung, 35.

many possibilities the particular decision that actualizes God's life-giving intentions—what Ignatius terms "that which is more conducive to the end for which we are created."[8] In the context of a theology of flourishing, discernment proceeds by "testing the spirits" in relationship to God and creation to determine what nurtures self-actualization, or deification, for persons and socio-ecological communities. In sum, discernment is a practice of contemplating and evaluating possibilities for action in dialogue with God and creation—and God *in* creation—to discover "what belief or way of acting or living is in harmony with *who we are* and *what reality is*," to use Stoeger's turn of phrase.[9]

Discernment begins with desire for God. It takes place in the movement of reaching out toward the love of God made manifest in created reality and in being grasped and drawn toward the fullness of life by that love. In practice, discernment arises naturally from dialogue with the material world because materiality mediates the Spirit's invitation to deification. Desire for God can thus be understood as desire for one's own flourishing and the flourishing of all creation. In other words, in discovering our truest desires—in our longing for God and our hopes for what the world can be—persons and communities also come to know who we *are* and who we are called to be. Here, it is important to note that, because desires arise in the embodied conditions of creaturely life, they are conditioned by *haecceitas* and thus "gendered and socially located."[10] The outcomes of a

---

[8] George Ganss, SJ, *The Spiritual Exercises of Saint Ignatius: A Translation and Commentary* (Chicago: Loyola Press, 1992), 32.

[9] William R. Stoeger, "Is There Common Ground in Practice and Experience of Science and Religion?" panel presentation, *Science and the Spiritual Quest Conference* (Berkeley, CA: Center for Theology and the Natural Sciences, 1998), 3.

[10] Kate Stogdon, "Life, Death, and Discernment: Ignatian Perspectives," in *Grace Jantzen: Redeeming the Present,* ed. Elaine Graham, 141–55 (New York: Routledge, 2010), 150.

Dialogue, Discernment, Decision 217

person's discernment will emerge in relation to, and never apart from, a person's embodied, embedded particularity.

As Pope Francis illustrates, discernment proceeds through a process of deep questioning that touches the depths of human experience and reaches out toward the needs of the world. In his 2024 encyclical *Dilexit Nos* he writes:

> Instead of running after superficial satisfactions and playing a role for the benefit of others, we would do better to think about the really important questions in life. Who am I, really? What am I looking for? What direction do I want to give to my life, my decisions and my actions? Why and for what purpose am I in this world? How do I want to look back on my life once it ends? What meaning do I want to give to all my experiences? Who do I want to be for others? Who am I for God? (no. 8)

Questions such as these lead persons and communities beyond inclinations that may be imparted by social conditioning, internalized forces of oppression, or the status quo, opening them to love that draws *haecceitas* to fulfillment. As George Aschenbrenner puts it, "These truest desires are exposed in the objective contour of the mystery of God's saving love as revealed by Christ. . . . These deepest, truest desires are ultimately God-given, beyond any other personal influence."[11]

Because it is guided by the "objective contour" of divine love made manifest in creation and human experience, discernment has the power to unmask forces of exploitation and death in a person's relationship with God and the world. As Stogdon explains, discernment "uncovers distortions of human power

---

[11] George Aschenbrenner, SJ, *Stretched for Greater Glory: What to Expect From the Spiritual Exercises* (Chicago: Loyola Press, 2004), 9.

218   *A Theology of Flourishing*

and reveals what divine empowerment looks like."[12] Elucidating this dimension of discernment in dialogue with the parable of the Sower, Joseph Tetlow notes how easy it can be even for mature adults to become tangled in the thorns of the "racism and nationalism infecting our culture the way iron absorbs radioactivity," even to the extent that they cannot love others.[13] He also acknowledges that "some of the thorns are in our Church policies," such that people of faith experience a "tension between what 'the Church teaches' and what they sense to be true in relationship with God, as this relationship is held in prayer and communion with others."[14] When discernment leads us to recognize powers that quench the Spirit and stifle flourishing, it may lead us, in faith, down pathways that diverge from those prescribed by social and ecclesial norms. We are indeed walking in fields of grain, and sometimes we must pick grain to be fed or to feed others. Sometimes, flourishing depends on protest, resistance, and conscientious disobedience.

Making a similar point with respect to social structures and political systems, Brackley—writing in the wake of the September 11, 2001, attacks on the World Trade Center—writes that discernment with respect to sociopolitical reality should be driven by a utopian vision that looks beyond "the short-sighted 'realism'" offered by the sociopolitical status quo. "Locked into the apparent possibilities of the present, *realpolitik* cannot move beyond the 'war on terror,' nuclear deterrents, razor wire, and free-market anarchy. It is clear-sighted about selfishness but blind to human goodness and, especially, to divine grace."[15] Freeing Christians from such short-sightedness and centering us on God's life-giving will, discernment takes up different questions: "What

---

[12] Stogdon, "Life, Death, and Discernment," 150.

[13] Joseph A. Tetlow, SJ, *Always Discerning: An Ignatian Spirituality for the New Millennium* (Chicago: Loyola Press, 2016), 41.

[14] Tetlow, 41.

[15] Brackley, *The Call to Discernment*, 165.

Dialogue, Discernment, Decision 219

kind of people do we want to be? What kind of society? What kind of church? What kind of economy do we want? What kind of government?"[16] When anchored in desire for the fullness of life, dialogue ensues, but such dialogue breaks out beyond prescribed possibilities to imagine forms of church and society that manifest greater harmony with God's will for all things.

Synthesizing dialogue and desire, discernment thus contemplates possible decisions and imaginable (and presently unimaginable) futures for the world with a view toward what fosters the fullest flourishing in a given time and place. Navigating an array of possible goods and bads through holistic attunement to oneself and to reality—integrating thought, feeling, contemplation, and conversation—renders discernment as personal, communal, and spiritual work that proceeds through what Tetlow names "an appreciative awareness of the constant interplay of complex human realities we refer to as head and heart and hands."[17]

All in all, then, discerning persons and communities aim to see things "in God's sight," not in blind obedience to social norms or ecclesial teachings, nor simplistically in terms of what is moral or sinful (recall Julian's claim that in God she saw no sin) but in terms of what leads to the fullest realization of who one is: what brings about a new inbreaking of *viriditas*, what fosters new creation. Invoking the Johannine vision of love in action, Tetlow makes the point well:

> We perceive the "facts" from a viewpoint fixed in faith in an ongoing Creator of all things seen and unseen. We look at the available options hopefully and lovingly, expecting to find values for the present life that will go beyond merely avoiding sin. What we want is to grow continually in the *image* and likeness of God who is love. So when we come

---

[16] Brackley, 166.
[17] Tetlow, *Always Discerning*, 5.

to decide what to do, we intend to *love, not in word or speech, but in truth and action* (1 John 3:18).[18]

Throughout this growth into God's image and likeness—what we may also term deification—flourishing emerges again the surest sign of the Spirit's presence. As persons and communities experience the joy that accompanies self-actualization, integration, and wholeness, they receive confirmation that God is truly at work in and among them. This brings us to decision.

Decision: Self-Actualization that Reaches to the Ends of Creation

From dialogue and contemplation a discerning person arrives at the point of decision. As the preceding analysis demonstrates, in a framework of flourishing, decision-making proceeds on the basis of discerning what cultivates fullness of life in the widest possible way. This orientation changes the question from, "Is this decision right or wrong?" according to prescribed conventions to, "Will this decision foster the fulfillment of God's life-giving will for me and for all creation? Will this action foster the liberation that enables me and others to experience fullness of life in communion with God and creation a whole?" In keeping with the overall arc of a theology of flourishing, this understanding of decision-making resituates the question, "Is this action sinful?" under the rubric of the fullness of life.

To be clear from the start, this is not license for moral relativism. Rather, this conception of discernment-driven decision-making takes with full seriousness what Joseph Ratzinger names the "non-arbitrary character and objectivity of conscience." Elaborating this principle, Ratzinger writes that conscience operates as "the inner complement and limit of the Church

---

[18] Tetlow, 18.

Dialogue, Discernment, Decision

principle. Over the pope as the expression of the binding claim of ecclesiastical authority there still stands one's own conscience, which must be obeyed before all else, if necessary even against the requirement of ecclesiastical authority."[19] The theological foundation for this understanding of conscience rests in the inviolability of the Spirit's work within the *haecceitas* of each creature. As persons and communities pursue their deepest desires in relationship and are deified in union with God, they will freely follow this inner law of conscience. As Congar puts it, "This freedom is not a license dependent on whim, which is an illusory freedom or a caricature of freedom that in fact destroys true freedom if it is taken too far." Rather, "the Christian into whom the Holy Spirit has poured the love of God will spontaneously observe a law which can be summed up in love."[20] Expressed in concrete action, love is the surest sign of the Spirit's work. And loving actions that foster the fulfillment of God's intentions will not be sinful, even if they contravene authority.

Here, the degree to which a decision manifests God's life-giving aims emerges as a basis for assessing the authenticity of discernment. This point is rendered especially important in light of the revolutionary character of Christ's love and the possibility that discernment may lead to decisions that diverge from established socio-ecclesial norms. Ultimately, God affirms the validity of any decision. Yet commentators note that feelings of lightness, joy, and wholeness—what the Ignatian tradition names consolation—confirm that the Spirit is at work. Through such consolation, Tetlow writes, "I can know that I really *believe* that God is creating me as I am and loves me as I am, when I am saying a great yes to myself, content with my life. . . . The idea

---

[19] Joseph Ratzinger, in *Commentary on the Documents of Vatican II,* vol. V: *Pastoral Constitution on the Church in the Modern World,* ed. Herbert Vorgrimler, trans. Walter Abbott (New York: Herder and Herder, 1969), 134.

[20] Yves M. J. Congar, *I Believe in the Holy Spirit,* vol. 2: *The Holy Spirit in the "Economy,"* trans. David Smith (New York: Seabury Press, 1983), 125.

222 *A Theology of Flourishing*

is that I can be happy and flourishing as long as I accept who I really am."[21] Consolation is the surest sign of the Spirit's presence in discernment and decision. As throughout Christian life, the interior freedom that emerges from authentic discernment confirms the validity of our decision-making, which expresses itself in a deeper capacity for love of self and love of neighbor.

Yet this is not only an individual matter. As Brackley explains, "Whereas Ignatius limits consolation to personal experience, consolation has social and political dimensions."[22] Indeed, because *haecceitas* is actualized relationally, authentic discernment is contextual and political; deciding what is most life-giving for an individual person also entails acting in a way that gives life to others and to creation as a whole. As Tetlow puts it, "Through discernment, we come to work with God working in the world."[23] By discovering their deepest desires in dialogue with God and the world, persons and communities actualize God's work by bringing the love of God, mediated through their unique gifts, to the needs of the world. In this way the self-actualization that accompanies a Spirit-guided decision breaks out beyond the individual, drawing others into God's deifying love, "evoking an endlessly recreative action in which human beings participate not as masters but as co-creators of an ecstatic outpouring of love."[24]

Therefore, given the integration of the individual and communal, of *haecceitas* and the contextual, a theology of flourishing also observes an intrinsic coherence between the subjective experience of consolation in the human heart and the objective realization of God's life-giving intentions through a deified person's life in the world. In practice, then, even when we are not conscious of it, the Spirit's movements in a person or community

---

[21] Tetlow, *Always Discerning*, 51.

[22] Brackley, *The Call to Discernment*, 204.

[23] Tetlow, *Always Discerning*, 15.

[24] Stogdon, "Life, Death, and Discernment," 149.

Dialogue, Discernment, Decision 223

will harmonize that person or community with God's life-giving intentions, leading to the discovery of new horizons for holiness and new ways of fostering God's life-giving aims. Here, in keeping with the revolutionary love of Christ Jesus, we "live the love that God has poured into humankind—by loving those whom God gives us and by taking care of anyone whose need calls on our gifts."[25] Together, the integration of subjective and objective confirmation of a decision reveals the fulfillment of the Spirit's aims. Ultimately, however, these confirmations are one and the same. A decision that gives life to the individual person or community will find confirmation in the life that person or community brings to the world and vice-versa. Love is the heart of discernment, and concrete acts of love are the surest sign of the Spirit's work of life within and among us.

The Ignatian maxim *ad majorem Dei gloriam*—for the greater glory of God—functions as an integrating principle for the approach to flourishing this chapter has proposed. Just as Irenaeus held that the glory of God is the living human person, so the fulfillment of dialogue and discernment in decisions that foster flourishing glorify the Creator of all. This glory—made manifest in the fulfillment of each person, creature, and creation as a whole—orients all things toward their final fulfillment in the fullness of life, wherein "all in the kingdom are filled with divine splendor and totally divinized in Christ, the refulgence of God."[26]

Guiding us toward this vision, the movement of dialogue, discernment, and decision deepens our self-engagement and our engagement with reality as a whole, leading us to discover God's life-giving will mediated in all things. In seeking to actualize this will, we continually ask Stoeger's question: "Is our self-engagement and our engagement with the larger reality of which we

---

[25] Tetlow, *Always Discerning*, 6.

[26] Jules J. Toner, *Discerning God's Will: Ignatius of Loyola's Teaching on Christian Decision Making* (Saint Louis: Institute of Jesuit Sources, 1991), 15.

are a part ultimately fruitful and life-giving or not—for ourselves and others?"[27] In discerning answers to this question and taking action in love, we come to perceive and reveal the Holy Spirit working all around us, inviting us to fulfillment, deifying us and all creation—drawing all things into the fullness of life. In all this our greatest consolation lies in the joy, wholeness, and integration that flourishing brings—the *viriditas* that breaks forth when we open our hearts and minds to the Spirit at work in every corner of creation. With this approach in place, I conclude by considering the implications of a theology of flourishing for praxis, seeking a Christianity that lives out *amor mundi*, love of the world, in service of the flourishing of all things.

---

[27] William R. Stoeger, SJ, "Rationality and Wonder: From Scientific Cosmology to Philosophy and Theology," in *Astronomy and Civilization in the New Enlightenment: Passions of the Skies: Analecta Husserliana: The Yearbook of Phenomenological Research*, vol. 107, ed. Anna-Teresa Tymieniecka and Attila Grandpierre (New York: Springer, 2011), 260.

Conclusion

Toward a Praxis of Flourishing

Having come to theology from a career as a liturgist and liturgical musician, reaching the end of a writing process like this one feels like an Easter Sunday afternoon. Our commemoration of the Paschal Mystery is complete. Narratives of creation, liberation, suffering, and resurrection have been proclaimed; redemption has been remembered in water, wine, and wheat; voices have been raised in hymns of praise; all things have been swept up in the feast of new creation. God's people emerge from this commemoration reminded that life can arise even from death, that peace and justice can reign where once violence and oppression held sway. We emerge reminded of the promise of the fullness of life that stands at the heart of a theology of flourishing and, indeed, of our Christian faith. After all the work of bringing this mystery to light—bringing all the elements of our remembrance together—Easter Sunday afternoon comes as a sudden, unexpected silence.

On one such afternoon, after one such Triduum at St. Mary Parish, I stepped out from the eucharistic chapel at the back of our church building into a small garden that lay between our ministry center and parish house. Roses and tulips, newly abloom, circled a small pond beneath a towering elm. Bees

226 *A Theology of Flourishing*

buzzed amid the buds, as they would a decade later during an outdoor Easter Vigil at Mission Santa Clara. As birds hopped about in the pond and sang in the elm's branches, I found myself suddenly attuned to creation's liturgy of praise—a liturgy that had been going on before and during our comparatively meager celebrations inside the church. I saw around me the same mystery I had celebrated with my siblings in faith: the glorious mystery of new creation—the joy of human flourishing united to the flourishing of innumerable other creatures through the death and resurrection of Christ and the *viriditas*—the greening power—of the Holy Spirit.

Animated by this vision of the glory of creation fully alive in God's presence, this book has aimed to retrieve from the riches of scripture and tradition a theology that takes flourishing—the fullness of life for all creation—as a starting point and center of gravity for Christian thought and praxis. Building on this *ressourcement*, or return to the sources of our faith, I have proposed a theology that places abundant life (John 10:10) at the heart of Christian theology and so fosters a praxis of revolutionary love that denounces injustice, degradation, and oppression and works in faith on behalf of the fulfillment of God's principal intention—that all things may flourish in the fullness of life. To conclude this work, I offer a few final thoughts on the praxis of a theology of flourishing and its implications for four questions in contemporary life.

Christianity as Contemplation in Loving Action

As a fruit of the practice of discernment, the Ignatian tradition speaks of forming people to be contemplatives in action. In light of the paradigm of dialogue, discernment, and decision proposed in the ninth chapter, I suggest that Christianity as a whole can be characterized in this way, as a means toward contemplation in loving action, contemplation that leads to a

Toward a Praxis of Flourishing

praxis of life-giving love of the world, *amor mundi*, on behalf of the fullness of life for all things. Given this vision, a theology of flourishing aims to cultivate two forms of contemplation, what I term *sentire cum humanum* and *sentire cum terra*, as a foundation for Christian life.[1]

Sentire cum humanum contemplates human experience, the *humanum*, through the lens of flourishing. Uniting thought and feeling (*sentir*), such contemplation requires radical hospitality, a willingness to listen deeply to others and respond in ways that foster the fullness of life. *Sentire cum humanum* entails a bold willingness to be truly present to and stay with suffering, discerning what one can do to foster others' flourishing through practices of compassionate care. On the level of communities, structures, and systems, *sentire cum humanum* is the bedrock of solidarity. It fosters awareness of how structures of oppression shape collective experience and enables us to imagine new possibilities for the human family. As Jantzen puts it, just as "the commonalities and multiplicities of oppression can be seen, by those engaged in the struggle for insight, as an invitation to solidarity," recognizing oppression provides a foundation for struggling "alongside one another to develop space for the woman subject, for the love of the world, embodied in our living communities."[2] In pursuing this vision, *sentire cum humanum* finds in narratives of suffering and survival, oppression and liberation, seeds for discernment and action that abolish systems of oppression, liberating persons to experience the fullness of life according to their beloved *haecceitas* and communities to flourish according to their own

---

[1] I first proposed the idea of *sentire cum terra* in an essay that places *Laudato Si'* in dialogue with Stoeger's writings and Ignatian spirituality. See Paul J. Schutz, "Cultivating a 'Cosmic Perspective' in Theology: Reading William R. Stoeger with *Laudato Si'*," *Theological Studies* 80, no. 4 (December 2019): 798–821.

[2] Grace M. Jantzen, *Becoming Divine: Towards a Feminist Philosophy of Religion* (Bloomington: Indiana University Press, 1999), 216.

228 *A Theology of Flourishing*

unique sociocultural and linguistic ways of being: their inviolable "thisness."

Sentire cum terra takes up a similar approach toward other-than-human creatures and ecological communities. Refusing to view nonhuman creatures as resources to be extracted and exploited or as inferior to humans, *sentire cum terra* contemplates creation as it is in its own integrity and discerns courses of action in view of the roles creatures play in the systems of life they inhabit, manifesting God's life-giving aims. As Wirzba states, within such a vision "an oak tree . . . is no longer simply a vertical log containing so many board feet of lumber. It is a vital member of a diverse ecosystem in which a bewildering array of geophysical, biochemical processes are at work so that it, along with other creatures, can flourish."[3] Crucially, this means seeing other creatures *as they are*, not *as we think they are*. This orientation also guides humans to recognize the unique, and uniquely limited, place we occupy in creation and positions us to hear other creatures on their terms, not ours. For indeed, as Eric Daryl Meyer observes, "Since many animals communicate regularly, we must acknowledge that they have something to say—even when it is not to us."[4] Informed by science and guided by prayerful discernment, *sentire cum terra* allows other-than-human creatures to speak to us from their *haecceitas*, calling us to act in ways that promote the fullness of life for all creatures and ecosystems in solidarity with and in equal relation to human systems.

This vision also requires being present to the reality of other-than-human suffering, with a particular focus on human

---

[3] Norman Wirzba, *The Paradise of God: Renewing Religion in an Ecological Age* (Oxford: Oxford University Press, 2007), 155.

[4] Eric Daryl Meyer, "They Fell Silent When We Stopped Listening: Apophatic Theology and 'Asking the Beasts,'" in *Turning to the Heavens and the Earth: Theological Reflections on a Cosmological Conversion*, ed. Julia Brumbaugh and Natalia Imperatori-Lee, 26–44 (Collegeville, MN: Liturgical Press, 2016), 32.

Toward a Praxis of Flourishing

practices that cause other-than-human creatures to suffer. To be clear, a theology of flourishing cannot explain, much less give value to, evolutionary suffering. To my mind, such suffering simply is. As Johnson observes, we can trust that as the source of life, God is present to this suffering, desiring that life come out of death.[5] We humans can also be present to animal suffering. We can stay with it and work on behalf of the alleviation of suffering for our other-than-human kin, especially those we willfully disregard to justify inhumane testing and farming practices.

When linked together, *sentire cum humanum* and *sentire cum terra* orient Christianity to see reality in holistic, socio-ecological perspective, offering fertile ground for contemplation and action. Pondering the interiority of a squirrel outside a window might lead us to ponder our own sense of self. The fragrance of basil might attune us to the "dearest freshness deep down things."[6] A wilting vine might attune us to the thirst of those who lack access to clean water while others drink from plastic water bottles that degrade ecosystems. Reflecting on the significance of water, the source of life, might also deepen contemplation of the living water that is Christ Jesus. For if God's life-giving action pervades every nook and cranny of the cosmos, then the creaturely work of building habitats, gathering food, and caring for the young manifests God's intentions among human and other-than-human creatures alike. Contemplating creation in this way may therefore enrich our understanding of our own creatureliness and open our eyes to new ways of fostering abundant life for all creation. As a unity, *sentire cum terra* and *sentire cum humanum* have the potential to bring about a transformation of Christian life that, in parallel with creation's own revelation of God's glory, breaks forth

---

[5] See Elizabeth Johnson, *Ask the Beasts: Darwin and the God of Love* (London: Bloomsbury, 2015), chap. 7.

[6] Gerard Manley Hopkins, "God's Grandeur."

230 *A Theology of Flourishing*

in the realization of Christ's command to "go and do likewise" (Lk 10:37) on behalf of the flourishing of *all*.

Amor Mundi: **The Praxis of Flourishing**

Guided by the contemplative practices of *sentire cum humanum* and *sentire cum terra*, a theology of flourishing enables us to see the interconnectedness of all creatures and behold with new clarity God's life-giving intentions at work in all things. This contemplation draws us into an inclusive vision that sees reality in the plural, with all things united to one another and to God in relationships of mutual flourishing. Santos explains:

> This integral inclusive vision of flourishing necessitates reciprocity and mutuality where all persons can learn from each other, challenge each other and work together towards enabling, experiencing and enjoying life in abundance. Flourishing can never be individualistic or experienced in isolation. It is always in relation to others in its concern for the wellbeing of all persons and the cosmos.[7]

Practically speaking, this vision enables us to see socio-ecological structures and systems, including our place within them, in their interrelatedness and interconnectedness, fostering what Pope Francis in *Laudato Si'* describes as a "sense of fraternity that excludes nothing and no one" (no. 92). At the same time this vision enables us to see the many ways in which Francis's hopes remain unrealized, stifled by individual and collective participation in structures of sin that—like the thief in John 10:10—kill, steal, and destroy. In either case, seeing the interconnectedness of

---

[7] Patricia H. Santos, "That All May Enjoy Abundant Life: A Theological Vision of Flourishing from the Margins," *Feminist Theology* 25, no. 3 (2017): 238.

Toward a Praxis of Flourishing

231

socioecosystems in the light of flourishing calls Christians to a revolutionary praxis of *amor mundi*, love of the world, that fosters the fullness of life—the glory for which all things were made.

Amor mundi proceeds with a critical sense of what gives life and what destroys it. As in theologies of liberation, *amor mundi* calls churches to denounce forces of death and announce the reign of God in word and deed, working to build a world in which all creatures may flourish in the fullness of what they are in accordance with the Spirit's aims.[8] Moreover, as a fundamental expression of Christian faith, this praxis calls churches to acknowledge their own responsibility for and complicity in injustice. Beyond just proclaiming salvation, churches must be willing to recognize and dismantle all sources of injustice and oppression, even those that lie within, as an expression of their faithfulness to a God who made all things and desires their fulfillment. Truly, as Johnson writes, "the church must be about the business of the reign of God in order for its thought about Jesus Christ to be true."[9] Anchored by a vision of creation fully alive, a theology of flourishing thus calls churches and all Christians to work on behalf of a socio-ecological order in which all things may flourish in communion with God and one another.

While this vision of the abolition of necrophilic logics is a utopian vision, this does not mean that conflict will cease. It means that churches and their members will learn to navigate conflicts lovingly, centered on what promotes the fullness of life in every moment. For, with fullness of life in mind, situations of conflict become sites of discernment, opportunities to contemplate and actualize God's life-giving intentions in difficult heres and nows. As such, while conflict may lead to the abolition of

---

[8] On annunciation and denunciation, see Gustavo Gutiérrez, *A Theology of Liberation: History, Politics, and Salvation,* rev. ed., trans. Sister Caridad Inda and John Eagleson (Maryknoll, NY: Orbis Books, 1988), 68–69; 150–54.

[9] Elizabeth Johnson, *Consider Jesus: Waves of Renewal in Christology* (New York: Crossroad, 1990), 62.

232   *A Theology of Flourishing*

systems and structures that perpetuate death, including those
that glorify war, abolition rooted in flourishing aims always to
deepen connections rather than destroy them.[10] Abolition tears
down walls that divide creatures, providing new opportunities
to attune ourselves to the radical interconnectedness that lies
beyond rhetoric and propaganda and discern new paths toward
the realization of God's life-giving intentions through a revolutionary praxis of love for the world.

Four Test Cases for a Theology of Flourishing

Since we have come this far together, it seems fitting to conclude
this work by reflecting on how the theological and praxiological
framework I have proposed bears on a few questions of contemporary concern that have become especially important in my
own research and practice. Others may apply this framework and
reach different conclusions. The reflections I offer here simply
aim to illustrate how a theology of flourishing might approach
and respond to issues affecting the contemporary church and
world.

Women's Ordination

Within the context of a theology of flourishing, the question
of women's ordination in the Roman Catholic Church takes
on new significance as a test of our attunement to experience
and confidence in the Spirit's work of new creation. As Johnson

---

[10] In other words, recognizing the inevitability of conflict must not be taken
as a justification for war. The abolition of necrophilic logics means an abolition
of war as a political strategy, profit-generating scheme, or show of might—in
a word, war as a *choice*. Seeking God's life-giving will amid conflict will never
involve weapons of war; to use instruments of death is always, even in the rare
case of a "just war" (if such a thing exists), to choose death over life, necrophilia
over flourishing.

Toward a Praxis of Flourishing

observes, in the context of ministry, attunement to experience reveals how women—though excluded by patriarchy from sacramental roles—have "consistently found ways to resist the official constriction of their lives, at times mounting public challenge in the spirit of prophecy."[11] Amid such a reality, the Spirit's work in baptism—the foundation of every vocation—elicits a critical observation. If "baptism does not discriminate," as Galatians 3:28 indicates, and if "this sacrament consecrates a female human being profoundly to God," then the grace of this sacrament of new creation naturally implies the possibility that women can be called to ordained ministry as agents of the Spirit's life-giving aims.[12]

Building on Johnson's analysis, a theology of flourishing asks whether the Holy Spirit's work of new creation could entail the possibility of women being called to ordained ministry and whether the admission of women to the priesthood and diaconate might provide new opportunities for women and all Christians to experience the fullness of life for which they are made. In other words, if ordaining women would actualize the Spirit's work and lead the whole faithful to encounter the mystery of divine love in new ways—in hearing the gospel proclaimed from new perspectives—then this question cannot be said to be permanently closed. In light of the proposed framework, this is preeminently a matter of discernment, not of teaching imposed from the outside.

For indeed, considering the question of women's ordination through a lens of flourishing resituates the interpretation of tradition within God's intention that all creatures may flourish and makes that intention the starting point and center of gravity for the question of who has access to holy orders. Such

---

[11] Elizabeth Johnson, *She Who Is: The Mystery of God in Feminist Theological Discourse* (New York: Crossroad, 1991), 122.

[12] Elizabeth A. Johnson, "'Your One Wild and Precious Life': Women on the Road of Ministry," *Theological Studies* 80, no. 1 (2019): 207–8.

234   *A Theology of Flourishing*

a shift calls us to reevaluate arguments about the "natural resemblance" of the priest's body to Jesus's male body and the
claim that the church has "no authority whatsoever" to ordain
women because Christ chose "his Apostles only from among
men."[13] Using the rubric of flourishing, the question changes:
What new possibilities is the Spirit offering us in view of both
tradition and women's narratives of discernment and the call
to serve? Crucially, this shift would mean that the only way to
declare the discussion of women's ordination permanently closed
is to assert that it is categorically impossible for the *Holy Spirit*
to call women to ordained ministry. If ecclesial leaders are willing to make such a claim about what the Spirit can and cannot
do, then the conversation will indeed by closed—not because
the Spirit cannot work such wonders but because we have so
hardened our hearts that we are willing to quench the Spirit and
foreclose possibilities for flourishing to defend patriarchy's hold
on church and society. And all the while, we proclaim that "for
God all things are possible" (Mt 19:26).

LGBTQ+ *Inclusion*

Against interpretations of Genesis that use the face-value meaning of the text as a basis for articulating a "natural law" that
justifies the marginalization of LGBTQ+ persons, a theology of
flourishing asks what fullness of life looks like in the embodied
haecceitas of queer people.[14] As with women's ordination, this

---

[13] On "natural resemblance," see Congregation for the Doctrine of the
Faith, *Inter Insigniores: On the Question of Admission of Women to the Ministerial
Priesthood* (October 15, 1976). On authority, see John Paul II, *Ordinatio Sacer-
dotalis* (May 22, 1994).

[14] I have previously written about this question in relationship to biblical
interpretation and theological method. See Paul J. Schutz, "En-Gendering Creation Anew: Rethinking Ecclesial Statements on Science, Gender, and Sexuality
with William R. Stoeger, SJ," *Horizons: The Journal of the College Theology Society*
48, no. 1 (June 2021): 34–68.

Toward a Praxis of Flourishing 235

question demands deep dialogue with experience, a willingness to let queer narratives disrupt long-held assumptions about what it means to be human. Rooted in the life-giving grace of baptism, this dialogue begins by acknowledging the real desire of queer persons to flourish *in the church*, to experience church as a space where they can seek God in their queerness—rather than as a place of exclusion, condemnation, and even violence. For, within a framework of flourishing, queer desire is a rightful foundation for discernment. This discernment may lead to the conclusion that queerness is an authentic, beloved, and integral expression of *haecceitas*, such that queer persons must be liberated to live authentically according to their *haecceitas* in church and society.[15]

As Jantzen observes, realizing this vision will not be easy given heterosexism's hold on the Christian imagination. She writes: "Certainly building a theology from within, enabling our queer shapes to emerge and flourish, is no easy option: it is sustained reflective work that is both costly and liberatory, the very opposite of careless relativism. It involves living always with the question: what do you long for most of all, and what are you doing to prevent it?"[16] As such, taking the question of what gives and obstructs fullness of life as a primary hermeneutical norm changes the context in which churches consider the question of queerness. If sustained dialogue and discernment produce

---

[15] I am not the first to link gender, sexuality, and *haecceitas* in this way. See Daniel P. Horan, "Beyond Essentialism and Complementarity: Toward a Theological Anthropology Rooted in *Haecceitas*," *Theological Studies* 75, no. 1 (2014), and *Catholicity and Emerging Personhood: A Contemporary Theological Anthropology* (Maryknoll, NY: Orbis Books, 2019). The writings of Todd Salzman and Michael Lawler also provide helpful resources for thinking about the concrete particularity of LGBTQ+ experience. See, for example, Todd A. Salzman and Michael G. Lawler, *Sexual Ethics: A Theological Introduction* (Washington, DC: Georgetown University Press, 2012).

[16] Grace M. Jantzen, "Contours of a Queer Theology," *Literature and Theology* 15, no. 3 (September 2001): 285.

opportunities for queer persons to actualize themselves in relationship with God and others, even in ways that run counter to traditional understandings, then we can conclude with confidence in the Holy Spirit that, as Craig Ford observes, "living into one's sex and gender identity is part of the larger journey towards fulfillment in one's relationship with one's self, with others, with the world, and with God."[17]

In theology, such discernment also provides a seedbed for theological anthropologies that bring empirical insights to bear on theological understandings of the human person. Here, it is vital to emphasize that the sciences do not offer theological answers in themselves; science is a dialogue partner for theology—and only that. Further, maintaining focus on flourishing demands that theology engage in such dialogue with a critical awareness of the ways science has been and continues to be used as an instrument of violence, as it was in the case of race-based eugenics and the sterilization of queer people and people with disabilities. Still, as Terrence Tilley notes, given the importance of scientific insights into phenomena like gender dysphoria and the link between sexual expression and the integrity of human persons and relationships, "We need an understanding of human nature that incorporates the sciences that portray natural, social and cultural evolution if we want to understand what it means to be human and to be flourishing humans."[18] If scientific knowledge enables theology to discern what is life-giving for LGBTQ+ persons, then theology has a responsibility to listen.

---

[17] Craig A. Ford Jr., "Transgender Bodies, Catholic Schools, and a Queer Natural Law Theology of Exploration," *The Journal of Moral Theology* 7, no. 1 (2018): 94. For a further study of this question, see Craig A. Ford Jr., "Our New Galileo Affair," *Horizons_*50, no. 2 (2023): 255–92.

[18] Terrence W. Tilley, "Challenges of Empirical Research for Theological Anthropology," in *Critical Questions in Contemporary Theology: Essays in Honour of Dermot A. Lane*, ed. Ethna Regan and Alan J. Kearns, 187–98 (New York: Peter Lang, 2024), 198.

Toward a Praxis of Flourishing

This discussion carries profound pastoral implications, as well. LGBTQ+ youth are four times more likely than their peers to attempt suicide.[19] Over 80 percent of trans people contemplate suicide, and over 40 percent of trans people have attempted suicide. Conversely, access to gender-affirming care causes these rates to drop by as much as 73 percent.[20] As Horan observes, in view of statistics like these the church's narrow anthropology manifests a "pastoral malpractice" that amounts to a death sentence for many LGBTQ+ persons.[21] Indeed, in light of such statistics, remaining silent or choosing to condemn LGBTQ+ persons amid the unspeakable suffering they endure amounts to saying that they are "better off dead"—an explicit affront to God's life-giving will.[22] Yet in receiving queer persons as they are in their beloved *haecceitas*, in staying with the suffering that too often accompanies queer experience, Christians exercise a preferential option for LGBTQ+ persons and stand in solidarity with them as they discern what it means to flourish, which is surely what God intends.

Environmental Racism

Because a theology of flourishing thinks holistically, linking social and ecological justice under the rubric of God's reign, it enables us to see clearly the intersection of social injustice and ecological degradation and so provides a resource for deepening analysis of complex issues from the standpoint of faith. Environmental

---

[19] "Facts About Suicide among LGBTQ+ Young People," *The Trevor Project* online (January 2024).

[20] Giuliana Grossi, "Suicide Risk Reduces 73% in Transgender, Nonbinary Youths with Gender-Affirming Care," *HCMLive* online (March 8, 2022).

[21] Daniel P. Horan, "Church's Anti-LGBTQ Policies Drive People Away— and the Policies Are Sinful, Too," *National Catholic Reporter,* September 22, 2022.

[22] For further reflection on this point, see Paul J. Schutz, "A Response to the Vatican Document 'Male and Female He Created Them,'" *National Catholic Reporter,* June 24, 2019.

238   *A Theology of Flourishing*

racism is one such issue. Illustrating what environmental racism is and how it functions, Aruna Gnanadason observes that communities of color are much more likely than white communities to be located near hazardous waste sites. The correlation is so significant that one can predict the location of communities of color using a map of hazardous waste dumps.[23] Enabled by global capitalist expansionism and a "not in my backyard" mentality, environmental racism links racial injustice and ecological degradation according to a necrophilic logic that exploits lands and peoples to the explicit benefit of white people and communities and the degradation of communities of color. Gnanadason explains:

> Dumping of toxic wastes and unaccountable dirty industries plague poor and minority communities in rich countries and poor developing nations and are a symptom of deep environmental racism. When the pollution of their own backyard becomes problematic, then waste needs to be disposed of elsewhere, either in the global commons of the oceans and the atmosphere or through their sale to Third World societies plagued by foreign debt.[24]

This socio-ecological reality unites the cry of the earth and the cry of the poor into a single cry of protest against a double degradation of life. Simply, such a double degradation should not be, especially in a world where Christians profess faith in a God who hears the cry of the poor and desires the fullness of life for all. In the face of such a reality a theology of flourishing demands protest and action on behalf of people of color and the earth, as both have a God-given right to flourish. Attunement to the

---

[23] Aruna Gnanadason, "The Integrity of Creation and Earth Community: An Ecumenical Response to Environmental Racism," *Union Seminary Quarterly Review* 58 (2004): 97–119 at 99.

[24] Gnanadason, "The Integrity of Creation," 108.

Toward a Praxis of Flourishing

239

reality of environmental racism thus elicits new opportunities for Christians to actualize the revolutionary love of Christ toward the transformation and abolition of systems that enslave and oppress. Such transformation aims to build a world in which all peoples, indeed all creatures, are enabled to flourish on their own terms in life-giving communion with their lands. In communion, people are empowered to bring their communities and cultures toward fulfillment according to God's intentions rather than the principles of extractive systems of exchange that kill, steal, and destroy.

Liturgy and Worship

To bring these reflections to a close, I return to liturgy, the place from which this study of flourishing began. In step with what I witnessed Sunday after Sunday at St. Mary, a theology of flourishing envisions the Eucharist—*when celebrated in fullness of heart, mind, and voice*—as a locus of individual and collective self-actualization and a training ground for the praxis of *amor mundi*. Admittedly, this account of worship puts a high premium on "full and active participation by all the people," what *Sacrosanctum Concilium* names "the aim to be considered before all else . . . the primary and indispensable source from which the faithful are to derive the true Christian spirit" (no. 14). Yet if active participation enables assemblies to encounter the living God and, by this encounter, be drawn into the grace of deification that leads to the fullness of life, then it is indeed indispensable—a foundation for flourishing. In such a case the eucharistic liturgy—through word, song, motion, and silence—has the potential to attune assemblies to the Spirit's presence and action in all things and form them to see every creature as made to flourish according to its *haecceitas*, guiding them toward contemplation in loving action on behalf of the fullness of life.

It can be difficult to specify how authentic participation facilitates such an encounter. In faith, we profess that, in our real

240   *A Theology of Flourishing*

presence to Christ in worship, Christ becomes really present to us. Christ calls to us in the depths of our hearts and minds, inviting us to join him in the deifying journey toward the fullness of who we are. Given what I witnessed and experienced at St. Mary, I have long been captivated by Aidan Kavanagh's suggestion, drawn from Urban Holmes, that "good liturgy borders on the vulgar" and "leads regularly to the edge of chaos."[25] In view of the radical in-breaking of divine love enacted through the eucharistic liturgy, I imagine the vulgarity and chaos of which Kavanagh speaks as markers of an encounter so profound and transformative that it unsettles facile, status quo sensibilities about the world and human identity and opens humans to being re-created by the Spirit as agents of new creation, who bring Christ's revolutionary love to the needs of the world. Kavanagh schematizes this transformation in a discussion of a gradual "adjustment" in the eucharistic assembly—a growth in holiness, a deification—that makes every liturgical act different from the one that preceded it because, when worship is authentic and the "true Christian spirit" is attained, the assembly never returns to the eucharistic table the same as it was before. Each liturgy facilitates a new, yet always authentic, encounter with the God who makes all things new. Kavanagh writes:

> In the liturgical instance, what has happened is an adjustment in the assembly of participants to its having been brought to the brink of chaos in the previous liturgical act. This adjustment causes the next liturgical act to be in some degree different from its predecessor because those who do the next act have been unalterably changed. . . . The growth is a function of adjustment to deep change caused

---

[25] Aidan Kavanagh, *On Liturgical Theology* (Collegeville, MN: Liturgical Press, 1994), 73.

in the assembly by its being brought regularly to the brink of chaos in the presence of the living God.[26]

In Kavanagh's understanding—an understanding I found to be true each Sunday as I stood united with my siblings in faith at St. Mary—good liturgy ultimately fosters a renewed sense of *orthodoxia*, not meaning "correct doctrine" but rather "right worship," what Kavanagh names "a life of communion in all God's holy things and among his holy persons . . . open unalterably to all people everywhere without let or hindrance."[27] Seen in this way, liturgy can be a seedbed for flourishing, an inroad that, in embodied word and action, leads toward the praxis of *amor mundi* on the model of the Word made flesh. Liturgy can make Christians agents of salvation: of the *viriditas* that makes all things new.

Near the end of *Ask the Beasts* Elizabeth Johnson declares, "A flourishing humanity on a thriving planet rich in species in an evolving universe, all together filled with the glory of God: such is the vision that must guide us at this critical time of Earth's distress, to practical and critical effect."[28] Sharing this vision for what can and must be, we have traced the precious thread of flourishing through the tapestry of our tradition. Once suppressed, we now see it woven through stories of creation, life and liberation; in God's collaboration with earth and in ineffable love enfleshed; in creation's glory and in care for others; in the *viriditas* of creation and in love that sees no sin; in human transcendence and the work of justice; in the Holy Spirit's stirrings in creation

---

[26] Kavanagh, 74.
[27] Kavanagh, 81.
[28] Johnson, *Ask the Beasts*, 286.

and in discerning human hearts; in all these places and more, we find this precious thread proclaiming a God who is life and who desires life—the fullness of life—for all creation. In this proclamation of life, we see salvation anew. Salvation is not an escape from this world but a deeper entry into the promise of abundant life here and now as we hope for the fulfillment of all things in perfect union with God. As we contemplate creation's wonders and act in love of the world, may God grant us the grace to discern our own paths toward the fullness of life and our own ways of fostering that fullness for others—as we walk, guided by the Spirit of life, with the one who came that all creation "may have life and have it abundantly" (Jn 10:10).

Index

Abraham, 54–55
Adam (*ha'adam*), 49–50, 53–54, 128
Adam, Margaret, 179–80
Against Heresies (Irenaeus), 95–102
Akiba, Rabbi, 80
alafia (well-being), 24
Allison, Dale, 79–80, 82, 83
Alter, Robert, 60
amor mundi
    Christian practice of, 6, 143, 201, 224
    liturgy as leading toward, 239, 241
    in a model of flourishing, 10
    as a praxis of flourishing, 226–27, 230–32
Anatolios, Khaled, 102–3
Anderson, Bernard, 68
Anselm of Canterbury, 119
anthropocentrism
    anthropocentric bias, 41–42, 44–45, 47–48
    eudaimonia as anthropocentric, 31
    in the Hebrew Bible, 37–38
    in Hildegard of Bingen, 118–19, 122

    in Irenaeus of Lyons, 96
    in Nicholas of Cusa, 143
    Saint-Maurice on, 129–30
Aquinas, Thomas, 52, 124, 125–26, 127
Arendt, Hannah, 6
Aschenbrenner, George, 217
Asian women's theology, 214–15
Ask the Beasts (Johnson), 241
Athanasius of Alexandria
    Contra Gentiles, 104
    Gregory and, 110–11
    maxim on becoming God, 102–3, 159–60
    in theology of flourishing, 91, 95, 102–5
Augustine of Hippo, 93

Bacon, Francis, 38–39
Basil of Caesarea, 45–46, 65
Bauckham, Richard, 38–39, 47, 69–70, 71, 90
Bauerschmidt, Frederick, 138
Behr, John, 101
Berry, Wendell, 174–75
Book of Divine Works (Hildegard), 115, 118
Brackley, Dean, 211, 218, 222

243

244   *Index*

Brown, Raymond, 70, 85–86, 87–88, 89
Brown, William, 40, 45, 58, 59, 61, 63
Brueggemann, Walter, 40, 56–57, 61

Canlis, Julie, 96
Cardman, Francine, 95
Cerinthianism, 85
Childs, Brevard, 79
Chung, Hyun Kyung, 213–15
circumcision, 72, 74
climate change, 13, 30
Clough, David, 43–44
Coblentz, Jessica, 195–96
Cone, James, 198
Congar, Yves, 186, 221
conscience, 220–21
consolation, 221–22, 224
Contra Gentiles (Athanasius), 104
Copeland, M. Shawn, 18, 19, 198
COVID-19 pandemic, 173–74
creation imagination, 58
crucified people, 167–68, 169
cultural cosmologies, 36–37
Cuomo, Chris, 3, 4

Davis, Ellen, 45
Deane-Drummond, Celia, xxv
decision, 205, 207, 216, 219, 220–24, 226
deification
    amor mundi, deified Christians practicing, 201
    cosmic deification, 148; 150

doctrine of deification, 94, 95, 97, 102, 105
early accounts of deification, 113, 114
fullness of life, as leading to, 99–100, 239
God's intent for deified creatures, 188–89
grace, deified humans as conduits of, 104–5
Gregory's account of, 105–6, 109–11, 159
as growth into God's image, 220
Holy Spirit's guidance toward, 208
as human participation in divine life, 166
inner law of conscience, the deified as following, 221
Irenaeus on the foundations of deification, 96
journey of deification, 199, 210
Kavanagh on growth in deification, 240
in the liberationist perspective, 167
Nicholas's account of, 138–39, 141, 159
self-actualization as part of, 176, 177
in theology of flourishing, 145, 205, 216, 222
Delio, Ilia, 68–69
dialogue
    contemplation in loving action, as leading to, 226

Index

245

decision, dialogue arriving at the point of, 220

discernment, as a context for, 208–15, 216, 218, 222

flourishing, understanding via, 176, 191, 205, 207, 219

queer community, dialogue with, 235–36

self-engagement, deepening through dialogue, 223

Dilexit Nos encyclical, 217

discernment

authenticity of discernment, assessing, 221

"being one's own" discerning while, 141

in Christian life, 25–26, 90, 170, 176

collective discernment, 202, 208

conflict situations as sites of, 231

constrained discernment, suffering due to, 199

dialogue as a context for, 208–15

flourishing as a foundation for, 200, 205, 233–34

Holy Spirit, discerning, 185, 188, 212, 215–20

as a human trait, 117, 118

in Ignatian tradition, 207, 226

Jesus Christ and, 138, 160

love at the heart of, 223

queerness, discerning the question of, 235–36

Rahner on discernment, 152, 154

in *sentire cum humanum*, 227

sentire cum terra as guiding, 228

Docetism, 85

dominion, 42, 43, 46–47

ecofeminism, 3, 4–6, 17. *See also* Jantzen, Grace

ecological theology, 13, 32

Ecology at the Heart of Faith (Edwards), 69

Edwards, Denis, 68–70, 101, 105, 118, 120–21

Eiesland, Nancy, 194, 195

Ellacuría, Ignacio

Rahner, as a student of, 112, 144, 145, 146, 162, 170

salvation, on its historicity, 165–69

in theology of flourishing, 169–70

Ellson, Sue, xiv

epektasis (spiritual growth), 107, 122

eudaimonia (well-being), 31

Faith in History and Society (Metz), 162

the fall, 6, 169

Christ as redeeming a corrupted world, 6, 128–29

creation as distinct from the fallen world, 15–16

incarnation before the fall, 126

materiality viewed as fallen, 5, 101

246   *Index*

punishment for fallen humanity, 54

salvation for a fallen people, 12, 114, 122, 129, 136

sin and the fallen created order, 178, 200, 203–4

Feminism and Ecological Communities (Cuomo), 3

feminist theology, 3, 24–25, 32, 129–30. *See also* ecofeminism

Fitzgerald, John, 75

flourishing. *See* theology of flourishing

Flourishing (Volf), 28

Ford, Craig, 236

Francis, Pope

on the bottom up/top down approach, 210–11

Dilexit Nos encyclical, 217

Laudato Si' encyclical, 42, 49, 178, 180, 186, 191, 230

synodal listening, emphasis on, 202

on the theology of welcoming, 209

Fretheim, Terence, 39–40, 50, 55, 64

Gager, John, 72

German Idealism, 162

Gilson, Étienne, 127

Gnanadason, Aruna, 238

Gnosticism, 86, 95, 101–2

good discomfort, 214–15

Gregory of Nyssa

on deification, 105–6, 108, 109–10, 111, 159

on *epektasis*, 107, 122

on the fulfillment of human life, 135–36

Life of Moses, 105–7, 111, 152

in theology of flourishing, 91, 95, 105–11, 113, 139

Grey, Mary, 18, 31, 187, 193

Griffith, Colleen, 193

Gunton, Colin, 179, 191, 193

Gutiérrez, Gustavo, 83

haecceitas (uniqueness)

Berry on all things flourishing in, 174

the contextual, integration with, 222

desires as conditioned by, 216

in discernment framework, 199, 205–6

Grey, reflections on, 193–94

Holy Spirit's work with, 190, 197, 208, 221

liturgy as offering attunement with, 239

love as drawing *haecceitas* to fulfillment, 217

mutual formation and, 179–80

of other-than-human creatures, 228

of queer persons, 234–35, 237

Rahner, analysis of, 147, 161

Scotus on, 124–25, 130–33, 143

self-actualization according to, 176, 189–92

in *sentire cum humanum* model, 227–28

Index

in theology of flourishing, 144, 145, 170, 174, 197
in theology of welcoming, 209
Hagar, 24, 195, 197
Hebrew Bible
abundant life proclaimed in, 67
"be fruitful and multiply" command, 41, 54, 61, 178
bloodless diet, prescribing, 43, 181
Eldad and Medad story, 188
forbidden fruit, 51, 179
Genesis 1, 36, 37–48, 50, 55, 59, 60, 63, 76, 116, 117, 174
Genesis 2, 36, 44, 48–54, 65
New Testament, claims of discontinuity with, 68
Psalm 19, 56–58, 61
Psalm 104, 56, 58–62
self-actualization and, 32
theme of order in, 103
in theology of flourishing, 35–36, 93
Wisdom literature, 36, 62–64
Hiebert, Theodore, 47
Hildegard of Bingen, 112, 113, 115–24, 133, 143, 190, 201
"Historical Roots of the Ecological Crisis" (White), 37–38
"Historicity of Christian Salvation" (Ellacuría), 166
Hollingsworth, Andrea, 141–42
Holmes, Urban, 240

Holy Spirit
actualization of queer folk and, 236
Christian attunement to, 175, 206, 207
deification through, 94, 201, 205, 209
discerning the Spirit, 79, 210, 212, 222
in eucharistic liturgy, 239
in the existential present, 192–93
as a guide for life, 242
haecceitas, working with, 190, 197, 208, 221
as harmonizing, 222–23
Hildegard of Bingen on, 122, 124, 143
Irenaeus on the Spirit, 95–96, 97, 99, 102
new possibilities, revealing, 26, 232–33, 234
radical otherness, welcoming, 200
in the reign of God, 231
self-actualization and, 98, 170, 205, 208, 222
in theology of flourishing, 19, 177, 183–89, 199, 203, 241
viriditas, work of, 176, 185, 202, 224, 226
will of the Spirit, discovering, 215–20
homonia (concord), 76, 77
Hopkins, Gerard Manley, xxi
Horan, Daniel, 13, 125, 132, 191, 237

248

Index

Horrell, David, 74–75

Hudson, Nancy, 139, 140, 142

Ignatius of Loyola
  discernment, Ignatian practice of, 207, 215–16, 226
  Ellacuría, Ignatian tradition of, 166, 167
  God, finding in all things, 153–54
  greater glory of God, maxim on, 223
  Spirit at work, on consolation as proof of, 221–22
image of God, 42, 47, 97, 219
individuation, principle of, 131, 132
Ingham, Mary Beth, 128, 131–32
Irenaeus of Lyons
  Against Heresies, 95–102
  Athanasius as inspired by, 103, 105
  creation account, 168
  on the fulfillment of human life, 135–36
  on the fullness of life, 97–98, 100, 142
  on the glorification of God, 176, 179, 204, 223
  Gregory as inspired by, 105, 110–11
Isasi-Díaz, Ada María, 189–90

Jantzen, Grace
  concerns raised by, 87, 108
  deification, on theologies of, 94, 138
  on discernment, 235–36

on divine wholeness, 136–37
  as an ecofeminist thinker, 3, 4–6, 17
  Hildegard of Bingen and, 118, 123–24
  Holy Spirit, reflecting on the work of, 185
  necrophilia, describing and defining, 5–6, 6–10, 130
  on oppression as an invitation to solidarity, 227
  on salvation, 7–10, 11, 12, 25, 50–51, 83
  on a theology of flourishing, 10, 16, 17, 19, 165
Jesus Christ
  abundance, promise of, 17, 23, 90
    Christian life, reimagining under abundance, 28
    discerning the promise of abundant life, 202, 212
    in the doctrine of salvation, 21
    Hebrew Bible, correspondence with, 67–68
    materiality, as anchored in, 85
    in theology of flourishing, 10, 11–12, 70, 130, 147, 176
  as avenged by the Father, 129–30
  in bottom-up/top-down approach, 210–11

Index

Cone on Christ as Black, 198
divine love of, 100, 152, 158, 176, 183, 217, 221, 223, 240
in doctrine of deification, 94, 199
enfleshment of, 69, 111, 165
 1 John, importance in, 84, 86–87, 97
 Athanasius on the incarnate body of Christ, 102–3
 cosmos, Christ's enfleshed connection to, 160–61
 as enlivening the world, 70
 the incarnate Word, 89, 90, 96
 Irenaeus on the Word made flesh, 97–98, 102
 presence of divine love, making possible, 182
 redemption, offering hope of, 149
faith in Christ, 72–75, 76, 84, 89, 169, 185
flourishing as expressed in the example of Christ, 93
fullness of life, proclaiming, 26, 27, 113, 164, 187
globalization, Christ in the context of, 29
"go and do likewise" command, 230
God's will revealed in, 18, 19
Hildegard on Jesus as the Word of God, 119
history of Jesus Christ, 168

human experience, sharing, 159–60
in liberation theologies, 170
as living water, 229
male Apostles of, 234
necrophilic logic as resulting in death of, 213
Passion of Christ, 134
as practicing love, 79–83, 86–89, 90–91, 152
praise as participation in Christ, 180
predestined Christ, 125, 128
Rahner on Christ as the climax of creation, 148
as redeemer, 15, 71, 85–86, 137, 142–43, 146, 150, 161, 186
in the reign of God, 231
as resurrected, 4, 5–6, 90, 169, 173, 182, 211, 226
as savior, 4–6, 15, 79, 96, 114, 161, 169
socioreligious status quo, transgressing, 215
suffering animals, connecting with, 181
Wisdom, as linked to, 62, 68, 69, 70–71, 95
Johnson, Elizabeth, 26, 231
 Ask the Beasts, 241
 on creation, 68–69, 177
 as an ecofeminist thinker, 17
 on God as She Who Is, 205
 on Jesus as setting law aside, 81–82
 poor women of color, on the flourishing of, 24–25

250   *Index*

on Scotus's Christology, 182
on self-actualization, 64
suffering, on God as present
    with, 229
on the symbol of God, 10–11,
    16
in theology of flourishing, 19
on the will of God, 12, 18
on women's ordination,
    232–33
Julian of Norwich
    Rahner as inspired by, 156,
        159
    on seeing in God's sight, 136–
        37, 174, 179, 219
    in theology of flourishing,
        112, 113, 115, 133–38, 201
    Wirzba as reflecting Julian's vi-
        sion, 182–83

Kavanagh, Aidan, 240–41
Kim, Grace Ji-Sun, 184
kingdom of God. *See* reign of
    God
Koester, Craig, xxv

Lash, Nicholas, 178, 184, 203
Laudato Si' encyclical, 42, 49,
    178, 180, 186, 191, 230
LGBTQ+ community, 24, 35–
    36, 234–37
liberation theologies, 32, 83, 107,
    167, 170, 231
Life of Moses (Gregory), 105–7,
    111, 152
Linahan, Jane, 184, 191, 200
Linzey, Andrew, 181
loving action, 219–20, 221,
    226–27

Luz, Ulrich, 80–81
lynching as America's cross, 198

Maier, Martin, 166
Marcionism, 68
Martin, Dale, 75–77
McGuckin, John, 109
mediated immediacy, 153
Meeks, Wayne, 75
mental depression, 195–96
Metz, Johann Baptist
    Ellacuría and, 167
    historical victims, on the suf-
        fering of, 163, 187
    Rahner, as a student of, 144,
        145, 146, 162–65, 170
    in theology of flourishing,
        112, 169
Mews, Constant, 119
Meyer, Eric Daryl, 228
Mission Santa Clara de Asís, 173,
    226
Moses, 55, 72, 105–6, 108–10,
    188, 190
mujerista theology, 189

necrophilia
    Christian indifference to, 177
    Genesis 2, necrophilic empha-
        sis in, 54
    human condition, viewing as
        fallen, 5–6
    natality as an antidote to,
        6–10, 64, 169
    necrophilic logic, 5, 181, 199,
        213, 231, 238
    Saint-Maurice, anticipating
        critique of, 130
Newman, John Henry, 181

Index

251

Nicholas of Cusa
  on deification, 159
  fulfillment, on orientation toward, 189
  haecceitas and, 131
  Scotus and, 152
  in theology of flourishing, 112, 113, 115, 133, 138–43, 201
nonviolence, 44
Norris, Richard, 101
nous (intellect), 94, 108

Oduyoye, Mercy, 23–24, 26, 27
On Learned Ignorance (Nicholas), 139, 141
On the Vision of God (Nicholas), 138, 141
ordination of women, 232–34
orthodoxia (right worship), 241

Pannenberg, Wolfhart, 183
parables
  the Good Samaritan, 80
  the Last Judgment, 82–83
  the Rich Young Man, 78, 109
  the Shepherd and the Gate, xxv
  the Sower, 218
Parousia (Second Coming), 83
patriarchy, 5, 53, 213
  biblical texts, patriarchal interpretation of, 65
  body and mind in the patriarchal view, 94
  church and society, hold on, 234
  colonization, intersecting with, 214

intellect and rationality, identifying with, 114
Johnson on the patriarchy, 11, 16
medieval European patriarchy, 123
punishment as resulting from, 52
racism as linked with, 155, 211
sacramental roles, keeping women from, 233
Perdue, Leo, 64
plasma (earthiness), 101
political theology, 164
praise, 46, 58, 59
  flourishing praise, 180
  God, praise for, 179, 205
  hymns of praise, 179, 225
  liturgy of praise, 226
  in Psalms, 57, 60–62, 67
preferential option for the poor, 24

quiddity, 139–40, 141

racism, 157, 211
  culture, as infecting, 218
  environmental racism, 198, 237–39
  feminist theology as addressing, 25
  structural racism, 24, 155
radah (rule), 47
radical hospitality, 24, 26, 194, 196, 200, 227
Rahner, Karl, 179, 192, 208
  categorical reality, on flourishing in, 210

252   *Index*

"Christology within an Evolutionary View of the
World," 147–48
Ellacuría as a student of, 112,
144, 145, 146, 162, 165–
69, 170
evolutionary Christology of,
145, 146–51
Metz as a student of, 144,
145, 146, 162–65, 170
redemption, on the essence
of, 161
self-transcendence, account
of, 176
in theology of flourishing,
143–44, 145, 147, 148,
154, 158, 164, 169–70
transcendental anthropology
of, 145–46, 151–58
transcendental Christology of,
159–60, 163
Ratzinger, Joseph, 220–21
reign of God, 18, 82, 182
abolition as opening space in,
215
churches, calling on to announce the reign, 231
Gregory, radical proclamation
of, 107
liberation from injustice under, 167
other-than-human flourishing
under, 30–31
praxis as active commitment
to the realization of, 166
reality, interpreting through
the lens of, 210–11
in theology of flourishing,
164–65, 168, 205, 237

working on behalf of, 6, 12,
182
Rhee, Helen, 29
Richard, Pablo, xxv
Rossing, Barbara, xxv
Rowson, Jonathan, 29, 31
ruah (divine wind), 39, 49, 62,
63, 64, 117, 184, 185–86,
187

Sacrosanctum Concilium constitution, 239
Saint-Maurice, Béraud de,
129–30
salvation, 178, 186
Athanasius on God's saving
work, 104
Christ as savior, 4–6, 15, 79,
96, 114, 161, 169
as creaturely fulfillment, 139
from a fallen world, 122, 129
flourishing as an expression of,
3, 4–6, 7–10, 85, 137
Gregory on salvation, 106,
110
heavenly salvation, 4, 5, 13, 15,
73, 83, 89, 93, 114, 127,
149, 158, 205
historicity of salvation, 152–
53, 165–69
Irenaeus on salvation, 97, 101
Jantzen on salvation, 7–10, 11,
12, 25, 50–51, 83
personal salvation, 5, 9, 10,
18–19, 93–94, 114
realized salvation, 86
resituating salvation, 16, 21,
130, 136, 143, 175, 203
self-actualization as part of, 32

Index

special knowledge, salvation via, 87–88
in Wisdom literature, 62
as a worldly task, 150–51, 157
Santmire, Paul, 13, 110
Santos, Patricia, 4, 230
sarx / en sarkì (flesh/enfleshment), 69, 73, 85, 86, 182
Schneiders, Sandra, 88
Scholastic theology, 124
Scivias (Hildegard), 115, 116
Scotus, John Duns
  haecceitas and, 130–33, 191
  Irenaeus and, 168
  Johnson on Christology of, 182
  Nicholas and, 139, 143
  Rahner as aligned with, 148, 152
  in theology of flourishing, 113, 115, 124–30, 140, 201
self-actualization, 152, 159, 195
  action on behalf of, 26–27
  of Christians, 214
  of creation, 35
  as creaturely fulfillment, 7, 141
  decision as self-actualization, 220–24
  as deification, 216
  as flourishing, 19, 22, 93, 113, 146, 176, 207, 208
  in friendship with God, 112
  as the fruit of redemption, 151
  haecceitas as a basis for, 189–92, 194
  in the Hebrew Bible, 42
  hermeneutics of the fullness of life as grounding, 32

Hildegard as an icon of, 123–24
Holy Spirit and, 98, 170, 205, 222
injustice as diminishing possibilities of, 199
joy as accompanying, 220
in Paul, 73, 78, 81
Rahner on, 154, 155, 161, 162
salvation, linking with, 18
sin as obstructing, 137, 156–57, 177
Wisdom as facilitating, 64
sentire cum humanum, 227, 229–30
sentire cum terra, 227, 228–30
Sheldrake, Philip, 133, 136, 137, 138
Showings, or Revelations of Divine Love (Julian), 134, 137
sin, 52, 135, 188
  created order, viewing as sinful, 178
  crime against the natural world as a sin, 180
  as a distortion of humanity, 179
  divine response to the reality of sin, 4
  flourishing and sin, relationship between, 50–54
  forces predisposed to sin, 162
  God as not seeing sin, 136–37, 179, 200, 219
  the incarnation, linking sin to, 125–29
  inner law of conscience, no sin in following, 221
  Jesus Christ as sinless, 160

254

justice under the rubric of sin, 168

justification for exploitation as sinful, 65

resituating sin, 16, 130, 143, 175, 203–4

salvation from sin, 5, 9, 13, 93–94, 114, 122, 137

self-actualization, sin obstructing, 137, 156–57, 177

structures of sin, 158, 230

in theology of flourishing, 205, 220, 241

soteriology, 4, 5, 8–9, 16, 114, 122, 130, 136, 169, 181, 203

Spirit. *See* Holy Spirit

St. Mary Catholic Church, 225–26, 239, 240, 241

Steenberg, Matthew, 100, 101

Stoeger, William, 22–23, 25, 26, 27, 37, 216, 223–24

Stogdon, Katie, 217–18

Strecker, Georg, 86, 87

Summa Theologica (Aquinas), 125–26

symbol of God, 10–11, 16

synodality, 202

ta pánta (whole creation), 45, 68, 71, 89, 164, 169

Tetlow, Joseph, 218, 219, 221–22

theological anthropologies, 145, 236

theology of flourishing, 91, 145

in categorical existence, 192–97

Christian history in, 21–22, 112, 143

commitment and limitations of, 27–32

contemplation, cultivating two forms of, 227–30

in covenantal history, 54–56

decision-making in, 220

dialogue as actualizing the vision of, 208–9, 211–12

discernment as a framework for, 207–8

divine intentions for flourishing, 64–66

early Christian resources on

Athanasius of Alexandria, 102–5

Gregory of Nyssa, 105–8, 111

Ireneus of Lyons, 95–102

environmental racism in, 237–39

fullness of life at the heart of, 197–99, 225

haecceitas as giving context to, 144, 222

in the Hebrew Bible

in creation texts, 37, 39, 48, 50–54, 64–65

in Psalms, 56, 58, 59

in Wisdom literature, 62, 64, 70

hermeneutics of

existential operation of sin, interpreting, 204

fullness of life, hermeneutics of, 22–27, 32, 35, 212

material conditions, critical evaluation of, 184

Index

mujerista theology as corresponding closely with, 190

oppression and injustice, focus on, 76

practical hermeneutics as interpreting religious truth claims, 165

suppressed strands of tradition, unearthing, 94

Holy Spirit as guiding, 183–89

"least of these," the flourishing of, 79–84, 90

LGBTQ+ inclusion in, 234–37

liturgy and worship in, 239–41

Medieval sources on, 113
  Hildegard of Bingen, 115–24
  John Duns Scotus, 124–33
  Julian of Norwich, 133–38
  Nicholas of Cusa, 138–43

moving toward a theology of flourishing, 169–70

nonviolence as a key norm for, 44

poor women of color and, 24–25

praxis of flourishing, 13, 68, 194, 196, 204–6, 226, 230–32, 232–41

preliminary understanding of, 17–19

Rahner on, 143–44, 145, 147, 148, 154, 158, 164, 169–70

reign of God, working toward, 204–5

salvation in, 3, 4–6, 7–10, 16, 50–51, 85

suffering, awareness of, 214, 228–29

symbol of creation, as rooted in, 36–37, 175–77, 177–82

theological symbols, measuring the adequacy of, 11–12

women's ordination, stance on, 232–34

word and deed as inseparable in, 88

See also self-actualization

theology of welcoming, 209

theophany, 55–56, 106

Tilley, Terrence, 236

tohu wabohu (watery void), 39, 116

Trible, Phyllis, 53, 65

Vawter, Bruce, 52

viriditas (greenness)
  Christians as agents of, 176–77, 241
  discerning a new inbreaking of, 219
  Hildegard of Bingen on, 120–23, 143
  Holy Spirit's work of, 185, 189, 202, 224, 226

Volf, Miroslav, 28–29, 30

Welker, Michael, 41

White, Lynn, 37–38
Wirzba, Norman
  on Christian imaginary, 12, 182–83
  on the doctrine of creation, 14–15
  garden imagery, utilizing, 48, 49–50

on love leading to self-actualization, 98
on *sentire cum terra* vision, 228
Wisdom. *See under* Hebrew Bible
womanist theologians, 198

Zimmerli, Walther, 62